Henry Jackson

The Fifth Book of the Nicomachean Ethics of Aristotle

Henry Jackson

The Fifth Book of the Nicomachean Ethics of Aristotle

ISBN/EAN: 9783337048501

Printed in Europe, USA, Canada, Australia, Japan

Cover: Foto ©Thomas Meinert / pixelio.de

More available books at **www.hansebooks.com**

ΠΕΡΙ ΔΙΚΑΙΟΣΥΝΗΣ.

THE FIFTH BOOK

OF THE

NICOMACHEAN ETHICS

OF

ARISTOTLE.

EDITED FOR THE SYNDICS OF THE UNIVERSITY PRESS

BY

HENRY JACKSON, M.A.
FELLOW OF TRINITY COLLEGE, CAMBRIDGE.

Cambridge:
AT THE UNIVERSITY PRESS.
LONDON: CAMBRIDGE WAREHOUSE, 17, PATERNOSTER ROW
CAMBRIDGE: DEIGHTON, BELL, AND CO.
1879

[All Rights reserved.]

PREFACE.

THE text of this edition of what, in deference to tradition, I have called on the title-page the Fifth Book of the Nicomachean Ethics, is founded upon a new collation of eight MSS. I cannot pretend that my researches in this direction have yielded much that is important. They have indeed enabled me to correct a few oversights in Bekker's text and critical notes, but they have thrown little light, if any, upon the difficulties of the treatise, and have convinced me that Bekker lost little by confining his attention to the four MSS. $K^b L^b M^b O^b$. I have however printed the results of my collation, in the hope that others may thereby be spared the repetition of an ungrateful labour.

Thinking, as many others have done, that the several parts of the Fifth Book do not stand in their proper order, I have with some hesitation adopted what seems to me a more intelligible arrangement than that of the received text. The chapter "On Dislocations in the Text", which forms a part of the Introduction, is based upon an article which I contributed to the *Journal of Philology* in 1875.

In the translation or paraphrase which stands opposite the text, my chief aim has been to show how I understand the drift and the several arguments of the original. Hence, wherever a Greek phrase seemed to be clearer than an English equivalent would have been, I have not scrupled to retain it in my version: and in general I have sacrificed neatness of expression to precision and perspicuity.

The necessity of justifying my interpretations has caused my notes to become in some parts, and especially in chapters 5, 8, and 9, disproportionately long. The substance of the commentary on chapter 5 appeared in 1872 in the *Journal of Philology*.

I believe that I have in all cases acknowledged my debts to previous commentators. But I should be ungrateful indeed if I did not make particular mention of my obligations to Sir Alexander Grant. It was in the pages of his edition that I first became acquainted with the Ethics, and however much I may differ from him in detail, I can never forget the help which, both as learner and as teacher, I have derived from his fresh and instructive work.

Professor Ramsauer's new edition did not reach me until my commentary was already in the press. As it was then too late to make use of his researches, I deferred the perusal of his work until my own little book should be out of my hands.

Finally it is my pleasant duty to offer my thanks to the Syndics of the University Press for their liberality in undertaking the publication of this book; to the authorities of the Bibliothèque Nationale at Paris, the Library of the Vatican, the Library of

St Mark at Venice, the Laurentian and Riccardian Libraries at Florence, the British Museum, and New College, Oxford, for their courtesy in allowing me to consult MSS. in their collections; and to my friends the Rev. W. M. Gunson, Fellow of Christ's College, Cambridge, Mr S. H. Butcher, Fellow of University College, Oxford, and Mr G. G. Greenwood of this College, with whom I have discussed many of the difficulties which beset this part of the Ethics.

H. J.

TRINITY COLLEGE, CAMBRIDGE.
November 9, 1878.

INTRODUCTION.

I. *On the Manuscripts.*

IN the critical notes to this edition I have recorded the readings of eight of the nine MSS. of the Ethics to which Bekker has assigned distinguishing letters. They are the following:

Q. Marcianus CC: "in folio membranaceus, foliorum 594, saeculi XV." Zanetti. Cf. Susemihl, *Politics* p. xxiv. This MS. (written by Joannes Rhosus in 1457) in general agrees exactly with M[b]. There are however occasional differences, sometimes one and sometimes the other exhibiting the conventional reading. I attach no value to Q, and in my general remarks on the MSS. have left it wholly out of account.

H[a]. Marcianus CCXIV: "in folio minori membranaceus, foliorum 240, saeculi circiter XI." Zanetti.

Bonitz made a collation of the whole of the Nic. Eth. in this MS.: "Kritische Ausbeute hat diese Collation so gut wie gar nicht ergeben, sondern nur bestätigt, was sich im Voraus vermuthen liess, dass Bekker Grund hatte, von der Collation der ganzen Handschrift abzusehen; sie ist an Fällen der Ungenauigkeit und an Auslassungen so reich, dass sie für Textesrecension der Nikomachischen Ethik sehr geringen Werth hat." *Aristot. Stud.* II. 8. I have nothing to say against this decided condemnation.

K[b]. Laurentianus LXXXI. 11: "codex membranaceus MS. in fol. minori seculi X nitidissimus et optimae notae, cum titulis singulorum librorum charactere vere quadrato et aureo exaratis. Constat foliis scriptis 181." Bandini.

I might have saved myself the trouble of collating this MS., as Bekker's collation has been most carefully revised by Schöll, whose corrections and additions are printed in Rassow's *Forschungen* p. 10 sqq. Numerous as are the readings which this MS. alone preserves, it is very incorrect, in the fifth book more so than several MSS. of less importance.

L^b. Parisiensis 1854: "cod. membr. Nic. Eth. cum scholiis varia manu eaque recentiori scriptis. Mich. Pselli esse verisimile est. Sec. XII." Catalogue. This MS. appears to me to be on the whole the most trustworthy authority for the text of the fifth book ("im fünften und zehnten Buche vielleicht als die zuverlässigste Quelle zu betrachten," says Rassow), though there are not very many instances in which it is alone in preserving a good reading.

M^b. Marcianus CCXIII: "in 4° membranaceus, fol. 276, saec. circ. XV." Zanetti. Though very incorrect this MS. occasionally preserves an important reading which would otherwise be lost. In the judgment of Bonitz (*Aristot. Stud.* II. 9) and Susemihl (*Politics* p. xxvi) it ranks for the Ethics only second in importance to K^b. So far as Bk. V is concerned, I think L^b more trustworthy than either.

N^b. Marcianus. Append. IV. 53: "bomb. fol. saec. XII." Waitz, *Organon* p. 3. I suspect that this was the MS. which was used by Aldus in printing the Nic. Eth. for his editio princeps. Lines have been drawn in the MS. to guide the copyist or printer in punctuation, and errors have been carefully corrected in the margin by the aid of some other MS. or MSS. In general the Aldine text exactly reproduces N^b together with the punctuation and emendations indicated by the corrector. I have admitted some three readings into my text on the sole authority of N^b. It is now well known that Bekker's collation of this MS. (as of H^a) is an incomplete one, and that it is the neglect of this fact which has led some scholars strangely to overrate its importance.

O^b. Riccardianus 46. More correct than M^b, O^b contributes fewer peculiar readings to the text than that MS. In this book however it does not seem to be as decidedly inferior to M^b as (according to the best authorities) it is elsewhere.

P^b. Vaticanus 1342. "Membr., kl. 4to oder 8vo, 133 Bl., Griechisch und Römisch paginirt. Kleine Schrift, viele Abkürzungen." Brandis.

In the *Journal of Philology*, 1876, VI. 208, I have endeavoured to show that the Cambridge MS. ('Eliensis') was copied from P^b, which must therefore have been written before 1279. Although apparently more closely connected with K^b than any other MS. and not so ancient, P^b is nevertheless less incorrect. I do not however find that it preserves any good readings which are not to be found in either $K^bL^bM^bN^b$ or O^b.

My own conclusions (as shown in the text which I have adopted) are, so far as Bk. V is concerned, briefly as follows:

1. That the MSS. collated (exclusive of Q which agrees too closely with M^b to be worth considering) stand in respect of correctness in the following order $L^bP^bO^bN^bK^bH^aM^b$, L^b being decidedly the most correct, and M^b decidedly the most incorrect;

2. That H^a and P^b contribute to the text nothing which is not to be found in one or other of the remaining five codices;

3. That when H^b and P^b are neglected there are about 43 places in which my reading depends upon one only of the remaining five MSS., the contributions of each being as follows: K^b 23, L^b 9, M^b 5, O^b and N^b 3 each;

4. That I am unable to distinguish families.

It will be remarked that these conclusions agree substantially with those of Rassow (*Forschungen* p. 8), and do not encourage the hope that in other parts of the Ethics an examination of the MSS. neglected by Bekker would yield considerable improvements upon his text.

Besides the MSS. above mentioned, I have also collated Bk. v. in two MSS. which are important only on the ground that they have been occasionally quoted by editors. One of them, now in the Library of the University of Cambridge, quoted by Zell as 'El.' i.e. 'Eliensis,' is, if I am not mistaken, a transcript from P^b (vide supra). It is dated 1279. See *Journal of Philology*, 1876, VI. 208 sqq., where I have given an account of it. The other, which is in the Library of New College, Oxford, quoted by Zell as C. N., seems to me to be a copy of Parisiensis 1853. Both codices have a lacuna extending from VIII. 11 § 7 to IX. 12 § 1, and if I may judge from the comparison of a few pages of the Parisian MS. with my collation of the Oxford one, they have the same readings, except where the Oxford MS. introduces a new blunder. I have also collated a few pages in Marcianus CCXII ("in 8º chartaceus, fol. 499, saeculi circiter XV" Zanetti), which appears to be a transcript from Q.

It will be understood that I have not in general recorded the corrections of later hands, that I have noted false accents and breathings only where they might seem to have some slight significance, and that I have neglected altogether the variations of the MSS. in respect of οὐθείς, οὐδείς, &c., of elisions, and of the ν ἐφελκυστικόν. I have not in general thought it necessary to call attention to discrepancies between Bekker's collation and my own. Finally, I have noted in the critical commentary all cases in which my text differs from that of Bekker.

II. *On Dislocations in the Text.*

Conceiving as others have done that the difficulty and the obscurity of this book are in a large measure due to dislocations in the text, I have with some hesitation decided to print the several parts of the treatise in what I suppose to be the true order. In this way I shall at any rate give the reader an opportunity of testing my rearrangement, whilst whatever may be thought of my attempt, I cannot well create a greater confusion than that which is to be found in the received text.

My main objections to the vulgate are two: (1) that the discussion of the ἀπορία περὶ τοῦ αὐτὸν αὑτὸν ἀδικεῖν is broken in two places by the intrusion of (*a*) 9 § 14—10 § 8, and (*b*) 11 §§ 7, 8, and (2) that 6 §§ 1—3 are wholly out of place in their present position between 5 § 19 and 6 § 4.

I proceed to examine these portions of the book with the double purpose of justifying the above statements, and of discovering how to dispose of the intrusive passages.

The opening words of ch. 9—ἀπορήσειε δ᾽ ἄν τις, εἰ ἱκανῶς διώρισται περὶ τοῦ ἀδικεῖσθαι καὶ ἀδικεῖν— appear to announce the beginning of a new division of the book, devoted to the consideration of ἀπορίαι with respect to ἀδικεῖν and ἀδικεῖσθαι. The first ἀπορία, discussed somewhat confusedly in §§ 1—7, is (*a*) 'can a man ἑκὼν ἀδικεῖσθαι?' The question having been answered in the negative, we are told in § 8 that two other ἀπορίαι remain to be investigated, (*b*) 'is it the distributor or the receiver who ἀδικεῖ?' and (*c*) 'can a man ἀδικεῖν αὑτόν?' The second of the two latter ἀπορίαι (which has been already referred to incidentally in § 4) having been separated from the first, in which at first sight it might seem to be involved, in § 9, the first is discussed and decided in §§ 10—13. Then follow three §§ (14—16), which have nothing to do with the ἀπορίαι announced for discussion, and which would appear to belong to a preliminary review of ἔνδοξα about universal δίκαιον and ἄδικον, such as that with which the book opens—else why the references, not merely to particular justice and injustice, but also to other virtues and vices? Next, § 17 limits the sphere of ἡ κατὰ μέρος δικαιοσύνη, and consequently has nothing to do either with §§ 14—16, or with §§ 8—13. Ch. 10 which follows investigates ἐπιείκεια and its relation to δικαιοσύνη, thus raising an entirely new matter. And now in ch. 11 §§

1—6, the third ἀπορία (which, I repeat, has been in 9 § 4 and § 9 referred to, but never considered) is formally discussed. Then, in 11 §§ 7, 8 it is debated whether ἀδικεῖν or ἀδικεῖσθαι is the worse. Next, § 9 recurs to the ἀπορία 'can a man ἀδικεῖν αὑτόν?' Finally § 10 concludes the book.

Thus the matters discussed in ch. 9—11 may be tabulated as follows:

(1) 9 §§ 1—7. The ἀπορία (a) Can a man ἑκὼν ἀδικεῖσθαι? discussed and decided.

(2) §§ 8, 9. The ἀπορίαι (b) Is it the distributor or the receiver who ἀδικεῖ? and (c) Can a man ἀδικεῖν αὑτόν? announced and distinguished.

(3) §§ 10—13. The ἀπορία (b) Is it the distributor or the receiver who ἀδικεῖ? decided.

(4) 9 §§ 14—16. Certain ἔνδοξα about universal justice enumerated and considered.

(5) 9 § 17. The sphere of particular justice determined.

(6) 10. Equity.

(7) 11 §§ 1—6. The ἀπορία (c) Can a man ἀδικεῖν αὑτόν? discussed and decided.

(8) 11 §§ 7, 8. Is ἀδικεῖν or ἀδικεῖσθαι the worse?

(9) § 9. The ἀπορία (c) Can a man ἀδικεῖν αὑτόν? finally dismissed.

(10) § 10. Conclusion of the book.

However we may hereafter dispose of the passages which I have enumerated on the right side of the page, there can be no doubt that those which I have placed on the left side gain in perspicuity if they are read in connection with one another. Even if I could offer no suggestion for the disposal of the two interpolations, i.e. 9 § 14—10 § 8 and 11 §§ 7, 8, I should still recommend this course. But I think that I can find places for the fragments which I have set aside. In the first place, it seems natural that the discussion of ἐπιείκεια, as a supplement to the investigation of δικαιοσύνη, should stand at the end of the book. I therefore propose to place it after 11 § 9, prefixing to it another fragment (6 § 3) of which I shall have something to say hereafter, and affixing 11 § 10 with which the book obviously concludes. Thus according to the numeration of the above tabular statement, (1), (2), (3), (7), (9), (6), (10) will stand in the order indicated.

It remains to determine the position of 9 §§ 14—16, 9 § 17, and 11 §§ 7, 8.

The first of these fragments, being an enumeration and examination of ἔνδοξα about justice and injustice in the large senses of those words, would seem to belong to the early part of the book. Now in 1 § 3 the author states and accepts provisionally the popular notion of justice and injustice: he then proceeds in § 4, οὐδὲ γὰρ τὸν αὐτὸν ἔχει τρόπον ἐπί τε τῶν ἐπιστημῶν καὶ δυνάμεων καὶ ἐπὶ τῶν ἕξεων. Does this sentence naturally succeed § 3? For my part, I think not. To say nothing of the harshness of the ellipse which Grant assumes,—"(and I have specified them thus) for it is not the same," &c.—the introduction of a doctrine of the schools in § 4, for no better purpose than to justify the form in which the popular notion of § 3 has been expressed, is surely very strange. Here then, after the words ὑποκείσθω ταῦτα, I propose to insert 9 §§ 14—16. (See paraphrase, p. 3.) It will be remarked (1) that a somewhat lengthy enumeration of popular views with accompanying criticisms is precisely what the author's declaration in § 2, that he will proceed κατὰ τὴν αὐτὴν μέθοδον τοῖς προειρημένοις, has led us to expect at the outset of the enquiry, whereas the addition of such an enumeration after the author's own view has been stated is not only useless, but also contrary to his ordinary practice ; and (2) that the doctrine of 1 § 4 is necessary to complete the argument of 9 § 16, as was seen by Michael Ephesius, who, though he does not suspect any displacement, is nevertheless careful in commenting on the latter passage to quote the former.

Again 9 § 17, which determines the kind of society in which ἡ κατὰ μέρος δικαιοσύνη can subsist, is obviously connected in thought with 1 § 9. Accordingly I propose to insert it after the words τὰ αὐτοῖς ἀγαθά, though I cannot allege any better reason than a general sense of superior fitness for placing it here, after the parenthetical remarks about prayer, rather than after τινὶ δ' οὐκ ἀεί. (See paraphrase, p. 7.)

It remains to find a place for 11 §§ 7, 8. In these §§, which have obviously nothing to do with the ἀπορίαι raised in ch. 9, ἀδικεῖν and ἀδικεῖσθαι being regarded as deviations from τὸ μέσον, it is asked which of the two is the worse? Now 5 §§ 17, 18 is the one place in which τὸ κατὰ μέρος δίκαιον (taken as a whole) is regarded as a μέσον. I therefore insert this fragment at the end of 5 § 18, after the words τοῦ δὲ ἀδικήματος τὸ μὲν ἔλαττον τὸ ἀδικεῖσθαί ἐστι, τὸ δὲ μεῖζον τὸ ἀδικεῖν.

Further, two minor changes appear to me to be necessary. Firstly, I cannot construe the clause καὶ ὥσπερ ὑγιεινὸν μὲν ἐν ἰατρικῇ εὐεκτικὸν δὲ ἐν γυμναστικῇ (11 § 7) in connection with its present surroundings. The best place which I can find for it is in 5 § 17 after the words ἀλλ' ὅτι μέσον ἐστίν, and accordingly I have printed it there in my text, though not without hesitation.

Secondly, I have introduced in 11 § 7, after οὐ γὰρ ἅπαν τὸ ἑκούσιον μετὰ ἀδικίας, the words ἐν οἷς δ' [qu. γὰρ] ἀδικία, καὶ τὸ ἀδικεῖν ἐν τούτοις, ἐν οἷς δὲ τὸ ἀδικεῖν, οὐ πᾶσιν ἀδικία, which, as Münscher has pointed out, *Quaest. Crit.* p. 84, are wholly irrelevant to 6 § 4[1]. Here again, though I am sure that the sentence is out of place where it stands, I cannot be sure that I have discovered the right position for it.

I turn now to 6 §§ 1—3. These sections, as is acknowledged by nearly all the scholars who have attempted to unravel the perplexities of this book, seriously interrupt the argument. As the text stands, 5 § 19 declares that the investigation of δικαιοσύνη, ἀδικία, δίκαιον and ἄδικον regarded καθόλου is now complete; while 6 § 4 begins an investigation of the kinds of δίκαιον called respectively πολιτικόν, δεσποτικόν, πατρικόν, οἰκονομικόν; and the introductory sentence—δεῖ δὲ μὴ λανθάνειν ὅτι τὸ ζητούμενόν ἐστι καὶ τὸ ἁπλῶς δίκαιον καὶ τὸ πολιτικὸν δίκαιον—carefully marks the connection of this inquiry with the inquiry concluded in ch. 5. Any intervening sentences must be either explanatory of the previous discussion, or explanatory by anticipation of 6 § 4 sqq., or, if purely parenthetical, complete in themselves. Now it is impossible to connect §§ 1—3 either with 5 § 19 or with 6 § 4: and when we consider them by themselves, apart from the context, we find that the author (1) in 6 §§ 1, 2, starting from the new assumption that ὁ ἀδικῶν is not necessarily ἄδικος, asks a question, demurs to the form of it, and alleges examples in justification of his objection, but does not restate the question or proceed to enunciate his doctrine, although in the words ἀλλ' οὐ διὰ προαιρέσεως ἀρχήν he has implicitly established a basis for it; and (2) in 6 § 3 introduces a reference to a former discussion, which reference is irrelevant not only to 6 §§ 1, 2, but also to 5 § 19 and 6 § 4[2]. I conceive then that the passage does not occupy its proper position, and that it consists of two distinct fragments, one of which,

[1] In the *Journal of Philology*, 1876, VI. p. 108, I placed these words in 6 § 1 after διοίσει.

[2] In the Latin version of Averroes' commentary no notice is taken of §§ 1—3, as is expressly noted in the margin of the Venetian edition of 1550. Michael Ephesius paraphrases §§ 1, 2, but not § 3.

J.   *b*

§§ 1, 2, belongs in thought, as Trendelenburg (*Historische Beiträge zur Philosophie* III. 421) has pointed out, to ch. 8, whilst the other, § 3, contains at first sight no hint of its origin. I proceed to deal with these fragments separately and in detail; and first with §§ 1, 2.

I have already said that the distinction between ὁ ἀδικῶν and ὁ ἄδικος, which is introduced as though it were familiar to the reader, is here imported into the discussion for the first time. I may now add that, whereas the words οὐ διὰ προαιρέσεως ἀρχὴν ἀλλὰ διὰ πάθος read as though the distinction between τὰ ἐκ προαιρέσεως and τὰ διὰ πάθος had been already enforced, that distinction has not been brought before us in connection with the present subject. It has also been stated that the author after asking the question ὁ ποῖα ἀδικήματα ἀδικῶν ἤδη ἄδικός ἐστιν ἑκάστην ἀδικίαν; objects to the form of the question, prepares to answer it in its spirit if not in its letter, but strangely stops short and drops the matter. Now in ch. 8 we find (1) that προαιρετά and ἀπροαίρετα (in which ὅσα διὰ θυμὸν καὶ ἄλλα πάθη ὅσα ἀναγκαῖα ἢ φυσικὰ συμβαίνει τοῖς ἀνθρώποις are included) are carefully distinguished in 8 § 5; (2) that the distinction between ὁ ἀδικῶν and ὁ ἄδικος is introduced, apparently as a novelty, in 8 § 8; and (3) that the very question asked in 6 § 1, not having been restated in the interval, is declared answered in 8 § 11, upon the principle hinted at but not distinctly enunciated in the former passage. Hence I infer that the fragment 6 §§ 1, 2 is to be inserted in ch. 8 somewhere between οὐ μέντοι πω ἄδικοι διὰ ταῦτα οὐδὲ πονηροί (§ 8) and ἂν δ' ἐκ προαιρέσεως βλάψῃ, ἀδικεῖ, κ.τ.λ. (§ 11): and on examination of the region thus defined I decide to place it in § 8 after βλάβῃ. (See paraphrase, p. 47.) The train of thought of 8 §§ 6—11 is then as follows:—' The βλάβαι which may occur in the several κοινωνίαι of society are three—ἀτύχημα (ὅταν παραλόγως ἡ βλάβη γένηται), ἁμάρτημα (ὅταν μὴ παραλόγως ἄνευ δὲ κακίας), ἀδίκημα (ὅταν εἰδὼς μὲν μὴ προβουλεύσας δέ). He who acts knowingly, but not of deliberate purpose, ἀδικεῖ but is not necessarily ἄδικος. *What are the acts then the commission of which makes the agent ἄδικος as well as ἀδικῶν? Not certain specified acts*, but acts done ἐκ προαιρέσεως (whence τὰ ἐκ θυμοῦ are rightly accounted ἀδικήματα which do not imply ἀδικία in the agent, for ὁ ὀργισθείς is εἰδώς but not προελόμενος).' Thus in this chapter ἄδικον, ἀδίκημα, and ἀδίκημα implying ἀδικία, are successively considered and defined. When the agent is not ἑκών, he ἄδικα πράττει. When the agent is ἑκών but not προελόμενος, he ἀδικεῖ and the act is an ἀδίκημα. When the agent is προελόμενος, he ἀδικεῖ καὶ ἄδικός ἐστιν. It will be observed, (1) that the fragment inserted accounts for the transition from the plurals ἄδικοι, πονηροί in 8 § 8 to the singulars ἄδικος, μοχθηρός in 8 § 9; and (2) that the phrase διὰ προαιρέσεως ἀρχήν in 6 § 1 leads up to the emphatic ἄρχει in the last sentence of the second of these sections. These coincidences may seem in some measure to confirm my conjecture.

So much for the first of the two fragments of which I suppose 6 §§ 1—3 to consist. It is more difficult to dispose of the second. We may however assume from the form of it—πῶς μὲν οὖν ἔχει τὸ ἀντιπεπονθὸς πρὸς τὸ δίκαιον εἴρηται πρότερον—that it is the beginning of a distinct paragraph, whilst it is evident that this allusion to the investigation of τὸ ἀντιπεπονθός would be specially appropriate at the beginning of a subsequent chapter upon an offshoot of justice. Indeed it is difficult to imagine any other circumstances under which the reminder would be required. I propose therefore to insert the fragment at the beginning of the chapter upon equity[1]. No inconsistency or awkwardness is created by the transfer. The opening sentence of ch. 10 will now run thus:

πῶς μὲν οὖν ἔχει τὸ ἀντιπεπονθὸς πρὸς τὸ δίκαιον εἴρηται πρότερον· περὶ δὲ ἐπιεικείας καὶ τοῦ ἐπιεικοῦς, πῶς

[1] According to Grant, Spengel so far anticipates me as to place ch. 10 after 6 § 3. In his *Aristotelische Studien* however Spengel adopts Hildenbrand's proposal to place 6 § 3—7 § 7 (with the omission of the word πρότερον) between 5 § 16 and 5 § 17.

ἔχει ἡ μὲν ἐπιείκεια πρὸς δικαιοσύνην τὸ δ' ἐπιεικὲς πρὸς τὸ δίκαιον, ἐχόμενόν ἐστιν εἰπεῖν· οὔτε γὰρ ὡς ταὐτὸν ἁπλῶς οὔθ' ὡς ἕτερον τῷ γένει φαίνεται σκοπουμένοις, κ.τ.λ.

I think that when these changes have been effected the several matters discussed in the book follow one another in a natural and orderly sequence. In ch. 1, (1) certain popular notions about justice and injustice are stated, criticized, and accepted, modified, or rejected: (2) the relations of the just and the unjust, the just and justice are considered: (3) the just is shown to include the lawful and the equal: (4) the just in the sense of the lawful is subdivided into τὸ κατὰ τὴν ὅλην ἀρετήν and τὸ ποιητικὸν καὶ φυλακτικὸν εὐδαιμονίας τῇ πολιτικῇ κοινωνίᾳ. In ch. 2, (1) our attention is directed to ἡ ἐν μέρει δικαιοσύνη, the discussion of which is necessary to the completeness of our theory of the virtues: (2) ἡ κατὰ μέρος δικαιοσύνη is subdivided into τὸ διανεμητικόν and τὸ διορθωτικόν. In ch. 3, distributive justice is shown to consist in that kind of equality which is attained by geometrical proportion. In ch. 4, corrective justice is shown to consist in that kind of equality which is attained by arithmetical proportion. In ch. 5, (1) commercial justice is shown to consist in that kind of equality which is attained by reciprocal proportion: (2) δικαιοσύνη is declared to be in some sense a mean, ἀδικεῖν and ἀδικεῖσθαι being extremes of which ἀδικεῖν is the worse: (3) the general investigation of δικαιοσύνη, ἀδικία, δίκαιον, and ἄδικον is declared complete. In ch. 6, we leave τὸ ἁπλῶς δίκαιον and proceed to consider τὸ πολιτικὸν δίκαιον together with τὰ καθ' ὁμοιότητα δίκαια, viz. δεσποτικόν, πατρικόν, οἰκονομικόν. In ch. 7, two elements of τὸ πολιτικὸν δίκαιον, viz. τὸ φυσικόν and τὸ νομικόν, are distinguished. In ch. 8, we pass on to the investigation of justice and injustice in the individual, who (1) οὐκ ἀδικεῖ unless he is ἑκών, (2) οὐ διὰ ταῦτα ἄδικός ἐστιν unless he acts ἐκ προαιρέσεως. In ch. 9 §§ 1—13 and ch. 11 §§ 1—6 and § 9, supplementary ἀπορίαι in regard to ἀδικεῖν and ἀδικεῖσθαι are discussed. In ch. 10, ἐπιείκεια and its relations to justice are considered. Finally, in 11 § 10, the investigation of δικαιοσύνη and the other ἠθικαὶ ἀρεταί is declared to be complete.

It now only remains for me to tabulate my arrangement of the book as follows:

   1 §§ 1—3. περὶ δὲ—ταῦτα.
   9 §§ 14—16. οἱ δ'—ὡδί.
   1 §§ 4—9. οὐδὲ γὰρ—ἀγαθά.
   9 § 17. ἔστι δὲ—ἐστιν.
   1 § 10—5 § 18. ὁ δ'—ἀδικεῖν.
   11 §§ 7, 8. φανερὸν—ἀποθανεῖν.
   5 § 19. περὶ—καθόλου.
   6 § 4—8 § 8. δεῖ δὲ—βλάβη.
   6 §§ 1, 2. ἐπεὶ—ἄλλων.
   8 § 9—9 § 13. ὅταν δ'—ἔλαβεν.
   11 §§ 1—6. πότερον—ἀδικεῖσθαι.
   11 § 9. κατὰ μεταφορὰν—τούτοις.
   6 § 3. πῶς μὲν—πρότερον.
   10 §§ 1—8. περὶ δὲ—ἕξις.
   11 § 10. περὶ μὲν—τοῦτον.

In the above statement I have not taken account of the two sentences ἐν οἷς δ' ἀδικία, καὶ τὸ ἀδικεῖν ἐν τούτοις, ἐν οἷς δὲ τὸ ἀδικεῖν, οὐ πᾶσιν ἀδικία, and καὶ ὥσπερ ὑγιεινὸν μὲν ἐν ἰατρικῇ εὐεκτικὸν δὲ ἐν γυμναστικῇ, because, though I am convinced that they ought not to stand in their present position (6 § 4 and 11 § 7), I do not feel much confidence in my attempt to find a place for them. On the same principle I have allowed them to stand in the text in their traditional positions, as well as in the places which I hesitatingly assign to them.

III. *On the relations of Book V. to the two Ethical treatises.*

Book V. being one of the three books which are common to the Nicomachean and the Eudemian Ethics, it is necessary that I should say something about its relation to the two treatises.

The principal[1] theories which have been entertained in regard to *N. E.* V. VI. VII. = *E. E.* IV. V. VI. are the following:

1. That these books, with the exception of the superfluous theory of pleasure at the end of VII., belong to the Nicomachean treatise: L. Spengel, *Abhandl. der k. bayer. Akad.* 1841:

2. That V. 1—10 belong to the Nicomachean treatise, V. 11. VI. VII. to the Eudemian: A. M. Fischer, *de Ethicis Nicomacheis et Eudemiis*, Bonn, 1847:

3. That all three books belong to the Eudemian treatise: H. A. J. Munro, *Journal of Classical and Sacred Philology*, 1855, II. 66—81.

For my own part, I give an unhesitating assent to the last of these three theories. I do not however propose on this occasion to investigate the whole question, but only so much of it as specially affects the fifth book, a limitation of the inquiry which would hardly be possible, had not Fischer taken up an intermediate position between the extreme theories of Spengel and Munro, holding that, while VI. and VII. belong to the *E. E.*, V. with the exception of the last chapter (ch. 11) belongs to the *N. E.* Assuming then that the detailed arguments which Fischer brings forward to prove the Eudemian origin of VI. and VII. are, as I think

[1] I imagine that Schleiermacher's paradoxical theory, that the Eudemian treatise, to which these books belong, is of superior authority to the Nicomachean, and the *Magna Moralia* of superior authority to both (*Philosophische Schriften* III. 306 sqq.) has not found many supporters.

them, absolutely conclusive, I proceed to consider his reasons for assigning V. 1—10 to the other treatise.

The following is, I think, a fair summary of his main argument:

"The discussion of the ἀπορία—πότερον ἐνδέχεται ἑαυτὸν ἀδικεῖν in ch. 11 is not only an 'ineptissima repetitio,' the question having been already settled in precisely the same way in 9 §§ 1—13, but also out of place, as it is impossible to justify the interposition of 9 §§ 14—17 and of ch. 10 (περὶ ἐπιεικείας). Both discussions cannot possibly be parts of the same work. Hence we are justified in assigning V. VI. VII. partly to one, partly to the other treatise; whereas had there been no such disturbance in the argument, we could hardly have refused to assign the whole to the *E. E.*, to which the superfluous theory of pleasure plainly belongs. That it is the second of the two discussions περὶ τοῦ αὐτὸν ἀδικεῖν, and not the first, which belongs to the *E. E.*, there can be no doubt; for, while the whole of the investigation of justice contained in cc. 1—9 is 'Aristotele dignissima,' and the last fragment of ch. 9 (§§ 14—17) 'pulcrae disquisitioni pulcerrimum finem imponit,' the superfluous ch. 11 exhibits 'anxiam illam argumentandi rationem qua haud raro in Eudemiis defatigamur,' and betrays the 'animum pusillum Eudemi, qui saepissime ad explicandas Nicomacheorum quaestiones non solum Aristoteleis argumentis utitur, sed de suo insuper hoc illudve adiicit, quo magis res conficiatur.' Thus ch. 11, together with VI. and VII., belongs to the Eudemian treatise, 'tota autem disquisitio de iustitia, omnibus suis partibus integra cum insequenti capite de aequitate locum suum in Nicomacheis obtinet.'"

It will be perceived that the whole of this argument rests upon the assumption that 11 §§ 1—6 are no more than a repetition of a previous discussion. Where then is this previous discussion to be found? According to Fischer in 9 §§ 1—7: "argumentatio capitis 15 [i.e. ch. 11] nil plane differt ab illa quae est in capite 11 [i.e. 9 §§ 1—7]; utroque loco notione spontanei adhibita demonstratur, iniuriam in se ipsum illatam esse nullam." I cannot however allow that this is a correct account of the substance of 9 §§ 1—7. In 9 § 4 indeed the question πότερον ἐνδέχεται αὐτὸν αὑτὸν ἀδικεῖν is mentioned, but the mention is an incidental one in connection with another ἀπορία, as the words ἔστι δὲ καὶ τοῦτο ἓν τῶν ἀπορουμένων, εἰ ἐνδέχεται αὐτὸν αὑτὸν ἀδικεῖν plainly show. Indeed Fischer himself, when he is speaking more precisely, seems to argue, not that the ἀπορία is here discussed, but rather that the resolution of it follows so directly from the διορισμὸς ὁ περὶ τοῦ ἑκουσίως ἀδικεῖσθαι that any discussion or even mention of it becomes unnecessary: "non dedita quidem opera hoc loco de quaestione αὐτὸν ἀδικεῖν disputatur, sed et hanc verbis eius postremis solvi nemo non videt; quodsi enim ἑκόντα ἀδικεῖσθαι absurdum est, iam per se liquet, αὐτὸν ἀδικεῖν non minus esse ineptum, quum illud ἀδικεῖν non possit nisi ἑκούσιον esse, id quod iamdudum demonstratum est. Itaque quaestio illa per se iam ideo evanescit, quod fieri non potest ut, quam quis iniuriam sibi ipse sua sponte inferat, eandem invitus a se patiatur. Pluribus verbis ad id demonstrandum non opus fuisse, satis liquet." But even if further discussion is unnecessary, it does not follow that we can dispense with all mention of the ἀπορία. The author ought at least to point out that further discussion is superfluous. He ought, in fact, to make the very remark which Fischer makes: and accordingly that remark occupies a prominent position in 11 §§ 1—6. At any rate the author himself does not think that the question has been "prorsus absoluta" in 9 §§ 1—7; for in § 8 we read— ἔτι δ' ὧν προειλόμεθα δύο ἔστιν εἰπεῖν, πότερόν ποτ' ἀδικεῖ ὁ νείμας παρὰ τὴν ἀξίαν τὸ πλεῖον ἢ ὁ ἔχων, καὶ εἰ ἔστιν αὐτὸν αὑτὸν ἀδικεῖν. That the ἀπορία has not been discussed hitherto, and will be discussed hereafter, could not well be stated more explicitly. Fischer indeed thinks "id tantum hoc loco agi, ut ex occasione quaestionis: πότερόν ποτ' ἀδικεῖ ὁ νείμας, κ.τ.λ. exemplum quoddam iniuriae in se ipsum illatae (dico exemplum: εἴ τις πλέον ἑτέρῳ ἢ ἑαυτῷ νέμει εἰδὼς καὶ ἑκών) quod solum iam superesse videri poterat, una cum hac quaestione absolvatur:" but for my own part I cannot allow that, when the author says 'two matters included in our programme have still to be spoken of,' he means 'it remains to consider in connection with another ἀπορία a case upon which we have already pronounced judgment.'

In brief, as I read the passage, 9 § 8 promises an answer to two questions, the second of which has been mentioned incidentally in § 4: § 9 shows that the two questions must be kept separate: §§ 10—13 discuss the former of them. Thus, that the argument may be complete, it is necessary that 9 § 13 should be immediately followed either by 11 §§ 1—6 or by a paragraph to the same effect; and as there are other grounds for supposing that the concluding pages of the book have been disarranged (to say nothing of other disturbances, the last paragraph of ch. 9 being, not an "epilogus qui totam disquisitionem de iustitia proprie sic dicta concludit," but rather a fragment or fragments of a preliminary investigation of justice in general), I unhesitatingly accept the former of these alternatives.

One other point in Fischer's argument summarized above remains to be noticed. He thinks that, whereas the concluding chapter exhibits the prolixity and the weakness which are characteristic of Eudemus, cc. 1—10 are worthy of Aristotle. It is always difficult to decide whether a given work is worthy of its reputed author, and especially in such a case as this, where the other claimant confessedly borrows both his style and his matter. I propose therefore to modify the question which Fischer here raises, and to inquire, not whether the fifth book (exclusive of ch. 11) is worthy of Aristotle, but whether it is consistent with the Nicomachean treatise. Now as to the style my own opinion is in complete accord with that of Munro, who holds that "the style of this book, last chapter and all, is precisely the same as that of the other two, and of the undisputed parts of the Eudemian Ethics." In regard to the substance of the book, I am not of course bound to show that it is wholly unaristotelian (as I may fairly assume that the Eudemian and Nicomachean accounts of justice were related to one another in precisely the same way as the Eudemian and Nicomachean accounts of the other virtues, i.e. that in general they agreed), but only that if any matter about which the two treatises are at variance is raised in this book, its doctrine is that of the *E. E.* If no such matter is raised here, Munro's theory does not necessarily fall to the ground: on the other hand, if it can be shown that, in dealing with any question, v. agrees with the *E. E.* in differing from the *N. E.*, this will be a strong reason for believing that v. does not belong to the latter. Now *N. E.* III. and *E. E.* II. differ, not inconsiderably, in the detail of the theory of the ἑκούσιον and the ἀκούσιον, and it will be found on examination that v. 8 agrees, in the minutest particulars, with the Eudemian statement: thus (1) the distinction made in *N. E.* III. 1 § 13 between οὐχ ἑκούσια and ἀκούσια is ignored in *E. E.* II. and in *N. E.* v. 8; (2) the view taken in *N. E.* v. 8 § 3 of πολλὰ τῶν φύσει ὑπαρχόντων, οἷον τὸ γηρᾶν ἢ ἀποθνήσκειν, that they are οὔθ' ἑκούσια οὔτ' ἀκούσια, is in exact accord with the statement made in *E. E.* II. 8 § 4, about the upward motion of the flame and the downward motion of the stone, ὅτι οὐ βίᾳ, οὐ μὴν οὐδ' ἑκούσια λέγεται, ἀλλ' ἀνώνυμος ἡ ἀντίθεσις, whilst *N. E.* III. 5 § 7 seems to indicate that the author of the *N. E.* had no such distinction in his mind; (3) in *N. E.* v. 8 and in *E. E.* II. 10 § 19 prominence is given to the legal classification of παθήματα as ἀκούσια, ἑκούσια and ἐκ προνοίας, which does not appear in the *N. E.*; (4) in v. 8 § 8 τὰ διὰ θυμόν are included amongst ὅσα εἰδὼς μὲν μὴ προβουλεύσας δέ, a classification which is at any rate not inconsistent with the doctrine of the *E. E.* (cf. *E. E.* II. 9 § 3), whilst in *N. E.* III. 1 § 14 it is expressly stated that ὁ ὀργιζόμενος is οὐκ εἰδὼς ἀλλ' ἀγνοῶν. I select these trifling instances of agreement and difference merely because they are capable of precise formulation; but I think that any one who takes the trouble to compare *N. E.* v. 8 as a whole with the last chapters of *E. E.* II. and the first chapters of *N. E.* III., will find the impression grow upon him that *N. E.* V. and *E. E.* II. are, and that *N. E.* V. and *N. E.* III. are not, the work of the same author.

For my own part, in proportion as I have become more familiar with *N. E.* V.=*E. E.* IV., the more certain I have become that, whereas its agreements with the rest of the *N. E.* are precisely what are to be expected from the general resemblance of the two treatises, its agreements with the rest of the *E. E.*, both in thought and in expression, indicate a more intimate connection.

One other argument is put forward, though cautiously, by Fischer: "in *E. E.* VII. 15 § 1 we read κατὰ μέρος μὲν οὖν περὶ ἑκάστης ἀρετῆς εἴρηται πρότερον· ἐπεὶ δὲ χωρὶς διείλομεν τὴν δύναμιν αὐτῶν, καὶ περὶ τῆς ἀρετῆς διαρθρωτέον τῆς ἐκ τούτων, ἣν ἐκαλοῦμεν ἤδη καλοκἀγαθίαν. The concluding sentence of this extract tells us that the word καλοκἀγαθία has been used in some previous part of the *E. E.*, whereas it is nowhere to be found in the extant treatise. The most likely place for its occurrence would be the book about justice. Hence the surviving discussion of justice, in which it does not appear, must belong not to the Eudemian, but to the Nicomachean work." To this argument Munro replies:—"But surely the word was more likely to have been mentioned in some one of the lost portions of this last book in which he treats of this virtue and its end and aim the right worship and contemplation of God." I think however that exception may be taken on other grounds. Apparently Fischer assumes that ἤδη in the phrase ἣν ἐκαλοῦμεν ἤδη καλοκἀγαθίαν is equivalent to πρότερον. Is this possible? I should have thought that the phrase must mean, not 'which in a previous passage we called καλοκἀγαθία,' but either 'which down to a time otherwise determined,' or 'which from a time otherwise determined, we called καλοκἀγαθία.' I suspect therefore that in place of ἐκαλοῦμεν we should read καλοῦμεν, and translate—'whereas we then distinguished the functions of the several virtues, we must now proceed to investigate the virtue which arises from their conjunction, which virtue we now [i.e. in this form] call καλοκαγαθία.' If so, the argument falls to the ground.

At this point it will be convenient to say something about a recent development of the theory of the Eudemian authorship of the three books. Grant, in his first edition of the Ethics, published in 1857, has accepted and justified Munro's theory, and in his second and third editions, published in 1866 and 1874 respectively, has made considerable additions to his chapter on the subject. In the second edition he hints a doubt whether the corresponding portion of the Nicomachean work was ever written, and in his third edition he seems decidedly to incline to the view that the Nicomachean work was left incomplete, and that the compiler of V. VI. VII., "not having before him any written exposition of this part of Aristotle's ethical system," "borrowed directly from other works of Aristotle's, such as the Politics and the Organon." At any rate, he thinks, "at the time when Aristotle wrote what were to be the concluding paragraphs of his treatise, he had not written the middle portion of the Nicomachean Ethics," and he "does not hesitate to pronounce a belief that the words 'as has before been said in the Ethics' in *Politics* II. ii. 4 and III. ix. 3" [which might seem to show that Aristotle had himself "by his own writing filled up the lacuna"] "are, in each case, the interpolated addition of either an editor or a copyist."

It will be convenient to examine first the evidence which Grant brings forward to prove that "Aristotle had not written the middle portion of the *Nic. Eth.*, at the time when he wrote what were to be the concluding paragraphs of his treatise." His argument is as follows:—

"That Aristotle, in summing up what he thought might be considered a complete ethical system, should have specified the leading topics of Books I.—IV. and VIII.—X. of his treatise, and should have omitted any mention of the subjects dealt with in Books V.—VII., seems a strong argument to prove that, at all events when he was writing Book X., he had not written the disputed middle books. Another argument in the same direction is, that while the three concluding books of the *Ethics* refer abundantly to Books I.—IV., they never make a single reference to Books V.—VII., though there was much opportunity for their doing so. For instance it seems peculiar that in all which is said about justice in Book VIII., there should be no allusion to the discussions of Book V., and that contemplation (θεωρία) should be treated of in Book X., without any recapitulation of what was said of the nature of Philosophic Wisdom (σοφία) in Book VI. That the treatise on Pleasure could have been written as it stands at the beginning of Book X., if Aristotle had previously written that other treatise on the same subject for what was to form Book VII. of the same work, is utterly impossible."

I proceed to consider these three arguments in their order.

Firstly, is it true that Aristotle "in summing up what he thought might be considered a complete ethical system omits any mention of the subjects dealt with in Books V.—VII."? The summary in question is to be found in x. 9 § 1: ἆρ' οὖν εἰ περὶ τούτων [sc. εὐδαιμονίας] καὶ τῶν ἀρετῶν, ἔτι δὲ καὶ φιλίας καὶ ἡδονῆς ἱκανῶς εἴρηται τοῖς τύποις, κ.τ.λ. Cf. also x. 6 § 1. Grant assumes that the phrase περὶ τῶν ἀρετῶν represents the subject-matter of II.—IV. to the exclusion of that of V. VI.; whereas it is obvious that the phrase includes the subject-matter of V. (περὶ δικαιοσύνης) and VI. (περὶ τῶν διανοητικῶν ἀρετῶν) as well as that of II.—IV. (περὶ τῶν ἄλλων ἀρετῶν). Thus Aristotle has not "omitted any mention of the subjects dealt with" in V. VI. In fact, if the Nicomachean equivalent of V. VI. had not been written, surely Aristotle would have avoided, instinctively or deliberately, the assertion that the virtues had been adequately treated. It is true that there is no mention of the subject of VII.: but the omission is not one which need surprise us. These summaries enumerate, not all the matters discussed in the treatise (else why is τὸ ἑκούσιον omitted?), but only so many of them as bear directly upon the subject of cc. 6—8, in which the ἀνθρώπινον ἀγαθόν is determined more precisely than was possible at the outset of the treatise. Now it is obvious that the theory of ἐγκράτεια and ἀκρασία, and that of ἡρωικὴ ἀρετή and θηριότης, are not directly connected with the subject of these chapters. Hence the silence of the two summaries is no proof that Aristotle had not written the equivalent of VII. I do indeed suspect, for reasons which I need not mention here, that Eudemus in the extant VII. treats this part of his subject at greater length than Aristotle had done, but this is a very different thing from saying that the corresponding Nicomachean book was never written. On the whole then the unqualified statement that 'the ἀρεταί have been adequately discussed' seems to me to indicate that Aristotle had already formulated his views about justice and the intellectual virtues: certainly it does not prove that he had not done so.

I pass on to speak of Grant's second argument. "The concluding books," he says, "never make a single reference to Books V.—VII." In particular he desiderates in VIII. some allusion to the theory of δικαιοσύνη, and in X. a recapitulation of what had been said about σοφία. But is he right in assuming that there are in VIII. IX. no allusions to the theory of justice? To say nothing of other passages in VIII. IX. which seem to show that Aristotle had made up his own mind about questions dealt with in V., such passages as *N. E.* VIII. 7 § 3 (οὐχ ὁμοίως δὲ τὸ ἴσον ἔν τε τοῖς δικαίοις καὶ ἐν τῇ φιλίᾳ φαίνεται ἔχειν· ἔστι γὰρ ἐν μὲν τοῖς δικαίοις ἴσον πρώτως τὸ κατ' ἀξίαν, τὸ δὲ κατὰ ποσὸν δευτέρως, κ.τ.λ.) and IX. I § I (ἐν πάσαις δὲ ταῖς ἀνομοιοειδέσι φιλίαις τὸ ἀνάλογον ἰσάζει καὶ σώζει τὴν φιλίαν, καθάπερ εἴρηται [sc. VIII. 13 § 1], οἷον καὶ ἐν τῇ πολιτικῇ τῷ σκυτοτόμῳ ἀντὶ τῶν ὑποδημάτων ἀμοιβὴ γίνεται κατ' ἀξίαν, καὶ τῷ ὑφάντῃ καὶ τοῖς λοιποῖς) seem to show, not only that he had elaborated the theory of commercial justice, but also that it was already familiar to the reader. Again in X. 7 § I we read—ἡ τούτου [sc. τοῦ ἀρίστου, εἴτε νοῦς τοῦτο εἴτε ἄλλο τι ὃ δὴ κατὰ φύσιν δοκεῖ ἄρχειν, κ.τ.λ.] ἐνέργεια κατὰ τὴν οἰκείαν ἀρετὴν εἴη ἂν ἡ τελεία εὐδαιμονία, ὅτι δ' ἐστὶ θεωρητική, εἴρηται. Nowhere in the acknowledged Nicomachean books has it been said that the ἐνέργεια of our noblest and best part is θεωρητική. Certainly not in I. 13 § 20 or I. 5 § 7, the passages quoted hesitatingly by Grant in his commentary, since I. 13 § 20 is a statement that some ἀρεταί are διανοητικαί, others ἠθικαί, whilst I. 5 § 7 is a purely anticipatory declaration, and anticipates, not the statement ὅτι ἡ τοῦ ἀρίστου ἐνέργεια κατὰ τὴν οἰκείαν ἀρετὴν θεωρητική ἐστιν, but the conclusion to which it leads us, that ἡ τελεία εὐδαιμονία is to be found in the θεωρητικὸς βίος. The reference then is to the missing books, and it is obvious that the remark in question would naturally occur in the investigation of the διανοητικαὶ ἀρεταί. If it is asked how it is that we find no such remark in the extant VI., the reason is not far to seek. With Eudemus it is not θεωρία, but καλοκαγαθία which is the centre of the system: hence in the investigation of the intellectual virtues he has no occasion to say that ἡ τοῦ ἀρίστου ἐνέργεια κατὰ τὴν οἰκείαν ἀρετὴν θεωρητική ἐστιν, whilst it would be strange indeed if the author of the *N. E.* had neglected the opportunity of making a remark which has so important a bearing upon his main argument. In fact x. 7 § 1 seems to me to prove that Aristotle had already written the middle books of the Nicomachean treatise, and at the same time to indicate that *N. E.* VI. = *E. E.* V. is not one of them.

Thirdly, Grant remarks that "the treatise on Pleasure could not have been written as it stands at the beginning of x., if Aristotle had previously written that other treatise on the same subject for what was to form Book VII. of the same work." This is of course perfectly true; it does not however prove that Aristotle had not written the middle portion of the *N. E.*, but only that *N. E.* VII. = *E. E.* VI. differs in some respects from the corresponding (lost) Nicomachean book[1].

If then Grant fails to prove that, when Aristotle wrote the concluding books, he had not written the middle portion of the

---

[1] In fact here, as in some other places, Grant seems to confound the two distinct questions, 'Had Aristotle, when he wrote *N. E.* x., already written the middle portion of the treatise?' and 'Had Aristotle, when he wrote *N. E.* x., already written *N. E.* V. VI. VII. = *E. E.* IV. V. VI.?'

treatise, the presumption is, in the absence of evidence to the contrary, that Aristotle completed his account of the moral virtues, and discussed the intellectual virtues, before he proceeded to treat of friendship in VIII. IX., and to sum up the results of the whole treatise in X. If the theory of the intellectual virtues had been unimportant, we might have imagined Aristotle deferring it to a more convenient moment: but as it is, it is the very keystone of the system. It is noticeable that Grant, who endeavours to explain how Aristotle came to defer the consideration of justice, does not attempt to show why he set aside the consideration of the intellectual virtues, a far more important matter.

Finally, Grant asks "Did Aristotle himself ever fill up by his own writing the lacuna which he had left in his Ethics?" and he would answer this question in the negative, on the grounds that "the remarks on Retaliation in the *Ethics* [v. v. 6] have all the appearance of being a development and improvement of those in the *Politics*" [II. ii. 4], and that *Nic. Eth.* v. iii. 4 "discusses the Law of Distribution in States (though a purely political question) with additional refinements beyond what we find in the *Politics.*" I am not prepared to allow that the doctrine of the passages cited from the *Ethics* is an advance upon that of the passages cited from the *Politics*: but even if it were so, Grant's point would not be proved; for, if, as he and I agree in supposing, V. VI. and VII. belong to the *E. E.*, the appearance in these books of refinements upon the doctrines of the *Politics* does not prove that their Nicomachean equivalents were never written, but only that the Eudemian treatise was written at a later date. Finally, it must not be forgotten that Grant by his own confession is obliged to suppose that at least two references to the *Ethics* have been interpolated in the *Politics*.

In brief, I hold with Munro that V. VI. and VII. were written by Eudemus, and are related to a lost portion of the Nicomachean treatise in precisely the same way in which the rest of the *E. E.* is related to the rest of the *N. E.*

ΗΘΙΚΩΝ ΝΙΚΟΜΑΧΕΙΩΝ Ε.

ΗΘΙΚΩΝ ΝΙΚΟΜΑΧΕΙΩΝ Ε.

1 Περὶ δὲ δικαιοσύνης καὶ ἀδικίας σκεπτέον, περὶ ποίας τε τυγχάνουσιν οὖσαι πράξεις, καὶ ποία μεσότης ἐστὶν
§ 2 ἡ δικαιοσύνη, καὶ τὸ δίκαιον τίνων μέσον· ἡ δὲ σκέψις ἡμῖν ἔστω κατὰ τὴν αὐτὴν μέθοδον τοῖς προειρημένοις.
§ 3 ὁρῶμεν δὴ πάντας τὴν τοιαύτην ἕξιν βουλομένους λέγειν δικαιοσύνην, ἀφ' ἧς πρακτικοὶ τῶν δικαίων εἰσὶ καὶ ἀφ' ἧς δικαιοπραγοῦσι καὶ βούλονται τὰ δίκαια· τὸν αὐτὸν δὲ τρόπον καὶ περὶ ἀδικίας, ἀφ' ἧς ἀδικοῦσι καὶ βούλονται τὰ ἄδικα. διὸ καὶ ἡμῖν πρῶτον ὡς ἐν
9 § 14 τύπῳ ὑποκείσθω ταῦτα. < οἱ δ' ἄνθρωποι ἐφ' ἑαυτοῖς οἴονται εἶναι τὸ ἀδικεῖν, διὸ καὶ τὸ δίκαιον εἶναι ῥᾴδιον. τὸ δ' οὐκ ἔστιν· συγγενέσθαι μὲν γὰρ τῇ τοῦ γείτονος καὶ πατάξαι τὸν πλησίον καὶ δοῦναι τῇ χειρὶ τὸ ἀργύριον ῥᾴδιον καὶ ἐπ' αὐτοῖς, ἀλλὰ τὸ ὡδὶ ἔχοντας ταῦτα ποιεῖν
9 § 15 οὔτε ῥᾴδιον οὔτ' ἐπ' αὐτοῖς. ὁμοίως δὲ καὶ τὸ γνῶναι τὰ δίκαια καὶ τὰ ἄδικα οὐδὲν οἴονται σοφὸν εἶναι, ὅτι περὶ ὧν οἱ νόμοι λέγουσιν οὐ χαλεπὸν συνιέναι. ἀλλ' οὐ ταῦτ' ἐστὶ τὰ δίκαια ἀλλ' ἢ κατὰ συμβεβηκός, ἀλλὰ πῶς πραττόμενα καὶ πῶς νεμόμενα δίκαια· τοῦτο δὲ πλέον ἔργον ἢ τὰ ὑγιεινὰ εἰδέναι, ἐπεὶ κἀκεῖ μέλι καὶ οἶνον

---

2 τε] om. K^b. ποία] ποῖα H^a. 4 ἔστω] ἐστὶν M^{b}Q. 6 ἀφ' ἧς πρακτικοί —ἀδικίας] om. Q. 8 τὸν—ἄδικα] om. K^b. 10 οἱ δ'—ὡδί.] 9 §§ 14—16 traieci. ἄνθρωποι] ἄνθρωπι M^b. ἄνθρωποι δὲ H^a. 11 τὸ δίκαιον] om. M^{b}Q. 12 τὸ] τοῦτο O^b. 13 πατάξαι] πειτάξαι Q. 14 ῥᾴδιον] ῥᾶον O^b. ῥᾳδίως Q. ὡδί] ὡς δεῖ pr. O^{b}P^h. ταῦτα] ταὐτὸ K^b. 19 νεμόμενα] γενόμενα H^{a}K^{b}M^{b}Q. διανεμόμενα O^b. δίκαια] om. M^{b}Q. πλέον] πλεῖον O^b. 20 μέλι] μὲν K^b. οἶνον] οἶνος Q.

[NICOMACHEAN] ETHICS V.

In regard to δικαιοσύνη and ἀδικία we have to inquire (1) what sort of actions they are concerned with, (2) in what sense δικαιοσύνη is a μεσότης, and (3) what the extremes are between which τὸ δίκαιον lies: and our inquiry shall be conducted in the same way as our previous investigations.

Now [firstly] we see that all men understand by δικαιοσύνη the ἕξις which makes men πρακτικοὶ τῶν δικαίων,—that is to say which makes them δικαιοπραγεῖν καὶ βούλεσθαι τὰ δίκαια; and in the same way by ἀδικία, the ἕξις which makes men ἀδικεῖν καὶ βούλεσθαι τὰ ἄδικα. Wherefore we may ourselves begin by assuming this to be roughly true. [Secondly] men conceive that τὸ ἀδικεῖν rests with themselves, and therefore that to be δίκαιος is easy: but this is not the case; for though it is easy and rests with ourselves to lie with another's wife, to strike our neighbour, and to give away our money, it is not easy nor does it rest with ourselves to do these things in a given ἕξις. [Thirdly] men assume in like manner that it requires no special wisdom to discriminate things δίκαια and things ἄδικα, because it is not difficult to apprehend such matters as are provided for by the laws: but it is only κατὰ συμβεβηκός that actions prescribed by law are identical with τὰ δίκαια; to be δίκαια, actions must be done and distributions must be made in a particular manner, and the knowledge required thereto is more difficult of attainment than the knowledge of what is salutary; whilst even in matters of health, though it is easy to know what honey, wine, hellebore, the

καὶ ἐλλέβορον καὶ καῦσιν καὶ τομὴν εἰδέναι ῥᾴδιον, ἀλλὰ πῶς δεῖ νεῖμαι πρὸς ὑγίειαν καὶ τίνι καὶ πότε, τοσοῦτον ἔργον ὅσον ἰατρὸν εἶναι. διʼ αὐτὸ δὲ τοῦτο καὶ τοῦ δικαίου οἴονται εἶναι οὐθὲν ἧττον τὸ ἀδικεῖν, ὅτι οὐθὲν ἧττον ὁ δίκαιος ἀλλὰ καὶ μᾶλλον δύναιτʼ ἂν ἕκαστον πρᾶξαι τούτων, καὶ γὰρ συγγενέσθαι γυναικὶ καὶ πατάξαι, καὶ ὁ ἀνδρεῖος τὴν ἀσπίδα ἀφεῖναι καὶ στραφεὶς ἐφʼ ὁποτεραοῦν τρέχειν. ἀλλὰ τὸ δειλαίνειν καὶ τὸ ἀδικεῖν οὐ τὸ ταῦτα ποιεῖν ἐστί, πλὴν κατὰ συμβεβηκός, ἀλλὰ τὸ ὡδὶ ἔχοντα ταῦτα ποιεῖν, ὥσπερ καὶ τὸ ἰατρεύειν καὶ τὸ ὑγιάζειν οὐ τὸ τέμνειν ἢ μὴ τέμνειν ἢ φαρμακεύειν ἢ μὴ φαρμακεύειν ἐστίν, ἀλλὰ τὸ ὡδί. > οὐδὲ γὰρ τὸν αὐτὸν ἔχει τρόπον ἐπί τε τῶν ἐπιστημῶν καὶ δυνάμεων καὶ ἐπὶ τῶν ἕξεων· δύναμις μὲν γὰρ καὶ ἐπιστήμη δοκεῖ τῶν ἐναντίων ἡ αὐτὴ εἶναι, ἕξις δʼ ἡ ἐναντία τῶν ἐναντίων οὔ· οἷον τῆς ὑγιείας οὐ πράττεται τὰ ἐναντία, ἀλλὰ τὰ ὑγιεινὰ μόνον· λέγομεν γὰρ ὑγιεινῶς βαδίζειν, ὅταν βαδίζῃ ὡς ἂν ὁ ὑγιαίνων. πολλάκις μὲν οὖν γνωρίζεται ἡ ἐναντία ἕξις ἀπὸ τῆς ἐναντίας, πολλάκις δὲ αἱ ἕξεις ἀπὸ τῶν ὑποκειμένων· ἐάν τε γὰρ ἡ εὐεξία ᾖ φανερά, καὶ ἡ καχεξία φανερὰ γίνεται, καὶ ἐκ τῶν εὐεκτικῶν ἡ εὐεξία καὶ ἐκ ταύτης τὰ εὐεκτικά· εἰ γάρ ἐστιν ἡ εὐεξία πυκνότης σαρκός, ἀνάγκη καὶ τὴν καχεξίαν εἶναι μανότητα σαρκὸς καὶ τὸ εὐεκτικὸν τὸ ποιητικὸν πυκνότητος ἐν σαρκί. ἀκολουθεῖ δʼ ὡς ἐπὶ τὸ πολύ, ἐὰν θάτερα πλεοναχῶς λέγηται, καὶ θάτερα πλεο-

---

1 ἐλλέβορον] ἐλέβορον HᵃKᵇLᵇMᵇQOᵇ.   2 νεῖμαι] εἶναι Kᵇ.   ὑγίειαν] ὑγείαν Hᵃ.   πότε] πότερον Hᵃ.   3 ἰατρόν] ἰατροῦ Kᵇ.   δι' αὐτό] διὰ ταὐτὸ Kᵇ.   4 ὅτι οὐθέν] ὅτι οὐχ KᵇPᵇ.   8 τὸ post καί] om. KᵇLᵇPᵇ.   10 ὡδί] ὧδε KᵇPᵇ.   ποιεῖν] om. MᵇQ.   11 ἢ μὴ τέμνειν] om. Nᵇ.   ἢ μὴ φαρμακεύειν] om. Oᵇ.   12 οὐδέ] οὔτε Kᵇ.   οὐ MᵇQ.   15 ἐναντία] αὐτὴ Hᵃ.   οὔ] δ' οὔ Pᵇ.   16 ἀπὸ—πράττεται] ἡ αὐτὴ εἶναι MᵇQ.   ἀπό] ὑπὸ Pᵇ.   17 ὑγιεινῶς] τὸ ὑγιεινῶς MᵇQ.   ὁ] om. MᵇQ.   20 εὐεξία] εὐξία Oᵇ.   εὐδοξία Q.   21 εὐεξία] εὐξία Oᵇ.   καὶ—εὐεκτικά] om. MᵇQ.   εὐεκτικῶν] εὐεκτικῶν εὐεκτικῶν Lᵇ.   23 εἶναι μανότητα σαρκός] μανότητα σαρκὸς εἶναι Mᵇ.   24 τὸ ante ποιητικόν] om. HᵃMᵇQ.   25 θάτερα] θάτερον Hᵃ.   θάτερα] θάτερον Hᵃ.

cautery, and the use of the knife are, to know how, for whom, and when, we should apply them with a view to health is no less an undertaking than it is to be a physician. [Fourthly] on the principle stated above, men assume that the δίκαιος can ἀδικεῖν as easily as δικαιοπραγεῖν, because he can do any particular ἄδικον as easily as any particular δίκαιον, if not more easily,—for example, lie with a woman, or strike a blow,—and the brave man can let go his shield and take to flight in this direction or in that: but δειλαίνειν and ἀδικεῖν consist, not in doing these things (except κατὰ συμβεβηκός), but in doing these things in a particular ἕξις, just as the practice of medicine or healing consists, not in using or not using the knife, in exhibiting or not exhibiting medicines, but in adopting either course on particular [i.e. scientific] grounds. The fact is that sciences and faculties differ from ἕξεις: for a faculty or a science is admitted to be the same for contraries, but one of two contrary ἕξεις does not deal with the matter of the other: for example, unhealthy things cannot be done with a healthy ἕξις, but only healthy things, for we say a man walks healthily, when he walks as a healthy man would.

Hence [as a faculty or a science is the same for contraries, though a ἕξις is not,] sometimes one of two contrary ἕξεις is known from the other, and sometimes the ἕξεις are known from things which are appropriate to them: for example, if we know what good condition of body is, we hence know also what bad condition of body is, and from things appropriate to good condition we know what good condition is, and from good condition, what are things appropriate to it; thus if good condition is firmness of flesh, bad condition must be flabbiness of flesh, and that which is appropriate to good condition that which produces firmness in flesh. And it follows in general that if one of the correlatives is used in several senses, the other is used in several senses

ναχῶς λέγεσθαι, οἷον εἰ τὸ δίκαιον, καὶ τὸ ἄδικον καὶ ἡ
§ 7 ἀδικία. ἔοικε δὲ πλεοναχῶς λέγεσθαι ἡ δικαιοσύνη καὶ ἡ
ἀδικία, ἀλλὰ διὰ τὸ σύνεγγυς εἶναι τὴν ὁμωνυμίαν αὐτῶν
λανθάνει καὶ οὐχ ὥσπερ ἐπὶ τῶν πόρρω δήλη μᾶλλον·
ἡ γὰρ διαφορὰ πολλὴ ἡ κατὰ τὴν ἰδέαν, οἷον ὅτι καλεῖται 5
κλεὶς ὁμωνύμως ἥ τε ὑπὸ τὸν αὐχένα τῶν ζῴων καὶ ᾗ τὰς
§ 8 θύρας κλείουσιν. εἰλήφθω δὴ ὁ ἄδικος ποσαχῶς λέγεται.
δοκεῖ δὲ ὅ τε παράνομος ἄδικος εἶναι καὶ ὁ πλεονέκτης
[καὶ ὁ ἄνισος]. ὥστε δῆλον ὅτι καὶ ὁ δίκαιος ἔσται ὅ τε
νόμιμος καὶ ὁ ἴσος. τὸ μὲν δίκαιον ἄρα τὸ νόμιμον καὶ τὸ 10
ἴσον, τὸ δ' ἄδικον τὸ παράνομον καὶ τὸ ἄνισον.
§ 9 ἐπεὶ δὲ καὶ πλεονέκτης ὁ ἄδικος, περὶ τἀγαθὰ ἔσται, οὐ
πάντα, ἀλλὰ περὶ ὅσα εὐτυχία καὶ ἀτυχία, ἃ ἐστὶ μὲν
ἁπλῶς ἀεὶ ἀγαθά, τινὶ δ' οὐκ ἀεί· (οἱ δ' ἄνθρωποι ταῦτα
εὔχονται καὶ διώκουσιν· δεῖ δ' οὔ, ἀλλ' εὔχεσθαι μὲν τὰ 15
ἁπλῶς ἀγαθὰ καὶ αὑτοῖς ἀγαθὰ εἶναι, αἱρεῖσθαι δὲ τὰ
9 § 17 αὑτοῖς ἀγαθά·) < ἔστι δὲ τὰ δίκαια ἐν τούτοις οἷς μέτεστι
τῶν ἁπλῶς ἀγαθῶν, ἔχουσι δ' ὑπερβολὴν καὶ ἔλλειψιν·
τοῖς μὲν γὰρ οὐκ ἔστιν ὑπερβολὴ αὐτῶν, οἷον ἴσως τοῖς
θεοῖς, τοῖς δ' οὐθὲν μόριον ὠφέλιμον, τοῖς ἀνιάτως κακοῖς, 20
ἀλλὰ πάντα βλάπτει, τοῖς δὲ μέχρι του· διὰ τοῦτ' ἀνθρώ-
1 § 10 πινόν ἐστιν. > ὁ δ' ἄδικος οὐκ ἀεὶ τὸ πλέον αἱρεῖται,
ἀλλὰ καὶ τὸ ἔλαττον ἐπὶ τῶν ἁπλῶς κακῶν· ἀλλ' ὅτι δοκεῖ

---

1 εἰ] εἰ καὶ Hᵃ.   δίκαιον καὶ τὸ ἄδικον καὶ ἡ ἀδικία] Lᵇ.   ἄδικον καὶ ἡ ἀδικία
KᵇPᵇ.   δίκαιον καὶ τὸ ἄδικον HᵃMᵇQNᵇOᵇ Bekker.   2 δικαιοσύνη καὶ ἡ ἀδικία]
δικαιοσύνη καὶ ἀδικία Pᵇ.   ἀδικία καὶ ἡ δικαιοσύνη MᵇQ.   3 σύνεγγυς] σύν-
εγκυς Nᵇ.   4 λανθάνει] λανθάνειν MᵇQ.   5 ἡ ante κατὰ] om. Lᵇ.
6 κλεὶς] κλεῖς KᵇLᵇ.   ὁμωνύμως] ὁμώνυμος Kᵇ.   8 δὲ] τε Oᵇ.
9 ὁ ἄνισος] ἄδικος Kᵇ.   10 ὁ ante ἴσος] om. Kᵇ.   μὲν] om. Lᵇ.
11 δ'] om. Kᵇ.   12 δὲ] γὰρ HᵃNᵇ.   καὶ] om. KᵇMᵇQᵇPᵇ.   περὶ]
καὶ περὶ Pᵇ.   τἀγαθὰ] τἀγαθὰ δὲ Hᵃ.   ἔσται, οὐ πάντα] οὐ πάντα
ἔσται Pᵇ.   οὐ πάντα (omisso ἔσται) Kᵇ.   13 εὐτυχία καὶ ἀτυχία] εὐτυχίαι καὶ
ἀτυχίαι Lᵇ.   17 ἐστι—ἐστιν] 9 § 17 traieci.   18 ἁπλῶς] ἁπλῶν Hᵃ.
δ' post ἔχουσι] δὲ καὶ HᵃMᵇQNᵇPᵇ.   καὶ ἔλλειψιν] ἐν τούτοις καὶ ἔλλειψιν
HᵃMᵇQNᵇPᵇ Bekker.   καὶ ἔλλειψιν ἐν τούτοις Oᵇ.   19 οὐκ] om. Kᵇ.   τοῖς
ante θεοῖς] om. HᵃMᵇQ.   20 ὠφέλιμον] ὠφέλιμον οἷον HᵃMᵇQ.   ἀνιάτως]
Kᵇ. ἀνιάτοις Hᵃ.   ἀνιάτοις καὶ LᵇMᵇQNᵇOᵇPᵇ.   21 πάντα βλάπτει] βλάπτει
πάντα Oᵇ.   23 ἀλλὰ] om. MᵇQ.   ἁπλῶς] ἁπλῶν Hᵃ.

also: for example, if τὸ δίκαιον, then also τὸ ἄδικον and ἡ ἀδικία. Now it appears that the terms δικαιοσύνη and ἀδικία are used in several senses, but their equivocation escapes detection in consequence of the close connection of their equivocal uses, whereas in the case of things widely different equivocation is comparatively obvious: thus the difference is considerable if it is one of shape; for example, the equivocal use of the word κλείς for the bone beneath the neck in animals and for the instrument with which we lock our doors. We have then to ascertain in how many senses we speak of ὁ ἄδικος. Now it is generally assumed that the term ἄδικος is applicable both to the violator of law (παράνομος) and to the grasping man (πλεονέκτης). Hence it is plain that the term δίκαιος will apply both to the law-fearing man (νόμιμος) and to the equal man (ἴσος). Τὸ δίκαιον then includes τὸ νόμιμον and τὸ ἴσον, and τὸ ἄδικον, τὸ παράνομον and τὸ ἄνισον.

And since the ἄδικος may be πλεονέκτης, he will be so in respect of goods; not all goods, but those on which good fortune and bad fortune depend, which goods, though always good ἁπλῶς, are not always so τινί;—([not seeing this] men pray for these goods and seek them; whereas they should rather pray that τὰ ἁπλῶς ἀγαθά may be good for them, and choose those things which are good for them:)—and δίκαια of this sort subsist among those who participate in τὰ ἁπλῶς ἀγαθά and can have too much or too little of them: for there are those who cannot have too much of them, (I mean of course the gods,) and those, (that is to say the incurably bad,) who cannot derive benefit from any share [however small], all goods being harmful to them, and again those to whom such goods are beneficial within limits: wherefore the sphere of τὸ δίκαιον is human society. But the ἄδικος does not always choose the larger share; in the case of τὰ ἁπλῶς κακά he chooses the less: nevertheless

καὶ τὸ μεῖον κακὸν ἀγαθόν πως εἶναι, τοῦ δ' ἀγαθοῦ ἐστὶν ἡ πλεονεξία, διὰ τοῦτο δοκεῖ πλεονέκτης εἶναι. ἔστι δ' ἄνισος· τοῦτο γὰρ περιέχει καὶ κοινόν. καὶ παράνομος· τοῦτο γὰρ [ἡ παρανομία ἤτοι ἡ ἀνισότης] περιέχει πᾶσαν ἀδικίαν καὶ κοινόν ἐστι πάσης ἀδικίας. ἐπεὶ δ' ὁ παράνομος ἄδικος ἦν ὁ δὲ νόμιμος δίκαιος, δῆλον ὅτι πάντα τὰ νόμιμά ἐστί πως δίκαια· τά τε γὰρ ὡρισμένα ὑπὸ τῆς νομοθετικῆς νόμιμά ἐστι, καὶ ἕκαστον τούτων δίκαιον εἶναί φαμεν. οἱ δὲ νόμοι ἀγορεύουσι περὶ ἁπάντων, στοχαζόμενοι ἢ τοῦ κοινῇ συμφέροντος πᾶσιν, [ἢ τοῖς ἀρίστοις] ἢ τοῖς κυρίοις ἢ κατ' ἀρετὴν ἢ κατ' ἄλλον τινὰ τρόπον τοιοῦτον. ὥστε ἕνα μὲν τρόπον δίκαια λέγομεν τὰ ποιητικὰ καὶ φυλακτικὰ εὐδαιμονίας καὶ τῶν μορίων αὐτῆς τῇ πολιτικῇ κοινωνίᾳ· προστάττει δ' ὁ νόμος καὶ τὰ τοῦ ἀνδρείου ἔργα ποιεῖν, οἷον μὴ λείπειν τὴν τάξιν μηδὲ φεύγειν μηδὲ ῥίπτειν τὰ ὅπλα, καὶ τὰ τοῦ σώφρονος, οἷον μὴ μοιχεύειν μηδ' ὑβρίζειν, καὶ τὰ τοῦ πράου, οἷον μὴ τύπτειν μηδὲ κακηγορεῖν, ὁμοίως δὲ καὶ τὰ κατὰ τὰς ἄλλας ἀρετὰς καὶ μοχθηρίας, τὰ μὲν κελεύων τὰ δ' ἀπαγορεύων, ὀρθῶς μὲν ὁ κείμενος ὀρθῶς, χεῖρον δ' ὁ ἀπεσχεδιασμένος. αὕτη μὲν οὖν ἡ δικαιοσύνη ἀρετὴ μέν ἐστι τελεία, ἀλλ' οὐχ ἁπλῶς ἀλλὰ πρὸς ἕτερον. καὶ διὰ τοῦτο πολλάκις κρατίστη τῶν ἀρετῶν εἶναι δοκεῖ ἡ δικαιοσύνη, καὶ οὔθ' ἕσπερος οὔθ' ἑῷος οὕτω θαυμαστός· καὶ παροιμιαζόμενοί φαμεν

---

1 μεῖον] μὴ K^{b}P^{b}L^b.   τοῦ—εἶναι] om. L^b.   ἐστὶν] om. O^b.   2 πλεονεξία] πλεονξία O^b.   3 καὶ παράνομος—ἀδικίας] om. K^b *Bekker*.   παράνομος] παράνομον H^a.   4 ἡ post ἤτοι] om. M^{b}QO^b.   7 πάντα τὰ νόμιμα] τὰ νόμιμα πάντα H^a.   πάντα νόμιμα (omisso τὰ) N^b.   ἐστί] ἔσται M^{b}Q.   τά τε] ταῦτα M^{b}Q.   11 ἢ ante κατ' ἀρετὴν] om. K^{b}L^b *Bekker*.   κατ' ἀρετὴν] om. K^b.   13 δίκαια] δίκαια μὲν Q.   14 εὐδαιμονίας] τῆς εὐδαιμονίας O^b *Bekker*.   16 λείπειν] λιπεῖν K^{b}L^{b}M^{b}QP^b.   17 τὰ τοῦ σώφρονος] ἃ τοῦ σώφρονος H^a.   19 κακηγορεῖν] κατηγορεῖν M^{b}QO^b.   καὶ τὰ κατὰ] L^b.   καὶ τὰ N^b.   καὶ κατὰ H^{a}K^{b}M^{b}QO^{b}P^b *Bekker*.   ἄλλας] om. P^b.   20 ὀρθῶς ante μὲν] ὀρθὸς M^{b}Q.   21 χεῖρον] χείρων L^{b}M^{b}Q.   αὕτη] ταύτῃ K^{b}P^b.   23 ἀλλὰ post ἁπλῶς] suprascr. L^b.   25 ἑῷος] ἕως N^b.   οὕτω θαυμαστός] οὔτε θαυμαστόν N^b.   καὶ] διὸ καὶ L^{b}M^{b}Q.   παροιμιαζόμενοι] παροιμιαζόμενοι N^b.

because the lesser evil is admitted to be in a manner a good, and πλεονεξία is concerned with what is good, the ἄδικος who so acts is therefore thought to be πλεονέκτης. And he is ἄνισος; for this is a comprehensive term which includes πλεονεξία. Further he is παράνομος; for this is a term which includes all ἀδικία and applies to it without exception.

And since the παράνομος is, as we have said, ἄδικος, and the νόμιμος, δίκαιος, it is plain that all νόμιμα are in a sense δίκαια; for νόμιμα are the determinations of νομοθετική, and we acknowledge that each of the determinations of νομοθετική is δίκαιον. Now the laws pronounce upon all subjects, endeavouring to hit either that which is for the common interest of all, or that which is for the interest of the governing class whether its position is determined by merit or in some other similar way. Hence in one sense we call things δίκαια which produce and secure happiness or the parts of happiness for the political community. But the law also enjoins conduct characteristic of the brave man,—for example, not to desert one's post, not to run away, not to throw away one's arms,—conduct characteristic of the temperate man,—for example, not to commit adultery, not to assault with violence,—conduct characteristic of the gentle man,—for example, not to strike, not to speak evil,—and similarly with the other virtues and vices, enjoining some things and forbidding others, the rightly established law doing this rightly, and the extemporized law with less propriety.

Hence this sort of δικαιοσύνη is perfect virtue, yet perfect virtue not ἁπλῶς but in relation to one's neighbour. And for this reason δικαιοσύνη is often thought to be the best of the virtues; neither the evening nor the morning star, it is thought, is so wonderful: indeed we use the proverb,

ἐν δὲ δικαιοσύνῃ συλλήβδην πᾶσ' ἀρετὴ ἔνι. <τελεία δ' ἐστὶν> ἀρετὴ ὅτι τῆς τελείας ἀρετῆς χρῆσίς ἐστι, <καὶ τελεία μάλιστα> ὅτι ὁ ἔχων αὐτὴν καὶ πρὸς ἕτερον δύναται τῇ ἀρετῇ χρῆσθαι, ἀλλ' οὐ μόνον καθ' αὑτόν· πολλοὶ γὰρ ἐν μὲν τοῖς οἰκείοις τῇ ἀρετῇ δύνανται
§ 16 χρῆσθαι, ἐν δὲ τοῖς πρὸς ἕτερον ἀδυνατοῦσιν. καὶ διὰ τοῦτο εὖ δοκεῖ ἔχειν τὸ τοῦ Βίαντος, ὅτι ἀρχὴ ἄνδρα δείξει·
§ 17 πρὸς ἕτερον γὰρ καὶ ἐν κοινωνίᾳ ἤδη ὁ ἄρχων. διὰ δὲ τὸ αὐτὸ τοῦτο καὶ ἀλλότριον ἀγαθὸν δοκεῖ εἶναι ἡ δικαιοσύνη μόνη τῶν ἀρετῶν, ὅτι πρὸς ἕτερόν ἐστιν· ἄλλῳ γὰρ τὰ
§ 18 συμφέροντα πράττει, ἢ ἄρχοντι ἢ κοινωνῷ. κάκιστος μὲν οὖν ὁ καὶ πρὸς αὑτὸν καὶ πρὸς τοὺς φίλους χρώμενος τῇ μοχθηρίᾳ, ἄριστος δ' οὐχ ὁ πρὸς αὑτὸν τῇ ἀρετῇ ἀλλ' ὁ
§ 19 πρὸς ἕτερον· τοῦτο γὰρ ἔργον χαλεπόν. αὕτη μὲν οὖν ἡ δικαιοσύνη οὐ μέρος ἀρετῆς ἀλλ' ὅλη ἀρετή ἐστιν, οὐδ' ἡ
§ 20 ἐναντία ἀδικία μέρος κακίας ἀλλ' ὅλη κακία. τί δὲ διαφέρει ἡ ἀρετὴ καὶ ἡ δικαιοσύνη αὕτη, δῆλον ἐκ τῶν εἰρημένων· ἔστι μὲν γὰρ ἡ αὐτή, τὸ δ' εἶναι οὐ τὸ αὐτό, ἀλλ' ᾗ μὲν πρὸς ἕτερον, δικαιοσύνη, ᾗ δὲ τοιάδε ἕξις ἁπλῶς, ἀρετή.

2 ζητοῦμεν δέ γε τὴν ἐν μέρει ἀρετῆς δικαιοσύνην· ἔστι γάρ τις, ὥς φαμεν. ὁμοίως δὲ καὶ περὶ ἀδικίας τῆς κατὰ
§ 2 μέρος. σημεῖον δ' ὅτι ἔστιν· κατὰ μὲν γὰρ τὰς ἄλλας μοχθηρίας ὁ ἐνεργῶν ἀδικεῖ μέν, πλεονεκτεῖ δ' οὐδέν, οἷον

'and in δικαιοσύνη all virtue is contained comprehensively.' And it is perfect virtue because it is the practice of perfect virtue—and perfect in a special sense because he who possesses it can practise his virtue towards another and not merely in himself: for there are many who can practise their virtue in their personal affairs, but are unable to do so in their relations to another. And for this reason the saying of Bias is generally approved, that 'office will show a man,' because the officer is ex hypothesi in relation to others and a member of a community. And it is for this same reason too, viz. because it implies relations with another, that δικαιοσύνη alone of the virtues is thought to be the good of others, as it does what is to the advantage of another, that other being either a ruler or an associate. Hence the worst man is one who practises his vice in relation to himself and in relation to his friends and not merely in relation to his neighbour, and the best is not one who practises his virtue in relation to himself but one who practises it in relation to another: for this is a work of difficulty. This sort of δικαιοσύνη then is not a part of virtue but universal virtue, and the contrary ἀδικία is not a part of vice but universal vice. How virtue and this sort of δικαιοσύνη differ, is plain from what has been said: for though they are the same, their εἶναι is not the same, the ἕξις viewed in relation to another being δικαιοσύνη, but viewed ἁπλῶς as a certain ἕξις, virtue.

What we have to investigate is the δικαιοσύνη which is a part of virtue;—that there is such a δικαιοσύνη, we assume;—and in like manner particular ἀδικία. Of the existence of particular ἀδικία, we have the following evidence: one who exhibits the other vices in action ἀδικεῖ μὲν πλεονεκτεῖ δ' οὐδέν; for example, one who throws away his shield ὁ ῥίψας τὴν ἀσπίδα διὰ δειλίαν ἢ κακῶς εἰπὼν διὰ χαλεπότητα ἢ οὐ βοηθήσας χρήμασι δι' ἀνελευθερίαν· ὅταν δὲ πλεονεκτῇ, πολλάκις κατ' οὐδεμίαν τῶν τοιούτων, ἀλλὰ μὴν οὐδὲ κατὰ πάσας, κατὰ πονηρίαν δέ γε τινά (ψέγομεν γὰρ) § 3 καὶ κατ' ἀδικίαν. ἔστιν ἄρα γε ἄλλη τις ἀδικία ὡς μέρος τῆς ὅλης, καὶ ἄδικόν τι ἐν μέρει τοῦ ὅλου ἀδίκου τοῦ παρὰ § 4 τὸν νόμον. ἔτι εἰ ὁ μὲν τοῦ κερδαίνειν ἕνεκα μοιχεύει καὶ προσλαμβάνων, ὁ δὲ προστιθεὶς καὶ ζημιούμενος δι' ἐπιθυμίαν, οὗτος μὲν ἀκόλαστος δόξειεν ἂν εἶναι μᾶλλον ἢ πλεονέκτης, ἐκεῖνος δ' ἄδικος, ἀκόλαστος δ' οὔ· δῆλον ἄρα § 5 ὅτι διὰ τὸ κερδαίνειν. ἔτι περὶ μὲν τἆλλα πάντα ἀδικήματα γίνεται ἡ ἐπαναφορὰ ἐπί τινα μοχθηρίαν ἀεί, οἷον εἰ ἐμοίχευσεν, ἐπ' ἀκολασίαν, εἰ ἐγκατέλιπε τὸν παραστάτην, ἐπὶ δειλίαν, εἰ ἐπάταξεν, ἐπ' ὀργήν· εἰ δ' ἐκέρδανεν, ἐπ' § 6 οὐδεμίαν μοχθηρίαν ἀλλ' ἢ ἐπ' ἀδικίαν. ὥστε φανερὸν ὅτι ἔστι τις ἀδικία παρὰ τὴν ὅλην ἄλλη ἐν μέρει, συνώνυμος, ὅτι ὁ ὁρισμὸς ἐν τῷ αὐτῷ γένει, ἄμφω γὰρ ἐν τῷ πρὸς ἕτερον ἔχουσι τὴν δύναμιν, ἀλλ' ἡ μὲν περὶ τιμὴν ἢ χρήματα ἢ σωτηρίαν ἢ εἴ τινι ἔχοιμεν ἑνὶ ὀνόματι περιλαβεῖν ταῦτα πάντα, καὶ δι' ἡδονὴν τὴν ἀπὸ τοῦ κέρδους, ἡ δὲ περὶ ἅπαντα περὶ ὅσα ὁ σπουδαῖος.

§ 7 ὅτι μὲν οὖν εἰσὶ δικαιοσύναι πλείους, καὶ ὅτι ἔστι τις καὶ ἑτέρα παρὰ τὴν ὅλην ἀρετήν, δῆλον· τίς δὲ καὶ ποία τις, § 8 ληπτέον. διώρισται δὴ τὸ ἄδικον τό τε παράνομον καὶ τὸ

1 ὁ ante ῥίψας] om. M^bQ. ἢ κακῶς] ἢ ὁ κακῶς H^aN^bP^b. 3 ἀλλὰ μὴν οὐδὲ] ἀλλὰ μὴν ἀλλ' οὐδὲ M^bQ. 4 ψέγομεν γάρ] om. H^a. ψεγομένην M^bQ. 5 ἀδικίαν] ἀδικίαν ψεγόμενος H^a. ἄρα γε] ἄρα γε P^b. ἀρά γε N^b. ἄρα (omisso γε) O^b. γὰρ K^b. ἄλλη τις] τις ἄλλη M^bQO^b. μέρος] μέρος τι L^bM^bQN^bO^bP^b. 7 ἔτι] ὅτι K^b. ἔτι δὲ O^b. μοιχεύει] μοιχεύοι N^b. 8 προσλαμβάνων] K^b. προσλαμβάνει H^aL^bM^bQ. προσλαμβάνοι N^bO^bP^b. 9 δόξειεν ἂν εἶναι μᾶλλον] δόξειεν ἂν μᾶλλον εἶναι O^b. μᾶλλον δόξειεν εἶναι P^b. μᾶλλον δόξει εἶναι K^b. 13 ἐγκατέλιπε] ἐγκατέλειπε M^b. ἐγκατέλοιπε P^b. 14 ἐπάταξεν] δ' ἐπάταξεν H^aK^bL^bN^bO^bQ. 17 ὁ] om. M^bQ. 18 ἢ χρήματα] ἢ καὶ χρήματα L^bM^bQ. καὶ χρήματα O^b. 19 ἢ σωτηρίαν] καὶ σωτηρίαν M^bQ. 20 τοῦ] om. O^b. 21 περὶ ἅπαντα] περὶ πάντα K^bP^b. om. M^bQ. 22 δικαιοσύναι] αἱ δικαιοσύναι K^bP^b. ἔστι om. O^b. 23 καὶ ante ἑτέρα] om. O^b. τίς] om. H^a. ποία] ποῖα Q. ὁποῖα H^a. ὁποιά N^b. ὁποία Bekker. 24 δὴ] δὲ H^aK^bM^bQ. τε] om. M^bQ.

through cowardice, or speaks evil through illnature, or refuses pecuniary aid through illiberality; but when a man πλεονεκτῇ, it often happens that he exhibits none of these, certainly not all, but yet a sort of vice, (for we censure him,) which vice is called ἀδικία. Hence there is besides universal ἀδικία another sort of ἀδικία which is a part of universal ἀδικία, and an ἄδικον which is a part of the universal ἄδικον which consists in the violation of law. Further if one man commits adultery with a view to gain and earns money by it, and another from desire at his own cost and to his own loss, the latter would appear to be intemperate rather than πλεονέκτης, the former ἄδικος but not intemperate: thus it is plain that gain is the motive of particular ἀδικία. Again in the case of all other ἀδικήματα there is always the further reference to some particular depravity; for example, if a man commits adultery, to intemperance, if he abandons his comrade, to cowardice, if he strikes another, to anger, but if a man derives gain unjustly, to no particular depravity besides ἀδικία. Hence it is plain that besides universal ἀδικία there is another sort of ἀδικία which is particular, συνώνυμος with the former because the definition has the same genus, both being occupied with a man's relations to his neighbour, but whereas the one is concerned with honour or property or safety or that, by whatever name we may call it, which comprehends all these, and is actuated by the pleasure derived from gain, the other is concerned with everything with which the virtuous man is concerned.

Thus it is plain that there are more kinds of δικαιοσύνη than one, and that there is another kind of δικαιοσύνη besides the universal virtue so called: we must now ascertain the genus and the differentia of particular δικαιοσύνη.

Now two kinds of ἄδικον have been distinguished, viz. τὸ παράνομον and τὸ ἄνισον, and two kinds of δίκαιον, viz. τὸ

ἄνισον, τὸ δὲ δίκαιον τό τε νόμιμον καὶ τὸ ἴσον. κατὰ μὲν οὖν τὸ παράνομον ἡ πρότερον εἰρημένη ἀδικία ἐστίν· § 9 ἐπεὶ δὲ τὸ ἄνισον καὶ τὸ παράνομον οὐ ταὐτὸν ἀλλ' ἕτερον ὡς μέρος καὶ ὅλον (τὸ μὲν γὰρ ἄνισον ἅπαν παράνομον, τὸ δὲ παράνομον οὐχ ἅπαν ἄνισον), καὶ τὸ ἄδικον καὶ ἡ ἀδικία οὐ ταὐτὰ ἀλλ' ἕτερα ἐκείνων, τὰ μὲν ὡς μέρη τὰ δ' ὡς ὅλα, (μέρος γὰρ αὕτη ἡ ἀδικία τῆς ὅλης ἀδικίας, ὁμοίως δὲ καὶ ἡ δικαιοσύνη τῆς δικαιοσύνης,)—ὥστε περὶ τῆς ἐν μέρει δικαιοσύνης καὶ περὶ τῆς ἐν μέρει ἀδικίας § 10 λεκτέον, καὶ τοῦ δικαίου καὶ τοῦ ἀδίκου ὡσαύτως. ἡ μὲν οὖν κατὰ τὴν ὅλην ἀρετὴν τεταγμένη δικαιοσύνη καὶ ἀδικία, ἡ μὲν τῆς ὅλης ἀρετῆς οὖσα χρῆσις πρὸς ἄλλον, ἡ δὲ τῆς κακίας, ἀφείσθω. καὶ τὸ δίκαιον δὲ καὶ τὸ ἄδικον τὸ κατὰ ταύτας φανερὸν ὡς διοριστέον· σχεδὸν γὰρ τὰ πολλὰ τῶν νομίμων τὰ ἀπὸ τῆς ὅλης ἀρετῆς πραττόμενά ἐστιν· καθ' ἑκάστην γὰρ ἀρετὴν προστάττει ζῆν καὶ καθ' § 11 ἑκάστην μοχθηρίαν κωλύει ὁ νόμος· τὰ δὲ ποιητικὰ τῆς ὅλης ἀρετῆς ἐστὶ τῶν νομίμων ὅσα νενομοθέτηται περὶ παιδείαν τὴν πρὸς τὸ κοινόν. περὶ δὲ τῆς καθ' ἕκαστον παιδείας, καθ' ἣν ἁπλῶς ἀνὴρ ἀγαθός ἐστι, πότερον τῆς πολιτικῆς ἐστιν ἢ ἑτέρας, ὕστερον διοριστέον· οὐ γὰρ ἴσως ταὐτὸν ἀνδρί τ' ἀγαθῷ εἶναι καὶ πολίτῃ παντί.

§ 12 τῆς δὲ κατὰ μέρος δικαιοσύνης καὶ τοῦ κατ' αὐτὴν δικαίου ἓν μέν ἐστιν εἶδος τὸ ἐν ταῖς διανομαῖς τιμῆς ἢ

---

1 τὸ δὲ—τὸ ἴσον] om. M^bQ.   2 μὲν οὖν] om. K^b.   πρότερον] προτέρα H^a.
3 τὸ ante ἄνισον] τῷ N^b.   3 παράνομον] παράνομον πλέον K^bP^b.   om. H^a.   πλέον
L^bM^bQN^b Bekker.   πλέον (παράνομον corr.) O^b.   4 καὶ] καὶ πρὸς K^b.   πρὸς
H^aL^bN^bO^bP^b Bekker. πρὸς τὸ M^bQ.   τὸ μὲν γὰρ ἄνισον ἅπαν παράνομον,
τὸ δὲ παράνομον οὐχ ἅπαν ἄνισον] τὸ μὲν γὰρ ἄνισον ἅπαν παράνομον, τὸ δὲ παράνομον οὐχ ἅπαν ἄνισον· τὸ μὲν γὰρ (καὶ τὸ μὲν M^bQ) πλέον ἅπαν ἄνισον, τὸ δ' ἄνισον
οὐ πᾶν (οὐχ ἅπαν M^bQ) πλέον M^bQO^bP^b.   τὸ μὲν γὰρ πλέον ἅπαν ἄνισον, τὸ δ'
ἄνισον οὐ πᾶν πλέον H^aK^bL^bN^b Bekker.   6 μέρη] μέρος H^a.   7 γὰρ] δ' M^bQ.
8 ὥστε] ὡς K^b.   ὥς N^b.   ὥστε καὶ M^bQ Bekker.   9 περὶ post καὶ] om. O^b.
10 τοῦ ante ἀδίκου] om. K^bP^b.   13 δὲ] om. M^bQ.   14 ταύτας] αὐτὰς L^b.
πάντας M^b.   γὰρ τὰ] γάρ τι M^b.   γάρ τοι Q.   15 τὰ ante ἀπὸ] om.
M^bQ.   πραττόμενα] πρᾱττόμενα margo O^b.   προστατόμενα P^b et corr. K^b.
16 προστάττει] προστάττειν Q.   20 πότερον] πότερα Q.   22 πολίτῃ] πολυτῃ N^b.
23 τοῦ κατ' αὐτὴν δικαίου] τοῦ κατὰ ταύτην δικαίου K^b.   δίκαιον τοῦ κατ' αὐτὴν L^b.

νόμιμον and τὸ ἴσον. Hence, whereas the ἀδικία spoken of above is coextensive with τὸ παράνομον, since τὸ ἄνισον and τὸ παράνομον are not identical but different, being related as part and whole,—(for τὸ ἄνισον is always παράνομον, but τὸ παράνομον is not always ἄνισον,)—and consequently the ἄδικα and ἀδικίαι belonging to them are in like manner not identical but different, the ἄδικον and the ἀδικία belonging to the one being parts, and the ἄδικον and the ἀδικία belonging to the other being wholes,—that is to say, the ἀδικία of which we are speaking being a part of universal ἀδικία, and in like manner the δικαιοσύνη of which we are speaking, a part of universal δικαιοσύνη,—we must now investigate particular δικαιοσύνη and particular ἀδικία, and the particular δίκαιον and the particular ἄδικον in like manner. At this point then we may dismiss the δικαιοσύνη, coextensive with universal virtue, which is the practice of universal virtue towards another, and the correlative ἀδικία which is the similar practice of universal vice. And it is obvious how the δίκαιον and ἄδικον which correspond to universal δικαιοσύνη and ἀδικία are to be determined: the great majority of the acts directed by law are the acts which spring from universal virtue, the law commanding us to live in the practice of each particular virtue and forbidding us to live in the practice of each particular vice, while those provisions which have been made by the legislature with regard to the education which fits a man for social life are means to the production of universal virtue. As to that particular education which produces simply a good man, we must hereafter determine whether it falls within the scope of political science or of some other: for it would seem that it is not in every case the same thing to be a good man and to be a good citizen.

But of particular δικαιοσύνη and the δίκαιον connected with it there are two sorts: one which is exhibited in dis-

χρημάτων ἢ τῶν ἄλλων ὅσα μεριστὰ τοῖς κοινωνοῦσι τῆς πολιτείας (ἐν τούτοις γὰρ ἔστι καὶ ἄνισον ἔχειν καὶ ἴσον ἕτερον ἑτέρου), ἓν δὲ τὸ ἐν τοῖς συναλλάγμασι διορθωτικόν. § 13 τούτου δὲ μέρη δύο· τῶν γὰρ συναλλαγμάτων τὰ μὲν ἑκούσιά ἐστι τὰ δ' ἀκούσια· ἑκούσια μὲν τὰ τοιάδε οἷον πρᾶσις ὠνὴ δανεισμὸς ἐγγύη χρῆσις παρακαταθήκη μίσθωσις, ἑκούσια δὲ λέγεται, ὅτι ἡ ἀρχὴ τῶν συναλλαγμάτων τούτων ἑκούσιος· τῶν δ' ἀκουσίων τὰ μὲν λαθραῖα, οἷον κλοπὴ μοιχεία φαρμακεία προαγωγεία δουλαπατία δολοφονία ψευδομαρτυρία, τὰ δὲ βίαια, οἷον αἰκία δεσμὸς 3 θάνατος ἁρπαγὴ πήρωσις κακηγορία προπηλακισμός. ἐπεὶ δ' ὅ τ' ἄδικος ἄνισος καὶ τὸ ἄδικον ἄνισον, δῆλον ὅτι καὶ § 2 μέσον τί ἐστι τοῦ ἀνίσου. τοῦτο δ' ἐστὶ τὸ ἴσον· ἐν ὁποίᾳ γὰρ πράξει ἐστὶ τὸ πλέον καὶ τὸ ἔλαττον, ἔστι καὶ τὸ § 3 ἴσον. εἰ οὖν τὸ ἄδικον ἄνισον, τὸ δίκαιον ἴσον· ὅπερ καὶ ἄνευ λόγου δοκεῖ πᾶσιν. ἐπεὶ δὲ τὸ ἴσον μέσον, τὸ δίκαιον § 4 μέσον τι ἂν εἴη. ἔστι δὲ τὸ ἴσον ἐν ἐλαχίστοις δυσίν. ἀνάγκη τοίνυν τὸ δίκαιον μέσον τε καὶ ἴσον εἶναι καὶ πρός τι, καὶ ᾗ μὲν μέσον, τινῶν (ταῦτα δ' ἐστὶ πλεῖον καὶ ἔλαττον), ᾗ δ' ἴσον ἐστί, δυοῖν, ᾗ δὲ δίκαιον, τισίν. § 5 ἀνάγκη ἄρα τὸ δίκαιον ἐν ἐλαχίστοις εἶναι τέτταρσιν· οἷς τε γὰρ δίκαιον τυγχάνει ὄν, δύο ἐστί, καὶ ἐν οἷς, [τὰ § 6 πράγματα,] δύο. καὶ ἡ αὐτὴ ἔσται ἰσότης, οἷς καὶ ἐν οἷς· ὡς γὰρ ἐκεῖνα ἔχει, οὕτω κἀκεῖνα ἔχει· εἰ γὰρ μὴ

---

1 κοινωνοῦσι] κοινοῦσι Nᵇ.   4 μέρη δύο] μέρη εἰσὶ δύο Lᵇ.   δύο μέρη Mᵇ.   συναλλαγμάτων] ἀδικημάτων KᵇLᵇMᵇQPᵇ.   5 μὲν τὰ] μὲν γὰρ τὰ Lᵇ.   8 τούτων] om. MᵇQ.   9 προαγωγεία] προαγωγία LᵇNᵇQPᵇ.   προσαγωγία Kᵇ et (σ eraso) Hᵃ.   δουλαπατία] δολοπατία Kᵇ.   δουλαπάτη Hᵃ.   11 κακηγορία] κατηγορία NᵇOᵇ.   13 ὁποίᾳ] ὁποῖα Hᵃ.   14 πράξει ἐστί] ἐστὶ πράξει Pᵇ.   ἔστι τὸ πλέον] om. (hiatu relicto) Hᵃ.   15 τὸ ἄδικον] om. (hiatu relicto) Hᵃ.   ὅπερ—πᾶσιν] om. MᵇQ.   16 δοκεῖ πᾶσιν] δοκοῦσιν Hᵃ.   μέσον τὸ] μέσον καὶ τὸ HᵃMᵇQ.   17 τι ἂν] ἄν τι KᵇOᵇPᵇ.   18 καὶ πρός τι] Lᵇ.   καὶ τισι καὶ πρός τι HᵃNᵇOᵇPᵇ.   καὶ τισίν Kᵇ.   καὶ πρός τι καὶ τισίν MᵇQ.   [καὶ πρός τι] καὶ τισίν Bekker.   19 ταῦτα] τὰ Pᵇ.   πλεῖον] πλέον Lᵇ.   20 ἐστί] om. Kᵇ.   23 ἔσται ἰσότης] ἰσότης ἔσται Pᵇ.   ἰσότης (omisso ἔσται) KᵇOᵇ.   24 ἔχει] ἔχοι Q.   ἔχει, οὕτω] Kᵇ.   ἔχει τὰ ἐν οἷς, οὕτω ceteri et Bekker.   μὴ ἴσοι] ἄνισοι Oᵇ.

tributions of preferment, property, or anything else which is divided amongst the members of the community, (for in such matters shares may be either unequal or equal,)—and another sort which rectifies wrong in the case of private transactions. This last sort has two subdivisions: for some transactions are voluntary, others involuntary; such transactions as selling, buying, lending at interest, pledging, lending without interest, depositing, letting for hire are voluntary, being called so because they are voluntarily entered into, whilst of involuntary transactions some are furtive, such as theft, adultery, poisoning, procuring, enticement of slaves, assassination, false witness, others violent, such as assault, imprisonment, murder, rape, maiming, slander, contumelious treatment.

Now since the ἄδικος is ἄνισος, and τὸ ἄδικον, ἄνισον, it is plain that there is a mean belonging to τὸ ἄνισον. This mean is τὸ ἴσον; for in any action which admits of τὸ πλέον and τὸ ἔλαττον, there is also τὸ ἴσον. Hence (1) if τὸ ἄδικον is ἄνισον, τὸ δίκαιον is ἴσον; a view which commends itself to all apart from argument. And (3) since τὸ ἴσον is a μέσον, τὸ δίκαιον will be a μέσον. Again (2) τὸ ἴσον subsists between two terms at the least. Hence τὸ δίκαιον must be a μέσον, an ἴσον, and πρός τι (relative): and inasmuch as it is a μέσον, it is between certain extremes, which are πλέον and ἔλαττον respectively; inasmuch as it is an ἴσον, it concerns two things; inasmuch as it is δίκαιον, it is relative to certain persons. It follows from this that τὸ δίκαιον implies four terms at the least; for the persons, for whom a distribution is δίκαιον, are two, and the things, of which distribution is made, are two: and if the persons are ἴσοι, the things will be ἴσα; since as the one person is to the other person, so is the one thing to the other thing, for if the persons are not ἴσοι they will not have

ἴσοι, οὐκ ἴσα ἕξουσιν, ἀλλ' ἐντεῦθεν αἱ μάχαι καὶ τὰ ἐγκλήματα, ὅταν ἢ ἴσοι μὴ ἴσα ἢ μὴ ἴσοι ἴσα ἔχωσι καὶ § 7 νέμωνται. ἔτι ἐκ τοῦ κατ' ἀξίαν τοῦτο δῆλον· τὸ γὰρ δίκαιον ἐν ταῖς διανομαῖς ὁμολογοῦσι πάντες κατ' ἀξίαν τινὰ δεῖν εἶναι, τὴν μέντοι ἀξίαν οὐ τὴν αὐτὴν λέγουσι πάντες ὑπάρχειν, ἀλλ' οἱ μὲν δημοκρατικοὶ ἐλευθερίαν, οἱ δ' ὀλιγαρχικοὶ πλοῦτον οἱ δ' εὐγένειαν, οἱ δ' ἀριστοκρα- § 8 τικοὶ ἀρετήν. ἔστιν ἄρα τὸ δίκαιον ἀνάλογόν τι. τὸ γὰρ ἀνάλογον οὐ μόνον ἐστὶ μοναδικοῦ ἀριθμοῦ ἴδιον, ἀλλ' ὅλως ἀριθμοῦ· ἡ γὰρ ἀναλογία ἰσότης ἐστὶ λόγων, καὶ ἐν § 9 τέτταρσιν ἐλαχίστοις. ἡ μὲν οὖν διῃρημένη ὅτι ἐν τέτταρσι, δῆλον. ἀλλὰ καὶ ἡ συνεχής· τῷ γὰρ ἑνὶ ὡς δυσὶ χρῆται καὶ δὶς λέγει, οἷον ὡς ἡ τοῦ πρώτου πρὸς τὴν τοῦ δευτέρου οὕτως ἡ τοῦ δευτέρου πρὸς τὴν τοῦ τρίτου· δὶς οὖν ἡ τοῦ δευτέρου εἴρηται· ὥστ' ἐὰν ἡ τοῦ δευτέρου τεθῇ § 10 δίς, τέτταρα ἔσται τὰ ἀνάλογα. ἔστι δὲ καὶ τὸ δίκαιον ἐν τέτταρσιν ἐλαχίστοις, καὶ ὁ λόγος ὁ αὐτός· διῄρηται γὰρ § 11 ὁμοίως, οἷς τε καὶ ἅ. ἔσται ἄρα ὡς ὁ πρῶτος ὅρος πρὸς τὸν δεύτερον οὕτως ὁ τρίτος πρὸς τὸν τέταρτον, καὶ ἐναλλὰξ

1 αἱ] ἐ Nᵇ. 2 ἢ ante ἴσοι] om. LᵇMᵇQPᵇ. ἴσοι μὴ ἴσα] μὴ ἴσα ἴσοι Kᵇ. om. Pᵇ. ἢ] ἢ (οἱ suprascripto) Pᵇ. ἢ μὴ ἴσοι ἴσα] om. LᵇMᵇQ. 3 νέμωνται] νέμωνται καὶ οἱ μὴ ἴσοι ἴσα Lᵇ. ἔτι] ἔτι καὶ Hᵃ. ἔστι δ' MᵇQ. τοῦτο—κατ' ἀξίαν] om. Nᵇ. 4 διανομαῖς] νομαῖς KᵇLᵇPᵇ et (suprascripto δια) Oᵇ. 5 δεῖν εἶναι] εἶναι δεῖν MᵇQ. 6 ὑπάρχειν] om. OᵇPᵇ. κατ' ἀξίαν τινὰ δεῖν εἶναι Kᵇ. μὲν δημοκρατικοὶ] δημοκρατικοὶ μὲν HᵃNᵇ. ἐλευθερίαν] om. (hiatu relicto) Hᵃ. 7 ὀλιγαρχικοὶ πλοῦτον] ὀλιγαρχικοὶ ἀρετήν. ἔστιν ἄρα τὸ δίκαιον ἀνάλογον πλοῦτον Nᵇ. πλοῦτον—ἀριστοκρατικοὶ] om. Pᵇ. οἱ δ' ἀριστο] om. (hiatu relicto) Hᵃ. 10 ἡ γὰρ] ἤ τε γὰρ MᵇOᵇ. ἐστί] τις ἐστὶν Nᵇ. λόγων] λόγου KᵇNᵇPᵇ. 11 ὅτι] om. Hᵃ. 13 χρῆται] χρήσεται HᵃLᵇMᵇQNᵇ. ὡς post οἷον] om. MᵇQ. πρώτου] ā LᵇMᵇQOᵇ. ū Bekker. 14 δευτέρου] β̄ LᵇMᵇQOᵇ. β Bekker. οὕτως] om. MᵇQ. καὶ Lᵇ. οὕτως καὶ Hᵃ Bekker. οὕτω καὶ Pᵇ. δευτέρου] β̄ LᵇMᵇQOᵇ. β Bekker. τρίτου] γ̄ LᵇMᵇQOᵇPᵇ. γ Bekker. 15 δευτέρου] β̄ LᵇMᵇQOᵇ. β Bekker. ἐὰν] ἂν HᵃNᵇOᵇ. ἡ τοῦ δευτέρου τεθῇ δίς] ἡ τοῦ β̄ τεθῇ δὶς LᵇMᵇQ. ἡ τοῦ β τεθῇ δὶς Bekker. ἡ τοῦ β̄ δὶς τεθῇ Oᵇ. τὸ δεύτερον δὶς τεθῇ Kᵇ. τὸ β̄ δὶς τεθῇ Pᵇ. 16 τέτταρα ἔσται] τέσσαρα ἔστι Mᵇ. τέτταρά ἐστι Q. τέτταρα (omisso ἔσται) Nᵇ. τά] ἀτά Nᵇ. 17 διῄρηται] διῄρηται KᵇQ. διῄρηται HᵃMᵇOᵇ. 18 ἔσται] om. Kᵇ. πρῶτος] ā LᵇMᵇQNᵇ. α Bekker. 19 δεύτερον] β̄ LᵇMᵇQNᵇOᵇ. β Bekker. οὕτως] οὕτω καὶ Pᵇ. τρίτος] γ̄ LᵇMᵇQNᵇOᵇ. γ Bekker. τέταρτον] δ̄ LᵇMᵇQNᵇOᵇ. δ Bekker. καὶ ἐναλλὰξ—τέταρτον] om. MᵇQ.

ἴσα; indeed all battles and complaints arise in consequence of ἴσοι having and possessing things which are not ἴσα, or persons who are not ἴσοι, things which are ἴσα. Again this is plain in the case of τὸ κατ' ἀξίαν (proportion); for all admit that in distributions τὸ δίκαιον should be determined κατ' ἀξίαν, though all do not acknowledge the same ἀξία, democrats taking as their ἀξία freedom, oligarchs wealth and sometimes birth, aristocrats excellence.

Hence τὸ δίκαιον is ἀνάλογόν τι. For τὸ ἀνάλογον is not peculiar to numerical quantity, but belongs to quantity generally, ἀναλογία being equality of ratios and having four terms at the least. That discrete ἀναλογία has four terms is plain: and so has continuous ἀναλογία; for it treats one term as two and repeats it; for example, with three lines, as the first term is to the second, so is the second to the third; thus the second term is repeated, and if the second term is so repeated, the ἀνάλογα will be four in number. And τὸ δίκαιον too has four terms at the least, and the ratio of the first to the second is the same as the ratio of the third to the fourth, for the persons and the things are similarly divided. Thus as the first term is to the second, so will the third be to the fourth; hence per-

ἄρα, ὡς ὁ πρῶτος πρὸς τὸν τρίτον ὁ δεύτερος πρὸς τὸν τέταρτον· ὥστε καὶ τὸ ὅλον πρὸς τὸ ὅλον· ὅπερ ἡ νομὴ συνδυάζει· κἂν οὕτως συντεθῇ, δικαίως συνδυάζει. ἡ ἄρα τοῦ πρώτου ὅρου τῷ τρίτῳ καὶ ἡ τοῦ δευτέρου τῷ τετάρτῳ σύζευξις τὸ ἐν διανομῇ δίκαιόν ἐστι· καὶ μέσον τὸ δίκαιον τοῦτ᾽ ἐστὶ τοῦ παρὰ τὸ ἀνάλογον, τὸ γὰρ ἀνάλογον μέσον, τὸ δὲ δίκαιον ἀνάλογον. καλοῦσι δὲ τὴν τοιαύτην ἀναλογίαν γεωμετρικὴν οἱ μαθηματικοί· ἐν γὰρ τῇ γεωμετρικῇ συμβαίνει καὶ τὸ ὅλον πρὸς τὸ ὅλον ὅπερ ἑκάτερον πρὸς ἑκάτερον. ἔστι δ᾽ οὐ συνεχὴς αὕτη ἡ ἀναλογία· οὐ γὰρ γίνεται εἷς ἀριθμῷ ὅρος, ᾧ καὶ ὅ. τὸ μὲν οὖν δίκαιον τοῦτο τὸ ἀνάλογον, τὸ δ᾽ ἄδικον τὸ παρὰ τὸ ἀνάλογον. γίνεται ἄρα τὸ μὲν πλέον τὸ δὲ ἔλαττον. ὅπερ καὶ ἐπὶ τῶν ἔργων συμβαίνει· ὁ μὲν γὰρ ἀδικῶν πλέον ἔχει, ὁ δ᾽ ἀδικούμενος ἔλαττον τοῦ ἀγαθοῦ. ἐπὶ δὲ τοῦ κακοῦ ἀνάπαλιν· ἐν ἀγαθοῦ γὰρ λόγῳ γίνεται τὸ ἔλαττον κακὸν πρὸς τὸ μεῖζον κακόν· ἔστι γὰρ τὸ ἔλαττον κακὸν μᾶλλον αἱρετὸν τοῦ μείζονος, τὸ δ᾽ αἱρετὸν ἀγαθόν, καὶ τὸ μᾶλλον μεῖζον.

4   τὸ μὲν οὖν ἓν εἶδος τοῦ δικαίου τοῦτ᾽ ἐστίν, τὸ δὲ λοιπὸν ἓν τὸ διορθωτικόν, ὃ γίνεται ἐν τοῖς συναλλάγμασι καὶ τοῖς ἑκουσίοις καὶ τοῖς ἀκουσίοις. τοῦτο δὲ τὸ δίκαιον ἄλλο εἶδος ἔχει τοῦ προτέρου. τὸ μὲν γὰρ διανεμητικὸν

---

1 πρῶτος] ᾱ L^bN^b. α *Bekker*. τρίτον] γ̄ L^bN^bO^bP^b. γ *Bekker*. ὁ ante δεύτερος] καὶ ὁ N^b. δεύτερος] β̄ L^bN^bO^b. β *Bekker*. 2 τέταρτον] δ̄ L^bN^bO^bP^b. δ *Bekker*. 3 κἂν—συνδυάζει] om. H^aM^bQ. 4 πρώτου] ᾱ L^bM^bQN^bP^b. α *Bekker*. τρίτῳ] γ̄ L^bM^bQN^bO^bP^b. γ *Bekker*. δευτέρου] β̄ L^bM^bQO^bP^b. β *Bekker*. τετάρτῳ] δ̄ L^bM^bQN^bO^bP^b. δ *Bekker*. 6 τοῦτ᾽—τὸ δὲ δίκαιον] om. M^bQ. τοῦ] τὸ H^aK^bL^bP^b. παρὰ] κατὰ H^a. γὰρ] μὲν γὰρ O^b. 8 μαθηματικοί] μαθητικοὶ L^b. 9 τὸ post πρὸς] om. M^b. ἑκάτερον post ὅπερ] ἑκάτερος H^a. 10 ἀναλογία] ἀνάλογος H^a. 11 ὅρος] ὁ ὅρος O^b. 12 τοῦτο] καὶ τοῦτο N^b. τούτῳ K^b. τὸ post τοῦτο] om. L^bN^b. 13 τὸ μὲν πλέον τὸ] τῷ μὲν πλέον τῷ H^aM^bQN^b. πλέον] πλεῖον H^aN^bO^b. 14 πλέον] πλεῖον H^aN^bO^b. 15 ἀνάπαλιν] τὸ ἀνάπαλιν O^b. 16 λόγῳ] λόγος H^a. τὸ ἔλαττον] καὶ τὸ ἔλαττον H^aM^bQN^b. 21 τοῖς συναλλάγμασι] τοῦ συναλλάγματος H^a. 22 καὶ τοῖς ἑκουσίοις καὶ τοῖς ἀκουσίοις] καὶ τοῖς ἀκουσίοις καὶ τοῖς ἑκουσίοις L^b. τοῖς ἑκουσίοις τε καὶ ἀκουσίοις M^bQ. 23 εἶδος ἔχει] ἔχει εἶδος M^b. εἶδος ἐστὶ N^b. ἐστὶ εἶδος H^a. προτέρου] πρότερον K^b. γὰρ] om. M^b. διανεμητικὸν] διανομητικὸν N^b.

mutando, as the first is to the third, so is the second to the fourth; and therefore also [componendo] the whole to the whole. Now this is the combination which the distribution effects, and the combination is effected δικαίως if the ἀνάλογα are so compounded. Hence the conjunction of the first term with the third, and that of the second term with the fourth is τὸ δίκαιον in distribution: and this δίκαιον is a mean between violations of τὸ ἀνάλογον, since τὸ ἀνάλογον is a mean, and τὸ δίκαιον is ἀνάλογον. This sort of ἀναλογία is called by mathematicians geometrical, for it is in geometrical ἀναλογία that the whole is to the whole as each to each. This ἀναλογία is not continuous, for person and thing do not constitute a single term.

Thus this sort of δίκαιον is τὸ ἀνάλογον, and the corresponding ἄδικον that which violates τὸ ἀνάλογον. Further τὸ ἄδικον violates τὸ ἀνάλογον either by excess or by defect; and this we find in fact, for ὁ ἀδικῶν has too much, ὁ ἀδικούμενος too little of the good in question. In the case of evil the contrary holds: for the lesser evil in comparison with the greater evil is reckoned a good; since the lesser evil is more desirable than the greater evil, and that which is desirable is a good, and that which is more desirable, a greater good.

This then is one sort of δίκαιον. The other is the corrective sort, which appears in private transactions both voluntary and involuntary. This sort of δίκαιον is of a different character from the former one. For, on the one hand the δίκαιον

δίκαιον τῶν κοινῶν ἀεὶ κατὰ τὴν ἀναλογίαν ἐστὶ τὴν εἰρημένην· καὶ γὰρ ἀπὸ χρημάτων κοινῶν ἐὰν γίγνηται ἡ διανομή, ἔσται κατὰ τὸν λόγον τὸν αὐτὸν ὅνπερ ἔχουσι πρὸς ἄλληλα τὰ εἰσενεχθέντα· καὶ τὸ ἄδικον τὸ ἀντικεί
§ 3 μενον τῷ δικαίῳ τούτῳ παρὰ τὸ ἀνάλογόν ἐστιν. τὸ δ᾽ ἐν τοῖς συναλλάγμασι δίκαιον ἐστὶ μὲν ἴσον τι, καὶ τὸ ἄδικον ἄνισον, ἀλλ᾽ οὐ κατὰ τὴν ἀναλογίαν ἐκείνην ἀλλὰ κατὰ τὴν ἀριθμητικήν. οὐθὲν γὰρ διαφέρει, εἰ ἐπιεικὴς φαῦλον ἀπεστέρησεν ἢ φαῦλος ἐπιεικῆ, οὐδ᾽ εἰ ἐμοίχευσεν ἐπιεικὴς ἢ φαῦλος· ἀλλὰ πρὸς τοῦ βλάβους τὴν διαφορὰν μόνον βλέπει ὁ νόμος, (καὶ χρῆται ὡς ἴσοις,) εἰ ὁ μὲν ἀδικεῖ ὁ δ᾽
§ 4 ἀδικεῖται, καὶ εἰ ὁ μὲν ἔβλαψεν ὁ δὲ βέβλαπται. ὥστε τὸ ἄδικον τοῦτο ἄνισον ὂν ἰσάζειν πειρᾶται ὁ δικαστής· καὶ γὰρ ὅταν ὁ μὲν πληγῇ ὁ δὲ πατάξῃ, ἢ καὶ κτείνῃ ὁ δ᾽ ἀποθάνῃ, διῄρηται τὸ πάθος καὶ ἡ πρᾶξις εἰς ἄνισα· ἀλλὰ
§ 5 πειρᾶται τῇ ζημίᾳ ἰσάζειν, ἀφαιρῶν τοῦ κέρδους. λέγεται γὰρ ὡς ἁπλῶς εἰπεῖν ἐπὶ τοῖς τοιούτοις, κἂν εἰ μή τισιν οἰκεῖον ὄνομα εἴη, τὸ κέρδος, οἷον τῷ πατάξαντι, καὶ ἡ
§ 6 ζημία τῷ παθόντι· ἀλλ᾽ ὅταν γε μετρηθῇ τὸ πάθος, καλεῖται τὸ μὲν ζημία τὸ δὲ κέρδος. ὥστε τοῦ μὲν πλείονος καὶ ἐλάττονος τὸ ἴσον μέσον, τὸ δὲ κέρδος καὶ ἡ ζημία τὸ μὲν πλέον τὸ δ᾽ ἔλαττον ἐναντίως, τὸ μὲν τοῦ ἀγαθοῦ πλέον τοῦ κακοῦ δ᾽ ἔλαττον κέρδος, τὸ δ᾽ ἐναντίον ζημία· ὧν ἦν μέσον τὸ ἴσον, ὃ λέγομεν εἶναι δίκαιον· ὥστε τὸ ἐπανορθωτικὸν

---

1 δίκαιον] om. K^bP^b. τὴν εἰρημένην] τῶν εἰρημένων H^a. 2 γίγνηται] γίνηται O^b. γένηται L^b. 3 τὸν ante λόγον] om. M^bQ. 4 πρὸς ἄλληλα τὰ εἰσενεχθέντα] εἰς ἄλληλα τὰ προσενεχθέντα P^b. εἰς ἄλληλα προσενεχθέντα K^b. 5 παρά] τὸ παρά K^bO^b. 7 ἐκείνην] ἔχει ἐκείνην P^b. 8 ἐπιεικῆς] ὁ ἐπιεικῆς M^bQ. φαῦλον] φαῦλα H^a. 9 ἀπεστέρησεν] ἀποστερήσει O^b. φαῦλος] ὁ φαῦλος M^bQ. εἰ] om. N^b. 10 πρὸς] πρὸ K^bN^b. διαφορὰν] ἀναφορὰν M^bQ. μόνον βλέπει] βλέπει μόνον K^bP^b. 12 καί] om. M^bQ. ὁ μὲν ante ἔβλαψεν] om. K^b Bekker. βέβλαπται] βλάπτεται M^bQO^b. 14 καὶ ante κτείνῃ] om. M^bQO^b. 18 εἴη] ἦ K^bP^b. δοκῇ O^b. τῷ] τὸ N^b. πατάξαντι] πατάξοντι H^a. 19 ὅταν] ὅτε H^a. 21 ἐλάττονος] τοῦ ἐλάττονος O^b. δὲ κέρδος] κέρδος δὲ L^b. 22 πλέω] πλεῖον P^b. ἔλαττον ἐναντίως] ἔλαττον καὶ ἡ ζημία τὸ μὲν πλέον τὸ δ᾽ ἔλαττον ἐναντίως O^b. 23 ἦν] ἦ Q. 24 λέγομεν] λέγεται τὸ μὲν H^a.

which distributes public possessions is always governed by the above-named ἀναλογία,—since, if the distribution is made from public funds, it will be in accordance with the ratio subsisting between the contributions,—and the ἄδικον opposed to this δίκαιον violates τὸ ἀνάλογον; and on the other hand the δίκαιον of private transactions, though it is ἴσον τι and the corresponding ἄδικον, ἄνισον, is regulated not by geometrical, but by arithmetical, ἀναλογία. For it makes no difference whether a good man defrauds a bad man or a bad one a good one, nor, whether it is a good man or a bad one who commits adultery, so that the law looks only to the degree of harm done, and, treating them as ἴσοι, considers whether the one ἀδικεῖ and the other ἀδικεῖται, whether the one harmed, and the other has been harmed. And consequently, this ἄδικον being ἄνισον, the juror endeavours to equalize it: i.e. when one man strikes and the other is struck, when one man kills and the other is killed, the action and the suffering have been divided into unequal portions, and the juror endeavours to equalize the profit and the loss by a deduction from the former. For, generally speaking, these terms are applied to all such cases, although in some they may not be strictly appropriate names, 'profit' to the striker for example, and 'loss' to the sufferer: but it is when the suffering comes to be estimated that the act of the one is called 'profit' and the suffering of the other 'loss'. Thus τὸ ἴσον is a mean between too much and too little, and profit and loss are, contrariwise, too much and too little, or too little and too much, too much good and too little evil being profit, too little good and too much evil being loss; and as τὸ ἴσον, which is conceived to be δίκαιον, is, as we said, a mean between them, τὸ δίκαιον in correction will

§ 7 δίκαιον ἂν εἴη τὸ μέσον ζημίας καὶ κέρδους. διὸ καὶ ὅταν ἀμφισβητῶσιν, ἐπὶ τὸν δικαστὴν καταφεύγουσιν· τὸ δ' ἐπὶ τὸν δικαστὴν ἰέναι ἰέναι ἐστὶν ἐπὶ τὸ δίκαιον· ὁ γὰρ δικαστὴς βούλεται εἶναι οἷον δίκαιον ἔμψυχον· καὶ ζητοῦσι δικαστὴν μέσον, καὶ καλοῦσιν ἔνιοι μεσιδίους, ὡς ἐὰν τοῦ § 8 μέσου τύχωσι τοῦ δικαίου τευξόμενοι. μέσον ἄρα τι τὸ δίκαιον, εἴπερ καὶ ὁ δικαστής. ὁ δὲ δικαστὴς ἐπανισοῖ, καὶ ὥσπερ γραμμῆς εἰς ἄνισα τετμημένης, ᾧ τὸ μεῖζον τμῆμα τῆς ἡμισείας ὑπερέχει, τοῦτ' ἀφεῖλε καὶ τῷ ἐλάττονι τμήματι προσέθηκεν. ὅταν δὲ δίχα διαιρεθῇ τὸ ὅλον, § 9 τότε φασὶν ἔχειν τὰ αὑτῶν, ὅταν λάβωσι τὸ ἴσον. < διὰ τοῦτο καὶ ὀνομάζεται δίκαιον, ὅτι δίχα ἐστίν, ὥσπερ ἂν εἴ τις εἴποι δίχαιον, καὶ ὁ δικαστὴς διχαστής. > < τὸ δ' ἴσον μέσον ἐστὶ τῆς μείζονος καὶ ἐλάττονος κατὰ τὴν ἀρι- § 10 θμητικὴν ἀναλογίαν. > ἐπὰν γὰρ δύο ἴσων ἀφαιρεθῇ ἀπὸ θατέρου πρὸς θάτερον δὲ προστεθῇ, δυσὶ τούτοις ὑπερέχει θάτερον· εἰ γὰρ ἀφῃρέθη μέν, μὴ προσετέθη δέ, ἑνὶ ἂν μόνον ὑπερεῖχεν· τοῦ μέσου ἄρα ἑνί, καὶ τὸ μέσον < τοῦ > § 11 ἀφ' οὗ ἀφῃρέθη ἑνί. τούτῳ ἄρα γνωριοῦμεν τί τε ἀφελεῖν δεῖ ἀπὸ τοῦ πλέον ἔχοντος, καὶ τί προσθεῖναι τῷ ἔλαττον ἔχοντι· ᾧ μὲν γὰρ τὸ μέσον ὑπερέχει, τοῦτο προσθεῖναι δεῖ τῷ ἔλαττον ἔχοντι, ᾧ δ' ὑπερέχεται, ἀφελεῖν ἀπὸ τοῦ § 12 μεγίστου. ἴσαι αἱ ἐφ' ὧν ΑΑ ΒΒ ΓΓ ἀλλήλαις· ἀπὸ τῆς ΑΑ ἀφῃρήσθω τὸ ΑΕ, καὶ προσκείσθω τῇ ΓΓ τὸ ἐφ' ᾧ

3 ἰέναι ἰέναι] ἰέναι K^bL^bM^bQN^b. ἐστὶν—βούλεται εἶναι] om. K^b. ὁ— ἔμψυχον] om. M^bQ. 5 μεσιδίους] μεσιδίκους (κ correcto) L^b. μεσιδίκην H^a. μεσοδίκην M^bQ. 6 τι] om. M^bQ. 9 καὶ] om. K^b. ἐλάττονι] ἐλάττωνι N^b. 10 προσέθηκεν] om. K^b. ὅταν] ὅτε H^a. διαιρεθῇ] διδιαιρεθῇ Q. 11 τὰ αὑτῶν] τὰ αὑτοῦ O^b. τὸ αὑτοῦ L^bP^b. τὸ αὑτοῦ H^aK^bN^b. τὸ αὑτὸ M^bQ. διὰ τοῦτο—διχαστής et τὸ δ' ἴσον—ἀναλογίαν] e coni. Rassow transposui. 12 ἂν] γὰρ ἂν L^b. om. M^bQ. 13 εἴ] om. K^b. εἴποι] εἴπη II^a. τὸ δ' ἴσον] om. N^b. 14 μείζονος καὶ ἐλάττονος] ἐλάττονος καὶ μείζονος M^b. 16 τούτοις] τοιούτοις O^b. 17 θάτερον] K^b. τὸ ἕτερον ceteri. ἀφῃρέθη] ἀφαιρέθη H^a. ἀφαιρεθῇ M^bQ. προσετέθη] προστεθῇ M^bQ. ἑνὶ ἂν] ἑνὶ γ' ἂν M^bQ. 18 μόνον] μόνῳ L^b. τοῦ] e coni. Zell inserui. 19 τε] om. K^b. 20 πλέον] πλεῖον M^bQ. προσθεῖναι] προστεθῆναι H^aL^bM^bQ. 21 ᾧ—ἔχοντι] om. H^aM^bQ. 23 αἱ ἐφ' ὧν] ἐφ' ὧν αἱ M^bQ. 24 ἀφῃρήσθω] ἀφαιρήσθω (?) M^b. ἀφῃρείσθω Q. ἀφαιρείσθω H^aL^bO^b. ἀφῄρηται K^b. προσκείσθω] πρόσκειται K^b. ᾧ] O^b. ὧν ceteri et Bekker.

be the mean between loss and profit. And this is the reason why when men dispute they have recourse to the juror: to go to the juror is to go to τὸ δίκαιον; for the juror is supposed to be a personification of τὸ δίκαιον, and men resort to a juror as to a mean, (some indeed calling jurors μεσίδιοι,) on the assumption that if they hit the mean they will obtain τὸ δίκαιον: τὸ δίκαιον is therefore a mean, seeing that the juror is one. Now the juror restores equality, and, to illustrate the matter by a line divided into two unequal parts, takes away that by which the greater segment exceeds the half of the whole line and adds it to the lesser segment. When the whole has been divided into two equal parts, men say they 'have their own', both having now got τὸ ἴσον. And this is the reason why δίκαιον is so called, because it is δίχα (equally divided), just as though one should call it δίχαιον, and [similarly] the δικαστής is a διχαστής. Here τὸ ἴσον is an arithmetical mean between the greater and the lesser lines. For when of two equals a part is taken from the one and added to the other, the second is in excess by twice the amount of the addition, since, if the part had been taken from the one but not added to the other, the second would have exceeded the first only by once the part taken away; so that the greater line exceeds the mean by once the part taken away, and the mean exceeds the segment from which a part was taken by once that part. By this process then we shall ascertain what we ought to take away from that which has too much, and what we ought to add to that which has too little: we must add to that which has too little that by which the mean exceeds it, and take from the greatest that by which the mean is exceeded. Let the lines AA', BB', CC' be equal to one another: let the segment AE

ΓΔ, ὥστε ὅλη ἡ ΔΓΓ τῆς ΕΑ ὑπερέχει τῷ ΓΔ καὶ τῷ ΓΖ· τῆς ἄρα ΒΒ τῷ ΓΔ. [ἔστι δὲ καὶ ἐπὶ τῶν ἄλλων τεχνῶν τοῦτο· ἀνῃροῦντο γὰρ ἄν, εἰ μὴ ἐποίει τὸ ποιοῦν, καὶ ὅσον καὶ οἷον καὶ τὸ πάσχον, ἔπασχε τοῦτο καὶ τοσοῦτον καὶ § 13 τοιοῦτον.] ἐλήλυθε δὲ τὰ ὀνόματα ταῦτα, ἥ τε ζημία καὶ τὸ κέρδος, ἐκ τῆς ἑκουσίου ἀλλαγῆς· τὸ μὲν γὰρ πλέον ἔχειν ἢ τὰ ἑαυτοῦ κερδαίνειν λέγεται, τὸ δ' ἔλαττον τῶν ἐξ ἀρχῆς ζημιοῦσθαι, οἷον ἐν τῷ ὠνεῖσθαι καὶ πωλεῖν καὶ § 14 ἐν ὅσοις ἄλλοις ἄδειαν ἔδωκεν ὁ νόμος· ὅταν δὲ μήτε πλέον μήτ' ἔλαττον ἀλλ' αὐτὰ δι' αὐτῶν γένηται, τὰ αὑτῶν φασὶν ἔχειν καὶ οὔτε ζημιοῦσθαι οὔτε κερδαίνειν.

ὥστε κέρδους τινὸς καὶ ζημίας μέσον τὸ δίκαιόν ἐστι τῶν παρὰ τὸ ἑκούσιον, τὸ ἴσον ἔχειν καὶ πρότερον καὶ ὕστερον.

5 δοκεῖ δέ τισι καὶ τὸ ἀντιπεπονθὸς εἶναι ἁπλῶς δίκαιον, ὥσπερ οἱ Πυθαγόρειοι ἔφασαν· ὡρίζοντο γὰρ ἁπλῶς τὸ § 2 δίκαιον τὸ ἀντιπεπονθός. τὸ δ' ἀντιπεπονθὸς οὐκ ἐφαρμόττει οὔτ' ἐπὶ τὸ διανεμητικὸν δίκαιον οὔτ' ἐπὶ τὸ διορθω-§ 3 τικόν· (καίτοι βούλονταί γε τοῦτο λέγειν καὶ τὸ Ῥαδαμάνθυος δίκαιον·

εἴ κε πάθοι τά τ' ἔρεξε, δίκη κ' ἰθεῖα γένοιτο·)

be taken away from the line AA' and the segment CD [equal to AE] be added to CC'; then the whole line DCC' exceeds EA' by CD and CZ, and therefore BB' by CD. These names 'loss' and 'profit' have come from voluntary exchange: for to have more than one's own is called 'to profit' and to have less than one had originally is called 'to lose,' for instance, in buying and selling, and in all other transactions which the law allows: but when men get just what they had at the outset, not more nor less, they say they 'have their own' and neither lose nor profit.

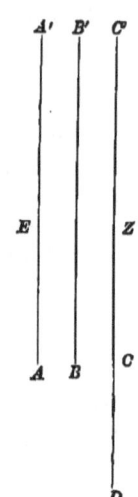

Thus τὸ [διορθωτικὸν] δίκαιον is a mean between a sort of profit and a sort of loss in matters which are not voluntary—the possession of exactly as much after the transaction as before it.

Some think with the Pythagoreans that τὸ ἀντιπεπονθός (retaliation) is without further qualification δίκαιον: for the Pythagoreans defined τὸ δίκαιον without qualification as τὸ ἀντιπεπονθός. But τὸ ἀντιπεπονθός does not accord either with δίκαιον in distribution or with δίκαιον in correction:—and yet they would have the δίκαιον of Rhadamanthus mean this; 'if a man suffers that which he did, right justice will be done:'—

§ 4 πολλαχοῦ γὰρ διαφωνεῖ· οἷον εἰ ἀρχὴν ἔχων ἐπάταξεν,
οὐ δεῖ ἀντιπληγῆναι, καὶ εἰ ἄρχοντα ἐπάταξεν, οὐ πληγῆναι
§ 5 μόνον δεῖ ἀλλὰ καὶ κολασθῆναι. ἔτι τὸ ἑκούσιον καὶ τὸ
§ 6 ἀκούσιον διαφέρει πολύ. ἀλλ' ἐν μὲν ταῖς κοινωνίαις ταῖς
ἀλλακτικαῖς συνέχει τὸ τοιοῦτον δίκαιον, τὸ ἀντιπεπονθός,
κατ' ἀναλογίαν καὶ μὴ κατ' ἰσότητα. τῷ ἀντιποιεῖν γὰρ
ἀνάλογον συμμένει ἡ πόλις· ἢ γὰρ τὸ κακῶς ζητοῦσιν·
εἰ δὲ μή, δουλεία δοκεῖ εἶναι, εἰ μὴ ἀντιποιήσει· ἢ τὸ εὖ·
εἰ δὲ μή, μετάδοσις οὐ γίνεται, τῇ μεταδόσει δὲ συμμέ-
§ 7 νουσιν. διὸ καὶ Χαρίτων ἱερὸν ἐμποδὼν ποιοῦνται, ἵν'
ἀνταπόδοσις ᾖ· τοῦτο γὰρ ἴδιον χάριτος· ἀνθυπηρετῆσαί
τε γὰρ δεῖ τῷ χαρισαμένῳ, καὶ πάλιν αὐτὸν ἄρξαι χαριζό-
§ 8 μενον. ποιεῖ δὲ τὴν ἀντίδοσιν τὴν κατ' ἀναλογίαν ἡ κατὰ
διάμετρον σύζευξις. οἷον οἰκοδόμος ἐφ' ᾧ Α, σκυτοτόμος
ἐφ' ᾧ Β, οἰκία ἐφ' ᾧ Γ, ὑπόδημα ἐφ' ᾧ Δ. δεῖ οὖν
λαμβάνειν τὸν οἰκοδόμον παρὰ τοῦ σκυτοτόμου τοῦ ἐκείνου
ἔργου, καὶ αὐτὸν ἐκείνῳ μεταδιδόναι τοῦ αὐτοῦ. ἐὰν οὖν
πρῶτον ᾖ τὸ κατὰ τὴν ἀναλογίαν ἴσον, εἶτα τὸ ἀντιπεπονθὸς γένηται, ἔσται τὸ λεγόμενον. εἰ δὲ μή, οὐκ ἴσον,
οὐδὲ συμμένει· οὐθὲν γὰρ κωλύει κρεῖττον εἶναι τὸ θατέρου
§ 9 ἔργον ἢ τὸ θατέρου· δεῖ οὖν ταῦτα ἰσασθῆναι. ἔστι δὲ
τοῦτο καὶ ἐπὶ τῶν ἄλλων τεχνῶν· ἀνῃροῦντο γὰρ < ἂν >, εἰ
μὴ ἐποίει τὸ ποιοῦν, καὶ ὅσον καὶ οἷον καὶ τὸ πάσχον,

---

2 οὐ δεῖ—ἐπάταξεν] om. P^b. δεῖ—οὐ] om. N^b. ἄρχοντα] ἀρχὴν ἔχοντα
O^b. 3 καὶ ante κολασθῆναι] om. K^b. ἑκούσιον καὶ τὸ ἀκούσιον] ἀκούσιον καὶ
τὸ ἑκούσιον H^aL^bN^b. ἑκούσιον (omissis καὶ τὸ ἀκούσιον) P^b. 5 ἀλλακτικαῖς]
συναλλακτικαῖς M^bQ. 6 ἀναλογίαν] ἀναλογίαν ἔχον M^bQ. 7 συμμένει] ἐμ-
μένει M^bQ. 10 Χαρίτων] χάριτος P^b. ἱερὸν] ἱερῶν N^b. ἕτερον P^b et (?) pr.
K^b. ἐμποδὼν] ἐκποδὼν M^bQ. 11 ἀνθυπηρετῆσαί τε] ἀνθυπηρετῆσαι H^aK^b
M^bQN^bP^b. 13 ποιεῖ δὲ] om. M^bQ. τὴν κατ' ἀναλογίαν] τῆς κατ' ἀναλογίαν
O^b. κατ' ἀναλογίαν (omisso τὴν) M^bQ. τῆς ἀναλογίας N^b. ἡ] ἢ M^bQ.
14 διάμετρον σύζευξις] τὸ μέτρον συζεύξεις M^bQ. οἷον] om. K^b. 15 ὑπόδημα]
ὑποδήματα O^b. 16 τοῦ ἐκείνου ἔργου] τὸ ἐκείνου ἔργον H^aM^bQP^b. 17 τοῦ
αὐτοῦ] K^bO^b. τοῦ αὐτοῦ H^aL^bM^bQN^bP^b. τὸ αὐτοῦ Bekker. 18 τὴν] om.
M^bQ. 19 γένηται] γενήσεται O^b. ἔσται] ἔτι H^a. 20 συμμένει] συμ-
μενεῖ O^b. συμμαίνει N^b. συμφέρει M^b. θατέρου ante ἔργον] θάτερον H^a.
21 οὖν] οὖν δὴ H^aN^bP^b. 22 ἂν] addit Bekker. om. codd. omnes. 23 ἐποίει]
εἴποι Q. καὶ ὅσον καὶ οἷον] τοιοῦτον καὶ τοσοῦτον M^bQ.

for in many cases the law of retaliation and the law of corrective justice do not agree; for example, if a man strikes being a magistrate, he ought not to be struck back, whilst if a man strikes a magistrate, he ought not only to be struck, but also to be chastised: furthermore there is a great difference between what is voluntary and what is involuntary. Nevertheless in commercial κοινωνίαι the bond of union is this sort of δίκαιον, viz. τὸ ἀντιπεπονθός, κατ' ἀναλογίαν (in the sense of reciprocal proportion), not κατ' ἰσότητα (in the sense of retaliation). In fact it is by proportionate requital that the city holds together: for men seek either to requite ill,—else, if they are not to requite it, they think themselves slaves, or to requite good,—else, there is no interchange, and it is by interchange that men hold together. And this is the reason why men set a shrine of the Graces in a prominent position, in order that there may be mutual requital: for this is a characteristic of grace, since it is right to make return to one who has shown grace, and then that he should begin again to show it.

Now proportionate return is secured by cross-conjunction. For example, let A be a builder, B a shoemaker, C a house, and D a shoe. Here the builder must receive from the shoemaker a portion of his work; and must give him a portion of his own. If then first there is proportionate equality of wares, and then τὸ ἀντιπεπονθός is effected, the result of which we speak will be attained. Otherwise the bargain is not ἴσον and does not hold: for there is nothing to prevent the work of the one from being superior to the work of the other: they must therefore be equalized. And this holds of the arts generally; for they would fall into disuse, if, besides acting, the agent did not receive an equivalent both

ἔπασχε τοῦτο καὶ τοσοῦτον καὶ τοιοῦτον· οὐ γὰρ ἐκ δύο
ἰατρῶν γίνεται κοινωνία, ἀλλ' ἐξ ἰατροῦ καὶ γεωργοῦ, καὶ
ὅλως ἑτέρων καὶ οὐκ ἴσων· ἀλλὰ τούτους δεῖ ἰσασθῆναι.
§ 10 διὸ πάντα συμβλητὰ δεῖ πως εἶναι, ὧν ἐστὶν ἀλλαγή.
ἐφ' ὃ τὸ νόμισμ' ἐλήλυθε, καὶ γίνεταί πως μέσον· πάντα 5
γὰρ μετρεῖ, ὥστε καὶ τὴν ὑπεροχὴν καὶ τὴν ἔλλειψιν, πόσα
ἄττα δὴ ὑποδήματ' ἴσον οἰκίᾳ ἢ τροφῇ. δεῖ τοίνυν ὅπερ
οἰκοδόμος πρὸς σκυτοτόμον, τοσαδὶ ὑποδήματα πρὸς οἰκίαν
ἢ τροφήν· (εἰ γὰρ μὴ τοῦτο, οὐκ ἔσται ἀλλαγὴ οὐδὲ κοι-
§ 11 νωνία·) τοῦτο δ', εἰ μὴ ἴσα εἴη πως, οὐκ ἔσται· δεῖ ἄρα 10
ἑνί τινι πάντα μετρεῖσθαι, ὥσπερ ἐλέχθη πρότερον· τοῦτο
δ' ἐστὶ τῇ μὲν ἀληθείᾳ ἡ χρεία, ἣ πάντα συνέχει· (εἰ γὰρ
μηθὲν δέοιντο ἢ μὴ ὁμοίως, ἢ οὐκ ἔσται ἀλλαγὴ ἢ οὐχ
ἡ αὐτή·) οἷον δ' ὑπάλλαγμα τῆς χρείας τὸ νόμισμα γέγονε
κατὰ συνθήκην· καὶ διὰ τοῦτο τοὔνομα ἔχει νόμισμα, ὅτι 15
οὐ φύσει ἀλλὰ νόμῳ ἐστί, καὶ ἐφ' ἡμῖν μεταβαλεῖν καὶ
§ 12 ποιῆσαι ἄχρηστον. ἔσται δὴ ἀντιπεπονθός, ὅταν ἰσασθῇ,
ὥστε ὅπερ γεωργὸς πρὸς σκυτοτόμον, τὸ ἔργον τὸ τοῦ
σκυτοτόμου πρὸς τὸ τοῦ γεωργοῦ. εἰς σχῆμα δ' ἀναλογίας οὐ δεῖ ἄγειν ὅταν ἀλλάξωνται (εἰ δὲ μή, ἀμφοτέρας 20
ἕξει τὰς ὑπεροχὰς τὸ ἕτερον ἄκρον), ἀλλ' ὅταν ἔχωσι τὰ
αὑτῶν· οὕτως ἴσοι καὶ κοινωνοί, ὅτι αὕτη ἡ ἰσότης δύναται
ἐπ' αὐτῶν γίνεσθαι· (γεωργὸς Α, τροφὴ Γ, σκυτοτόμος Β,
τὸ ἔργον αὐτοῦ τὸ ἰσασμένον Δ·) εἰ δ' οὕτω μὴ ἦν ἀντι-
§ 13 πεπονθέναι, οὐκ ἂν ἦν κοινωνία. ὅτι δ' ἡ χρεία συνέχει 25
ὥσπερ ἕν τι ὄν, δηλοῖ ὅτι ὅταν μὴ ἐν χρείᾳ ὦσιν ἀλλήλων,

1 καὶ τοιοῦτον] om. K^b. 3 καὶ ante οὐκ] om. M^bQ. 4 πάντα] ταῦτα K^b. συμβλητά] ξυμβλητὰ M^bQ. πως] πῶς H^aN^b. 5 ὅ] K^b. ceteri ᾧ. 6 μετρεῖ, ὥστε καὶ] μετρίωστε καὶ K^b. ἔλλειψιν] ἔλλειψιν, μετρεῖ δηλονότι τὸ νόμισμα P^b. 7 ἄττα] om. K^b. δὴ] δεῖ N^b. ἴσον—ὑποδήματα] om. M^bQ. ὅπερ] ὅπερ ὁ L^bN^bO^bP^b. 8 τοσαδὶ] τόσαδε K^b. τόσα δὴ L^b. 11 πρότερον] καὶ πρότερον O^b. 12 ἐστί] ὅτι K^b. ἢ ante πάντα] om. K^b. 13 ἢ post ὁμοίως] om. H^aM^bQ. 16 οὐ] οὐχὶ L^b. μεταβαλεῖν] μεταβάλλειν H^aK^bM^bQN^bO^b. 18 ὅπερ] ὅπερ δὴ ὁ P^b. τὸ post ἔργον] om. H^aL^bM^bQN^b. 19 ἀναλογίας οὐ δεῖ ἄγειν] οὐ δεῖ ἄγειν ἀναλογίας P^b. οὐ διάγειν ἀναλογίας K^b. 21 ὑπεροχάς] ὑπερβολὰς K^b. τά] τὸ K^bP^b. 22 αὑτῶν] αὐτῶν H^aK^bL^bN^bO^b. 23 αὐτῶν] αὐτῷ H^a. Α] τὸ ᾶ K^bL^b. 26 ὅταν] ὁπόταν O^b.

in quantity and quality for what the recipient receives: for it is not two physicians between whom κοινωνία finds place, but a physician and a husbandman, and generally those who are not ἴσοι, but different: these have to be equalized. Hence all things which are exchanged must be somehow commensurable: and that they may be so, men have introduced τὸ νόμισμα, which serves as a sort of medium; for it measures all things, and therefore the excess and the defect, —that is to say, determines how many shoes are equivalent to a given house or a given quantity of food. Hence, as a builder to a shoemaker, so must so many shoes be to a house or a given quantity of food (otherwise there will be no exchange, and no κοινωνία), and this proportion will not be secured unless the articles are somehow equal. Hence, as was said above, all things must be measured by a single standard. This standard is in reality demand, which holds all things together; (for if the builder and the shoemaker do not require anything, or do not require correspondingly, there will be either no exchange, or an exchange of a different sort): but demand is conventionally represented by νόμισμα, which is therefore so called, because it is not φύσει but νόμῳ, so that it is in our power to change it and to make it useless. Ἀντιπεπονθός then will take place when an equality is established so that as husbandman is to shoemaker, so is the shoemaker's ware to the husbandman's. The reference to the proportional formula must be made, not after the exchange (otherwise there will be two extremes, one of which possesses both the excesses [of 4 § 10]), but when they still retain their own wares: in this way they are ἴσοι and κοινωνοί, because it is possible in their case to establish the proper equality: (husbandman A, food C, shoemaker B, his ware equated to the food D:) while if ἀντιπεπονθός could not be established in this way, there would be no κοινωνία. That demand holds things together as a single standard, is indicated

ἢ ἀμφότεροι ἢ ἅτερος, οὐκ ἀλλάττονται, ὥσπερ ὅταν οὗ ἔχει αὐτὸς δέηταί τις, οἷον οἴνου διδόντες σίτου ἐξαγωγήν. § 14 δεῖ ἄρα τοῦτο ἰσασθῆναι. ὑπὲρ δὲ τῆς μελλούσης ἀλλαγῆς, εἰ νῦν μηδὲν δεῖται, ὅτι ἔσται ἐὰν δεηθῇ, τὸ νόμισμα οἷον ἐγγυητής ἐσθ' ἡμῖν· δεῖ γὰρ τοῦτο φέροντι εἶναι λαβεῖν. πάσχει μὲν οὖν καὶ τοῦτο τὸ αὐτό· οὐ γὰρ ἀεὶ ἴσον δύναται· ὅμως δὲ βούλεται μένειν μᾶλλον. διὸ δεῖ πάντα τετιμῆσθαι· οὕτω γὰρ ἀεὶ ἔσται ἀλλαγή, εἰ δὲ τοῦτο, κοινωνία. τὸ δὴ νόμισμα ὥσπερ μέτρον σύμμετρα ποιῆσαν ἰσάζει· οὔτε γὰρ ἂν μὴ οὔσης ἀλλαγῆς κοινωνία ἦν, οὔτ' ἀλλαγὴ ἰσότητος μὴ οὔσης, οὔτ' ἰσότης μὴ οὔσης § 15 συμμετρίας. τῇ μὲν οὖν ἀληθείᾳ ἀδύνατον τὰ τοσοῦτον διαφέροντα σύμμετρα γενέσθαι, πρὸς δὲ τὴν χρείαν ἐνδέχεται ἱκανῶς. ἓν δή τι δεῖ εἶναι, τοῦτο δ' ἐξ ὑποθέσεως· διὸ νόμισμα καλεῖται· τοῦτο γὰρ πάντα ποιεῖ σύμμετρα· μετρεῖται γὰρ πάντα νομίσματι. οἰκία Α, μναῖ δέκα Β, κλίνη Γ. τὸ δὴ Α τοῦ Β ἥμισυ, εἰ πέντε μνῶν ἀξία ἡ οἰκία, ἢ ἴσον· ἡ δὲ κλίνη δέκατον μέρος τὸ Γ τοῦ Β· § 16 δῆλον τοίνυν πόσαι κλῖναι ἴσον οἰκίᾳ, ὅτι πέντε. ὅτι δ' οὕτως ἡ ἀλλαγὴ ἦν πρὶν τὸ νόμισμα εἶναι, δῆλον· διαφέρει γὰρ οὐδὲν ἢ κλῖναι πέντε ἀντὶ οἰκίας, ἢ ὅσου αἱ πέντε κλῖναι.

§ 17 τί μὲν οὖν τὸ ἄδικον καὶ τί τὸ δίκαιόν ἐστιν, εἴρηται.

by the fact that, when there is no demand on the part of both for mutual assistance, or at least on the part of one, they do not exchange: whereas, when B wants what A has, they exchange, giving, for example, the privilege of exporting corn in return for wine; this bargain then has to be equalized. But if we do not require a thing now, τὸ νόμισμα is to us a sort of guarantee of future exchange, a pledge that it shall take place if at another time we require the thing: for it must be possible for the trader on producing the νόμισμα to obtain the ware. Of course τὸ νόμισμα is subject to the same laws as the wares themselves,—it is not always of the same value: nevertheless it tends to be more constant in value than they. All things therefore ought to have a value assigned to them: for so there will always be exchange, and if so, a κοινωνία. Thus τὸ νόμισμα is a sort of measure which makes things commensurable and reduces them to equality: for there would be no κοινωνία if there were no exchange, and no exchange if there were no equality, and no equality if there were no commensurability. Thus though it is in reality impossible for things so widely different to become commensurable, it is possible in an adequate degree by reference to demand. Hence there must be a single standard, and this determined by agreement, whence it is called νόμισμα. This νόμισμα makes all things commensurable, all things being measured by it. Let A be a house, B ten minas, C a bed. Now A is half B, if the house is worth or equivalent to five minas, and the bed C is the tenth part of B: it is plain then how many beds are equivalent to a house, viz. five. That this was the way in which exchange was effected before currency existed, is clear; for it makes no difference whether five beds are given for a house, or the price of the five beds.

We have now defined ἄδικον, and δίκαιον, and from our

διωρισμένων δὲ τούτων δῆλον ὅτι ἡ δικαιοπραγία μέσον ἐστὶ τοῦ ἀδικεῖν καὶ ἀδικεῖσθαι· τὸ μὲν γὰρ πλέον ἔχειν τὸ δ᾽ ἔλαττον ἐστίν. ἡ δὲ δικαιοσύνη μεσότης τίς ἐστιν, οὐ τὸν αὐτὸν δὲ τρόπον ταῖς ἄλλαις ἀρεταῖς, ἀλλ᾽ ὅτι μέσου ἐστίν, < καὶ ὥσπερ ὑγιεινὸν μὲν ἐν ἰατρικῇ εὐεκτικὸν δὲ ἐν γυμναστικῇ· > ἡ δ᾽ ἀδικία τῶν ἄκρων. καὶ ἡ μὲν δικαιοσύνη ἐστὶ καθ᾽ ἣν ὁ δίκαιος λέγεται πρακτικὸς κατὰ προαίρεσιν τοῦ δικαίου, καὶ διανεμητικὸς καὶ αὐτῷ πρὸς ἄλλον καὶ ἑτέρῳ πρὸς ἕτερον, οὐχ οὕτως ὥστε τοῦ μὲν αἱρετοῦ πλέον αὑτῷ ἔλαττον δὲ τῷ πλησίον τοῦ βλαβεροῦ δ᾽ ἀνάπαλιν, ἀλλὰ τοῦ ἴσου τοῦ κατ᾽ ἀναλογίαν, ὁμοίως δὲ καὶ ἄλλῳ πρὸς ἄλλον. ἡ δ᾽ ἀδικία τοὐναντίον τοῦ ἀδίκου· τοῦτο δ᾽ ἐστὶν ὑπερβολὴ καὶ ἔλλειψις τοῦ ὠφελίμου ἢ βλαβεροῦ παρὰ τὸ ἀνάλογον. διὸ ὑπερβολὴ καὶ ἔλλειψις ἡ ἀδικία, ὅτι ὑπερβολῆς καὶ ἐλλείψεώς ἐστιν, ἐφ᾽ αὑτοῦ μὲν ὑπερβολῆς μὲν τοῦ ἁπλῶς ὠφελίμου, ἐλλείψεως δὲ τοῦ βλαβεροῦ· ἐπὶ δὲ τῶν ἄλλων τὸ μὲν ὅλον ὁμοίως, τὸ δὲ παρὰ τὸ ἀνάλογον, ὁποτέρως ἔτυχεν. τοῦ δὲ ἀδικήματος τὸ μὲν ἔλαττον τὸ ἀδικεῖσθαί ἐστι, τὸ δὲ μεῖζον τὸ ἀδικεῖν.

< φανερὸν δὲ καὶ ὅτι ἄμφω μὲν φαῦλα, καὶ τὸ ἀδικεῖσθαι καὶ τὸ ἀδικεῖν· τὸ μὲν γὰρ ἔλαττον τὸ δὲ πλέον ἔχειν ἐστὶ τοῦ μέσου· [καὶ ὥσπερ ὑγιεινὸν μὲν ἐν ἰατρικῇ εὐεκτικὸν δὲ ἐν γυμναστικῇ] ἀλλ᾽ ὅμως χεῖρον τὸ ἀδικεῖν· τὸ μὲν

definitions of them it is plain that δικαιοπραγία is a μέσον between ἀδικεῖν and ἀδικεῖσθαι, the former consisting in having too much, the latter in having too little. Δικαιοσύνη is a μεσότης, not in the same way as the other virtues, but in the sense of having a μέσον for its result, in fact like ὑγιεινόν in medicine and εὐεκτικόν in gymnastic, the extremes being similarly the results of ἀδικία. Furthermore δικαιοσύνη is a ἕξις in virtue of which the δίκαιος is said to be πρακτικὸς κατὰ προαίρεσιν τοῦ δικαίου, καὶ διανεμητικός whether between himself and another, or between two others, not in such a way that he shall have more and his neighbour less of what is desirable, and contrariwise of what is harmful, but so that he and his neighbour shall have τὸ ἴσον τὸ κατ' ἀναλογίαν, and in like manner when the distribution is between two others. Ἀδικία on the other hand is similarly related to τὸ ἄδικον, τὸ ἄδικον being excess and defect of what is beneficial or harmful, in violation of τὸ ἀνάλογον. Wherefore ἀδικία is excess and defect in the sense that its results are excess and defect, that is to say, in the case of the offender, excess of what is generally speaking beneficial and defect of what is harmful, and in the case of others, in general as in the former case, though the deviation from τὸ ἀνάλογον may be either on the side of excess or on that of defect. In the ἀδίκημα defect constitutes ἀδικεῖσθαι, excess ἀδικεῖν. Plainly both are bad, both τὸ ἀδικεῖσθαι and τὸ ἀδικεῖν; for τὸ ἀδικεῖσθαι is to have less, and τὸ ἀδικεῖν to have more, than the mean: nevertheless τὸ ἀδικεῖν is the worse of the two; for τὸ ἀδικεῖσθαι does not imply κακία and

γὰρ ἀδικεῖν μετὰ κακίας καὶ ψεκτόν, καὶ κακίας ἢ τῆς τελείας καὶ ἁπλῶς ἢ ἐγγύς, (οὐ γὰρ ἅπαν τὸ ἑκούσιον μετὰ ἀδικίας, <ἐν οἷς δ' ἀδικία, καὶ τὸ ἀδικεῖν ἐν τούτοις, ἐν οἷς δὲ τὸ ἀδικεῖν, οὐ πᾶσιν ἀδικία, >) τὸ δ' ἀδικεῖσθαι ἄνευ κακίας καὶ ἀδικίας. καθ' αὑτὸ μὲν οὖν τὸ ἀδικεῖσθαι ἧττον φαῦλον, κατὰ συμβεβηκὸς δ' οὐθὲν κωλύει μεῖζον εἶναι κακόν. ἀλλ' οὐδὲν μέλει τῇ τέχνῃ, ἀλλὰ πλευρῖτιν λέγει μείζω νόσον προσπταίσματος· καίτοι γένοιτ' ἄν ποτε θάτερον κατὰ συμβεβηκός, εἰ προσπταίσαντα διὰ τὸ πεσεῖν συμβαίη ὑπὸ τῶν πολεμίων ληφθῆναι καὶ ἀποθανεῖν. >

περὶ μὲν οὖν δικαιοσύνης καὶ ἀδικίας, τίς ἑκατέρας ἐστὶν ἡ φύσις, εἰρήσθω τοῦτον τὸν τρόπον, ὁμοίως δὲ καὶ περὶ δικαίου καὶ ἀδίκου καθόλου. δεῖ δὲ μὴ λανθάνειν ὅτι τὸ ζητούμενόν ἐστι καὶ τὸ ἁπλῶς δίκαιον καὶ τὸ πολιτικὸν δίκαιον. τοῦτο δ' ἐστὶ κοινωνῶν βίου πρὸς τὸ εἶναι αὐτάρκειαν, ἐλευθέρων καὶ ἴσων ἢ κατ' ἀναλογίαν ἢ κατ' ἀριθμόν· ὥστε ὅσοις μὴ ἔστι τοῦτο, οὐκ ἔστι τούτοις πρὸς ἀλλήλους τὸ πολιτικὸν δίκαιον, ἀλλά τι δίκαιον καὶ καθ' ὁμοιότητα. ἔστι γὰρ δίκαιον οἷς καὶ νόμος πρὸς αὐτούς· νόμος δ', ἐν οἷς ἀδικία· ἡ γὰρ δίκη κρίσις τοῦ δικαίου καὶ τοῦ ἀδίκου· [ἐν οἷς δ' ἀδικία, καὶ τὸ ἀδικεῖν ἐν τούτοις, ἐν οἷς δὲ τὸ ἀδικεῖν, οὐ πᾶσιν ἀδικία·] τοῦτο δ' ἐστὶ τὸ πλέον αὑτῷ νέμειν τῶν ἁπλῶς ἀγαθῶν, ἔλαττον δὲ τῶν ἁπλῶς κακῶν. διὸ οὐκ ἐῶμεν ἄρχειν ἄνθρωπον, ἀλλὰ τὸν λόγον, ὅτι ἑαυτῷ τοῦτο

1 ψεκτόν, καὶ κακίας] ψεκτὸν ἦν καὶ κακίας Nᵇ. ψεκτὸν ἦν καὶ τῆς κακίας HᵃMᵇQ. τῆς post ἢ] om. Lᵇ. 2 καὶ post τελείας] om. Kᵇ. ἐγγύς] σύνεγγυς Oᵇ. ἅπαν] πᾶν KᵇPᵇ. 7 εἶναι] om. HᵃKᵇLᵇNᵇOᵇPᵇ. μέλει] μέλλει Hᵃ. 9 προσπταίσαντα] προσπταίσαντος MᵇQ. 10 καὶ] ἢ KᵇOᵇ. 14 δικαίου] τοῦ δικαίου Bekker. 6 §§ 1, 2] vide infra, post 8 § 8. 6 § 3] vide infra, 10 § 1. 15 καὶ τὸ ἁπλῶς—ἐστιν] om. MᵇQ. καὶ post δίκαιον] om. KᵇLᵇNᵇ. 16 ἐστὶ] ἐπὶ Kᵇ. ἐστιν ἐπὶ Oᵇ Bekker. κοινωνῶν] κοινωνὸν HᵃMᵇQ. κοινα Pᵇ. 20 ἀλλά τι δίκαιον] ἀλλά τι δίκαιον ἀλλά τι δίκαιον Hᵃ. καὶ ante καθ'] om. Hᵃ. 21 οἷς] ἐν οἷς Oᵇ. αὐτούς] Mᵇ. αὐτοὺς ceteri et Bekker. 22 κρίσις] κρίσις ἐστὶ LᵇOᵇ. 24 αὐτῷ] αὑτῷ Kᵇ. αὑτῶ HᵃNᵇ. 26 τὸν λόγον] τῶν λόγων Nᵇ. τὸν νόμον MᵇQ.

ἀδικία in the sufferer, whereas τὸ ἀδικεῖν is blameworthy and implies κακία, which κακία is either τελεία καὶ ἁπλῶς or almost so. ([The qualification is required] because an ἀδίκημα voluntarily committed does not necessarily imply ἀδικία; where there is ἀδικία, there is ἀδικεῖν, but where there is ἀδικεῖν, there is not always ἀδικία.) Thus in itself τὸ ἀδικεῖσθαι is the lesser evil; still it may be κατὰ συμβεβηκός the greater. With this however theory is not concerned: theory reckons pleurisy a more serious infirmity than a sprain; but a sprain may be κατὰ συμβεβηκός worse than a pleurisy, should it chance that a man in consequence of a sprain falls, and in consequence of the fall is taken by the enemy and put to death.

So much may be said in explanation of the nature of δικαιοσύνη and ἀδικία, and in like manner of δίκαιον and ἄδικον regarded καθόλου. But it must not be forgotten that what we seek is not merely τὸ ἁπλῶς δίκαιον, but also τὸ πολιτικὸν δίκαιον, i.e. the δίκαιον of free and (proportionately or actually) equal citizens living together with a view to the satisfaction of wants. Where this is not the case, πολιτικὸν δίκαιον does not exist, but only a sort of δίκαιον, so called καθ' ὁμοιότητα. For δίκαιον subsists among those who have law to govern their mutual dealings; and law, where there is ἀδικία, δίκη being the determination of δίκαιον and ἄδικον, and ἄδικον consisting in the appropriation of too large a share of what is generally speaking good or too small a share of what is generally speaking bad. Hence we do not allow a particular man to rule, preferring the formula of law, because a particular man

ποιεῖ καὶ γίνεται τύραννος. ἔστι δ' ὁ ἄρχων φύλαξ τοῦ
§ 6 δικαίου, εἰ δὲ τοῦ δικαίου, καὶ τοῦ ἴσου· ἐπεὶ δ' οὐθὲν
αὑτῷ πλέον εἶναι δοκεῖ, εἴπερ δίκαιος, (οὐ γὰρ νέμει πλέον
τοῦ ἁπλῶς ἀγαθοῦ αὑτῷ, εἰ μὴ πρὸς αὑτὸν ἀνάλογόν
ἐστιν· διὸ ἑτέρῳ πονεῖ, καὶ διὰ τοῦτο ἀλλότριον εἶναί 5
φασιν ἀγαθὸν τὴν δικαιοσύνην, καθάπερ ἐλέχθη καὶ πρό-
§ 7 τερον,)—μισθὸς ἄρα τις δοτέος, τοῦτο δὲ τιμὴ καὶ γέρας·
§ 8 ὅτῳ δὲ μὴ ἱκανὰ τὰ τοιαῦτα, οὗτοι γίνονται τύραννοι. τὸ
δὲ δεσποτικὸν δίκαιον καὶ τὸ πατρικὸν οὐ ταὐτὸν τούτοις
ἀλλ' ὅμοιον· οὐ γὰρ ἔστιν ἀδικία πρὸς τὰ αὑτοῦ ἁπλῶς, 10
τὸ δὲ κτῆμα καὶ τὸ τέκνον, ἕως ἂν ᾖ πηλίκον καὶ χωρισθῇ,
§ 9 ὥσπερ μέρος αὑτοῦ. αὑτὸν δ' οὐθεὶς προαιρεῖται βλάπτειν, διὸ οὐκ ἔστιν ἀδικία πρὸς αὑτόν, οὐδ' ἄρα ἄδικον
οὐδὲ δίκαιον τὸ πολιτικόν· κατὰ νόμον γὰρ ἦν, καὶ ἐν
οἷς ἐπεφύκει εἶναι νόμος· οὗτοι δ' ἦσαν οἷς ὑπάρχει 15
ἰσότης τοῦ ἄρχειν καὶ ἄρχεσθαι. διὸ μᾶλλον πρὸς γυ-
ναῖκά ἐστι δίκαιον ἢ πρὸς τέκνα καὶ κτήματα· τοῦτο γάρ
ἐστι τὸ οἰκονομικὸν δίκαιον· ἕτερον δὲ καὶ τοῦτο τοῦ
7 πολιτικοῦ. τοῦ δὲ πολιτικοῦ δικαίου τὸ μὲν φυσικόν ἐστι
τὸ δὲ νομικόν, φυσικὸν μὲν τὸ πανταχοῦ τὴν αὐτὴν ἔχον 20
δύναμιν, καὶ οὐ τῷ δοκεῖν ἢ μή, νομικὸν δὲ ὃ ἐξ ἀρχῆς
μὲν οὐθὲν διαφέρει οὕτως ἢ ἄλλως, ὅταν δὲ θῶνται, διαφέρει, οἷον τὸ μνᾶς λυτροῦσθαι, ἢ τὸ αἶγα θύειν ἀλλὰ μὴ
δύο πρόβατα, ἔτι ὅσα ἐπὶ τῶν καθ' ἕκαστα νομοθετοῦσιν,

2 εἰ δὲ τοῦ δικαίου] om. M^bQ.   3 πλέον post νέμει] om. P^b.   4 τοῦ ἁπλῶς ἀγαθοῦ αὑτῷ] αὑτῷ τοῦ ἁπλῶς ἀγαθοῦ L^b.   αὑτῷ] αὑτῷ L^bN^bQ.   αὑτὸν] ἑαυτὸν Q.   5 πονεῖ] ποιεῖ Bekker.   εἶναί φασιν ἀγαθὸν] ἀγαθὸν εἶναί φασιν H^aM^bQ.   6 καὶ] om. H^a.   7 ἄρα τις] τις ἄρα H^aM^bQO^b.   8 ὅτῳ] ὅσοις O^b.   τὰ τοιαῦτα] ταῦτα H^aM^bQN^bO^b.   9 ταὐτὸν] ταυτὸ O^b.   τούτοις] τούτων H^a.   10 αὑτοῦ] αὐτοῦ H^aL^bN^b.   11 τὸ ante τέκνον] om. K^bL^b.   χωρισθῇ] μὴ χωρισθῇ H^aL^bM^bQ Bekker.   12 αὑτὸν] αὐτὸν H^aN^b.   13 αὑτὸν] αὐτὸν H^aK^bM^bQ.   ἄδικον] ἀδικία ὂν K^b.   16 γυναῖκα] τὴν γυναῖκα M^bQ.   17 κτήματα] κτῆμα L^b.   18 οἰκονομικὸν] οἰκονομικὸν καὶ N^b.   δὲ] δέ ἐστι N^bP^b.   καὶ ante τοῦτο] om. H^aM^bQ.   19 τοῦ δὲ πολιτικοῦ] om. K^b.   μὲν] μὲν γὰρ K^b.   20 νομικόν] νόμιμον K^bP^b.   νομικόν, καὶ L^b.   21 οὐ τῷ] οὕτω K^bM^bQ.   νομικὸν] νόμιμον K^b.   ὃ] om. M^bQ.   22 ὅταν δὲ θῶνται, διαφέρει] om. P^b.   23 οἷον] οὕτως ἢ ἄλλως οἷον K^b.

rules in his own interest and becomes a tyrant. The magistrate is the guardian of τὸ δίκαιον, and therefore of τὸ ἴσον: and since it is assumed that if he is δίκαιος, he has no more than his share,—for he does not apportion to himself more of what is generally speaking good unless such a share is proportionate to his claims, so that it is in the interest of another that he is at the pains of the distribution, (which is the reason why δικαιοσύνη is said to be the good of others, as was remarked before,)—a reward must be given to the magistrate in the shape of honour and privilege; and when magistrates do not receive a sufficiency of such things, they become tyrants.

The δίκαιον of master and slave (δεσποτικόν) and that of father and son (πατρικόν) resemble, but are not identical with, that of the free and equal: for there is no ἀδικία in the strict sense of the word towards what is one's own; and the slave, and the child until he reaches a certain age and becomes independent, are as it were parts of oneself. Again no one deliberately chooses to harm himself, and therefore a man cannot show ἀδικία towards himself; it follows that he cannot exhibit towards himself πολιτικὸν ἄδικον or δίκαιον, since, as we said before, these depend upon law, and subsist only among those with whom law is a natural institution, that is to say, as we explained, those who have equality in ruling and being ruled. Hence δίκαιον subsists rather between man and wife than between father and children or master and slave: this, [the δίκαιον of man and wife,] is the δίκαιον of the household, and even this is different from the δίκαιον of the polity.

Of the πολιτικὸν δίκαιον there are two kinds, the one natural, the other conventional; that being natural which everywhere has the same import and does not depend upon enactment, and that conventional which in the first instance is decided indifferently one way or another, but when once decided is not a matter of indifference: for example, that a mina shall be the prisoner's ransom, that a sacrifice shall consist of a goat and not of two sheep, and all prescriptions for

§ 2 οἷον τὸ θύειν Βρασίδᾳ, καὶ τὰ ψηφισματώδη. δοκεῖ δ᾽ ἐνίοις εἶναι πάντα τοιαῦτα, ὅτι τὸ μὲν φύσει ἀκίνητον καὶ πανταχοῦ τὴν αὐτὴν ἔχει δύναμιν, ὥσπερ τὸ πῦρ καὶ ἐνθάδε καὶ ἐν Πέρσαις καίει, τὰ δὲ δίκαια κινούμενα § 3 ὁρῶσιν. (τοῦτο δ᾽ οὐκ ἔστιν οὕτως ἔχον, ἀλλ᾽ ἔστιν ὥς. καίτοι παρά γε τοῖς θεοῖς ἴσως οὐδαμῶς· παρ᾽ ἡμῖν δ᾽ ἔστι μέν τι καὶ φύσει, κινητὸν μέντοι πᾶν.) ἀλλ᾽ ὅμως § 4 ἔστι τὸ μὲν φύσει τὸ δ᾽ οὐ φύσει· ποῖον δὲ φύσει τῶν ἐνδεχομένων καὶ ἄλλως ἔχειν, καὶ ποῖον οὐ ἀλλὰ νομικὸν καὶ συνθήκῃ, εἴπερ ἄμφω κινητὰ ὁμοίως, δῆλον. καὶ ἐπὶ τῶν ἄλλων ὁ αὐτὸς ἁρμόσει διορισμός· φύσει γὰρ ἡ δεξιὰ κρείττων, καίτοι ἐνδέχεται πάντας ἀμφιδεξίους γε- § 5 νέσθαι. τὰ δὲ κατὰ συνθήκην καὶ τὸ συμφέρον τῶν δικαίων ὅμοιά ἐστι τοῖς μέτροις. οὐ γὰρ πανταχοῦ ἴσα τὰ οἰνηρὰ καὶ σιτηρὰ μέτρα, ἀλλ᾽ οὗ μὲν ὠνοῦνται, μείζω, οὗ δὲ πωλοῦσιν, ἐλάττω· ὁμοίως δὲ καὶ τὰ μὴ φυσικὰ ἀλλ᾽ ἀνθρώπινα δίκαια οὐ ταὐτὰ πανταχοῦ, ἐπεὶ οὐδ᾽ αἱ πολιτεῖαι, ἀλλὰ μία μόνον πανταχοῦ κατὰ φύσιν ἡ ἀρίστη. § 6 τῶν δὲ δικαίων καὶ νομίμων ἕκαστον ὡς τὰ καθόλου πρὸς τὰ καθ᾽ ἕκαστα ἔχει· τὰ μὲν γὰρ πραττόμενα πολλά, § 7 ἐκείνων δ᾽ ἕκαστον ἕν· καθόλου γάρ. διαφέρει δὲ τὸ ἀδίκημα καὶ τὸ ἄδικον, καὶ τὸ δικαίωμα καὶ τὸ δίκαιον. ἄδικον μὲν γάρ ἐστι τῇ φύσει ἢ τάξει· αὐτὸ δὲ τοῦτο, ὅταν πραχθῇ, ἀδίκημά ἐστι, πρὶν δὲ πραχθῆναι, οὔπω,

individual cases, e. g. the sacrifice in honour of Brasidas, and the provisions of a psephism. Some maintain that all δίκαια are of this conventional sort, because what is by nature is invariable and has the same effect everywhere, as for example fire burns both here and in Persia; whereas they see that δίκαια vary. (That δίκαια vary, though not true without limitation, is true in a manner. With the gods indeed, it is perhaps not true at all; but with men, though there is a δίκαιον which is by nature, all δίκαια are variable.) Nevertheless there is a δίκαιον which is natural, as well as a δίκαιον which is non-natural: and it is easy to see what regulations which might have been otherwise are natural, and what regulations are not natural but legal and conventional, the two sorts being all the time equally variable. And in all other matters the same distinction will hold: for by nature the right hand is the stronger; still all may become ambidextrous. In fact δίκαια which are determined by convention and convenience resemble standard measures: for the measures of wine and corn are not equal in all places, being larger in wholesale, and smaller in retail, markets; and in like manner δίκαια which are not natural but of human appointment are not the same in all places, inasmuch as constitutions are not the same, though in all places there is one only which is natural, i. e. the perfect constitution.

Each δίκαιον or νόμιμον stands to individual acts in the relation of universal to particulars: for the things done are many, and each δίκαιον or νόμιμον is one, because universal.

There is a difference between the ἀδίκημα and the ἄδικον, the δικαίωμα and the δίκαιον: for whereas a thing is ἄδικον by nature or by appointment, the thing in question when it is done is an ἀδίκημα; before it is done it is not an ἀδίκημα but

ἀλλ' ἄδικον. ὁμοίως δὲ καὶ δικαίωμα. (καλεῖται δὲ μᾶλλον δικαιοπράγημα τὸ κοινόν, δικαίωμα δὲ τὸ ἐπανόρθωμα τοῦ ἀδικήματος.) καθ' ἕκαστον δὲ αὐτῶν, ποῖά τε εἴδη καὶ πόσα καὶ περὶ ποῖα τυγχάνει ὄντα, ὕστερον ἐπισκεπτέον.

8 ὄντων δὲ τῶν δικαίων καὶ ἀδίκων τῶν εἰρημένων, ἀδικεῖ μὲν καὶ δικαιοπραγεῖ, ὅταν ἑκών τις αὐτὰ πράττῃ· ὅταν δ' ἄκων, οὔτ' ἀδικεῖ οὔτε δικαιοπραγεῖ ἀλλ' ἢ κατὰ συμβεβηκός· οἷς γὰρ συμβέβηκε δικαίοις εἶναι ἢ § 2 ἀδίκοις, πράττουσιν. (ἀδίκημα δὲ καὶ δικαιοπράγημα ὥρισται τῷ ἑκουσίῳ καὶ ἀκουσίῳ· ὅταν γὰρ ἑκούσιον ᾖ, ψέγεται, ἅμα δὲ καὶ ἀδίκημα τότ' ἐστίν· ὥστ' ἔσται τι ἄδικον μὲν ἀδίκημα δ' οὔπω, ἐὰν μὴ τὸ ἑκούσιον § 3 προσῇ. λέγω δ' ἑκούσιον μέν, ὥσπερ καὶ πρότερον εἴρηται, ὃ ἄν τις τῶν ἐφ' αὑτῷ ὄντων εἰδὼς καὶ μὴ ἀγνοῶν πράττῃ μήτε ὃν μήτε ᾧ μήτε οὗ < ἕνεκα >, οἷον τίνα τύπτει καὶ τίνι καὶ τίνος ἕνεκα, κἀκείνων ἕκαστον μὴ κατὰ συμβεβηκὸς μηδὲ βίᾳ, ὥσπερ εἴ τις λαβὼν τὴν χεῖρα αὐτοῦ τύπτοι ἕτερον, οὐχ ἑκών, οὐ γὰρ ἐπ' αὐτῷ. ἐνδέχεται δὲ τὸν τυπτόμενον πατέρα εἶναι, τὸν δ' ὅτι μὲν ἄνθρωπος ἢ τῶν παρόντων τις γινώσκειν, ὅτι δὲ πατὴρ ἀγνοεῖν. ὁμοίως δὲ τὸ τοιοῦτον διωρίσθω καὶ ἐπὶ τοῦ οὗ ἕνεκα, καὶ περὶ τὴν πρᾶξιν ὅλην. τὸ δὴ ἀγνοούμενον, ἢ μὴ ἀγνοούμενον μὲν μὴ ἐπ' αὐτῷ δ' ὄν, ἢ βίᾳ, ἀκούσιον.)

1 ἄδικον] ἄδικον ὅτι (τι Κᵇ) ὅταν πραχθῇ ἀδίκημα ἐστίν ΚᵇLᵇNᵇOᵇPᵇ.   2 μᾶλλον δικαιοπράγημα τὸ κοινόν] τὸ κοινὸν μᾶλλον δικαιοπράγημα HᵃMᵇQNᵇ.   δὲ] om. Hᵃ.   3 ποῖά] ποῖα Nᵇ.   4 τυγχάνει] τυγχάνοι Pᵇ.   6 τῶν ante δικαίων] om. MᵇQ.   εἰρημένων] προειρημένων Oᵇ.   7 ὅταν—ἀλλ' ἢ] τις ἀλλὰ MᵇQ.   9 εἶναι ἢ ἀδίκοις] ἢ ἀδίκοις εἶναι Oᵇ.   12 ἔσται τι ἄδικον] ἄδικόν τι ἔσται HᵃMᵇQNᵇ.   13 δ' οὔπω, ἐὰν] οὔπω ἐστὶν ἐὰν MᵇQ.   ἐὰν] ἂν HᵃKᵇLᵇPᵇ.   14 μὲν] om. MᵇQ.   15 αὑτῷ] ἑαυτῷ HᵃMᵇQOᵇ.   16 πράττῃ] πράττοι Mᵇ.   πράττῃ—οἷον] om. Nᵇ.   ὃν] ὁ ΚᵇPᵇ.   ᾧ] ὡς corr. Κᵇ.   οὗ] ὃν corr. ΚᵇPᵇ.   ἕνεκα] addit Bekker. om. codd. omnes.   17 τύπτει] τύπτειν Κᵇ.   καὶ τίνι] om. Κᵇ.   ἕκαστον] ἑκάτερον Κᵇ. ἑκάτεον Pᵇ.   19 τύπτοι] τύπτει HᵃLᵇMᵇQOᵇ.   ἑκών] ἑκὼν δὲ HᵃMᵇQNᵇOᵇPᵇ.   ἐπ' αὐτῷ] ἐφ' ἑαυτῷ Oᵇ.   21 δὲ πατὴρ] δ' ὁ πατὴρ Oᵇ.   22 τὸ ante τοιοῦτον] om. Q.   τοῦ] Κᵇ. τῶν ceteri.   24 ἐπ' αὐτῷ] ἐφ' αὐτῷ LᵇPᵇ. ἐφ' αὑτῷ Nᵇ. ἐφ' ἑαυτῶ Oᵇ.   ἀκούσιον] ἑκούσιον Nᵇ.

only ἄδικον. So too with a δικαίωμα. (More correctly the general term is δικαιοπράγημα, δικαίωμα being the correction of the ἀδίκημα.)

We must enumerate hereafter the several kinds of δίκαια and νόμιμα, and describe them and the things with which they are concerned.

And whereas δίκαια and ἄδικα are what has been said, a man ἀδικεῖ or δικαιοπραγεῖ when he voluntarily does ἄδικα or δίκαια: but when he does those acts involuntarily, he neither ἀδικεῖ nor δικαιοπραγεῖ except κατὰ συμβεβηκός, for such an one does acts which are κατὰ συμβεβηκὸς δίκαια or ἄδικα. (That an act is or is not an ἀδίκημα or δικαιοπράγημα is determined by its voluntariness or involuntariness: for when an act is voluntary it is blamed, and is at the same time an ἀδίκημα: so that there will be an act which is ἄδικον, but not yet an ἀδίκημα, if voluntariness is lacking. Here by a voluntary act I mean, as has been said above, anything which being within his power a man does knowingly and not in ignorance of the person, the instrument, or the result,—for example whom he strikes, what he strikes with, and with what result,—doing any such act neither κατὰ συμβεβηκός nor under compulsion; whereas if B were to take A's hand and strike C, A would not strike voluntarily, the act not being in his own power. But it is possible that the person struck should be the father of the striker, and that the striker should know that the other was a human being or even one of the bystanders, and yet be ignorant that it was his father. The same sort of distinction may be made in like manner in regard to the result, and with reference to the act generally. Now an act done in ignorance, or an act which, though not done in ignorance, is not under the agent's control, or is done under compulsion,

πολλὰ γὰρ καὶ τῶν φύσει ὑπαρχόντων εἰδότες καὶ πράττομεν καὶ πάσχομεν, ὧν οὐθὲν οὔθ' ἑκούσιον οὔτ' ἀκούσιόν ἐστιν, οἷον τὸ γηρᾶν ἢ ἀποθνήσκειν· ἔστι δ' ὁμοίως ἐπὶ τῶν ἀδίκων καὶ τῶν δικαίων καὶ τὸ κατὰ συμβεβηκός· καὶ γὰρ ἂν τὴν παρακαταθήκην ἀποδοίη τις ἄκων καὶ διὰ φόβον, ὃν οὔτε δίκαια πράττειν οὔτε δικαιοπραγεῖν φατέον ἀλλ' ἢ κατὰ συμβεβηκός· ὁμοίως δὲ καὶ τὸν ἀναγκαζόμενον καὶ ἄκοντα τὴν παρακαταθήκην μὴ ἀποδιδόντα κατὰ συμβεβηκὸς φατέον ἀδικεῖν καὶ τὰ ἄδικα πράττειν. τῶν δὲ ἑκουσίων τὰ μὲν προελόμενοι πράττομεν τὰ δ' οὐ προελόμενοι, προελόμενοι μὲν ὅσα προβουλευσάμενοι, ἀπροαίρετα δὲ ὅσα ἀπροβούλευτα. τριῶν δὲ οὐσῶν βλαβῶν τῶν ἐν ταῖς κοινωνίαις, τὰ μὲν μετ' ἀγνοίας ἁμαρτήματά ἐστιν, ὅταν μήτε ὃν μήτε ὃ μήτε ᾧ μήτε οὗ ἕνεκα ὑπέλαβε πράξῃ· ἢ γὰρ οὐ βαλεῖν ἢ οὐ τούτῳ ἢ οὐ τοῦτον ἢ οὐ τούτου ἕνεκα ᾠήθη, ἀλλὰ συνέβη οὐχ οὗ ἕνεκα ᾠήθη, οἷον οὐχ ἵνα τρώσῃ ἀλλ' ἵνα κεντήσῃ, ἢ οὐχ ὅν, ἢ οὐχ ᾧ· ὅταν μὲν οὖν παραλόγως ἡ βλάβη γένηται, ἀτύχημα, ὅταν δὲ μὴ παραλόγως, ἄνευ δὲ κακίας, ἁμάρτημα· ἁμαρτάνει μὲν γὰρ ὅταν ἡ ἀρχὴ ἐν αὐτῷ ᾖ τῆς ἀγνοίας, ἀτυχεῖ δ' ὅταν ἔξωθεν. ὅταν δὲ εἰδὼς μὲν μὴ προβουλεύσας δέ, ἀδίκημα, οἷον ὅσα τε διὰ θυμὸν καὶ ἄλλα πάθη ὅσα ἀναγκαῖα ἢ φυσικὰ συμβαίνει τοῖς ἀνθρώποις· ταῦτα γὰρ βλάπτοντες καὶ ἁμαρτάνοντες ἀδικοῦσι μέν,

is involuntary.) For there are many natural processes which we perform and experience with full knowledge, but which do not fall either under the head of voluntary or under that of involuntary, for example growing old, or dying: and in like manner there is a κατὰ συμβεβηκός in the case of things ἄδικα and δίκαια: thus a man may restore the deposit unwillingly and under the influence of fear, and such a one should not be said δίκαια πράττειν or δικαιοπραγεῖν except κατὰ συμβεβηκός: and in like manner one who under compulsion and unwillingly retains the deposit should be said κατὰ συμβεβηκὸς ἀδικεῖν and τὰ ἄδικα πράττειν. Of voluntary acts we do some of deliberate purpose, others without deliberate purpose, of deliberate purpose when we have previously debated what we shall do, without deliberate purpose when we have not so debated. And whereas there are three sorts of harm which may be done in κοινωνίαι, things done ignorantly are ἁμαρτήματα when the object, the act, the instrument, or the result is other than the agent supposed: for instance, he had thought that he would not strike, or that he would not strike with this weapon, or that he would not strike this person, or that the blow would not have this effect, and the result was other than he had expected (thus he did not strike with intent to cut, but with intent to prick), or the person or the weapon was different. Now when the harm is done contrary to expectation, it is an ἀτύχημα; but when, though it is not contrary to expectation, there is no malice, it is a ἁμάρτημα; that is to say, when the origin of the ignorance is in the agent, he ἁμαρτάνει, but when it is external to him, he ἀτυχεῖ. When however a man harms another knowingly but without previous deliberation, it is an ἀδίκημα; for instance, harms done under the influence of anger or any other unavoidable or natural passion to which men are liable: when men do harm (βλάπτοντες) or misconduct themselves (ἁμαρτά-

καὶ ἀδικήματά ἐστιν, οὐ μέντοι πω ἄδικοι διὰ ταῦτα οὐδὲ πονηροί· οὐ γὰρ διὰ μοχθηρίαν ἡ βλάβη· < ἐπεὶ δ' ἔστιν ἀδικοῦντα μήπω ἄδικον εἶναι, ὁ ποῖα ἀδικήματα ἀδικῶν ἤδη ἀδικός ἐστιν ἑκάστην ἀδικίαν, οἷον κλέπτης ἢ μοιχὸς ἢ λῃστής; ἢ οὕτω μὲν οὐδὲν διοίσει, (καὶ γὰρ ἂν συγγένοιτο γυναικὶ εἰδὼς τὸ ᾗ, ἀλλ' οὐ διὰ προαιρέσεως ἀρχὴν ἀλλὰ διὰ πάθος· ἀδικεῖ μὲν οὖν, ἄδικος δ' οὐκ ἔστιν, οἷον οὐ κλέπτης, ἔκλεψε δέ, οὐδὲ μοιχός, ἐμοίχευσε δέ· ὁμοίως δὲ καὶ ἐπὶ τῶν ἄλλων,) > ὅταν δ' ἐκ προαιρέσεως, ἄδικος καὶ μοχθηρός; διὸ καλῶς τὰ ἐκ θυμοῦ οὐκ ἐκ προνοίας κρίνεται· οὐ γὰρ ἄρχει ὁ θυμῷ ποιῶν, ἀλλ' ὁ ὀργίσας. ἔτι δὲ οὐδὲ περὶ τοῦ γενέσθαι ἢ μὴ ἀμφισβητεῖται, ἀλλὰ περὶ τοῦ δικαίου· ἐπὶ φαινομένῃ γὰρ ἀδικίᾳ ἡ ὀργή ἐστιν· οὐ γὰρ ὥσπερ ἐν τοῖς συναλλάγμασι περὶ τοῦ γενέσθαι ἀμφισβητοῦσιν, ὧν ἀνάγκη τὸν ἕτερον εἶναι μοχθηρόν, ἂν μὴ διὰ λήθην αὐτὸ δρῶσιν· ἀλλ' ὁμολογοῦντες περὶ τοῦ πράγματος, περὶ τοῦ ποτέρως δίκαιον ἀμφισβητοῦσιν· ὁ δ' ἐπιβουλεύσας οὐκ ἀγνοεῖ. ὥστε ὁ μὲν οἴεται ἀδικεῖσθαι, ὁ δ' οὔ. ἂν δ' ἐκ προαιρέσεως βλάψῃ, ἀδικεῖ καὶ κατὰ ταῦτ' ἤδη τὰ ἀδικήματα ὁ ἀδικῶν ἄδικος, ὅταν παρὰ τὸ ἀνάλογον ᾖ ἢ παρὰ τὸ ἴσον. ὁμοίως δὲ καὶ δίκαιος, ὅταν προελόμενος δικαιοπραγῇ, δικαιοπραγεῖ δέ, ἂν μόνον ἑκὼν πράττῃ. τῶν δ' ἀκουσίων τὰ μέν ἐστι συγγνωμονικὰ τὰ δ' οὐ συγγνωμονικά· ὅσα μὲν γὰρ μὴ μόνον ἀγνοοῦντες ἀλλὰ καὶ δι' ἄγνοιαν ἁμαρτάνουσι, συγ-

2 οὐ γὰρ] οὐδὲ HᵃMᵇQNᵇ.   ἐπεί—ἄλλων] 6 §§ 1, 2 traieci.   3 ποῖα] ποῖα δ' Pᵇ.   6 διὰ ante προαιρέσεως] om. Kᵇ.   7 διὰ ante πάθος] om. MᵇQ.   πάθος] πάθη Hᵃ.   8 οὐ ante κλέπτης] οὐδὲ HᵃLᵇMᵇQNᵇOᵇ Bekker.   9 δὲ post ὁμοίως] om. Pᵇ.   10 μοχθηρός] πονηρός MᵇQ.   διὸ] διὸ καὶ Lᵇ.   προνοίας] προαιρέσεως MᵇQ.   11 θυμῷ ποιῶν] θυμοποιῶν Kᵇ.   12 οὐδὲ] οὐ MᵇQ.   περὶ] παρὰ Hᵃ.   13 περὶ] παρὰ Hᵃ.   φαινομένῃ] φερομένῃ Pᵇ.   ἡ] om. Mᵇ.   14 ἐν] om. Kᵇ.   περὶ] παρὰ Hᵃ.   γενέσθαι] γίνεσθαι Mᵇ.   15 ἀμφισβητοῦσιν] ἀμφισβητεῖται MᵇQ.   16 ἂν] εἰ Oᵇ.   αὐτὸ] αὐτῶν HᵃMᵇ   17 τοῦ ποτέρως] δὲ τοῦ ποτέρως pr. Kᵇ.   19 ἂν] ἐὰν KᵇLᵇPᵇ.   20 ἄδικος] ὁ ἄδικος Pᵇ.   21 παρὰ] περὶ Lᵇ.   ᾖ] om. MᵇQ.   22 δίκαιος] ὁ δίκαιος Lᵇ.   δικαιοπραγεῖ] δικαιοπραγῇ Mᵇ.   23 μόνον] om. Q.   μὲν] μὴ MᵇQ.

νοντες) in this manner, they ἀδικοῦσιν and the acts are ἀδικήματα, but the perpetrators are not necessarily ἄδικοι or πονηροί, the harmful act not being the result of μοχθηρία. But seeing that a man may be ἀδικῶν and yet not necessarily ἄδικος, what are the ἀδικήματα the commission of which makes a man necessarily ἄδικος of any particular ἀδικία—for example, a thief, an adulterer, or a brigand? Shall we not rather say that the distinction is not of this sort [i.e. does not lie in the acts],—(for a man may have intercourse with a woman knowing who she is, yet not of deliberate purpose, but under the influence of passion: such an one ἀδικεῖ without being ἄδικος, thieving, for example, yet not being a thief, committing adultery, yet not being an adulterer, and so forth),—[but lies in the person], and that it is when a man ἀδικῇ of deliberate purpose that he is ἄδικος and μοχθηρός?

Hence actions prompted by anger are rightly held not to have been done ἐκ προνοίας. For it is not ὁ θυμῷ ποιῶν who begins the quarrel, but ὁ ὀργίσας. Moreover the issue is one not of fact but of δίκαιον, anger arising at apparent ἀδικία: i.e. the parties do not dispute the fact, as they do in συναλλάγματα, where one or other must be μοχθηρός,—unless they do it through forgetfulness; but, agreeing about the fact, they disagree as to the side on which right lies (ποτέρως δίκαιον). On the other hand ὁ ἐπιβουλεύσας (the vengeful man) is obviously not ignorant of the fact. Thus whereas ὁ θυμῷ ποιῶν may plead his belief that he has been wronged, ὁ ἐπιβουλεύσας cannot do so.

But if a man harms another of deliberate purpose, he ἀδικεῖ and is moreover ἄδικος, provided that the act violates proportion or equality. In like manner a man is δίκαιος when he δικαιοπραγῇ of deliberate purpose, whilst he δικαιοπραγεῖ if he acts voluntarily though not, perhaps, deliberately.

Of involuntary harmful acts some are excusable, others are not. Those ἁμαρτήματα which men do not only in ignorance, but owing to ignorance, are excusable, but those

γνωμονικά, ὅσα δὲ μὴ δι' ἄγνοιαν, ἀλλ' ἀγνοοῦντες μὲν διὰ πάθος δὲ μήτε φυσικὸν μήτ' ἀνθρωπικόν, οὐ συγγνωμονικά.

9 ἀπορήσειε δ' ἄν τις εἰ ἱκανῶς διώρισται περὶ τοῦ ἀδικεῖσθαι καὶ ἀδικεῖν, πρῶτον μὲν εἰ ἔστιν ὥσπερ Εὐριπίδης εἴρηκε, λέγων ἀτόπως

μητέρα κατέκταν τὴν ἐμήν, βραχὺς λόγος.
ἑκὼν ἑκοῦσαν, ἢ οὐχ ἑκοῦσαν οὐχ ἑκών;

πότερον γὰρ ὡς ἀληθῶς ἔστιν ἑκόντα ἀδικεῖσθαι, ἢ οὒ ἀλλ' ἀκούσιον ἅπαν, ὥσπερ καὶ τὸ ἀδικεῖν πᾶν ἑκούσιον; καὶ ἆρα πᾶν οὕτως ἢ ἐκείνως, ὥσπερ καὶ τὸ ἀδικεῖν πᾶν § 2 ἑκούσιον, ἢ τὸ μὲν ἑκούσιον τὸ δ' ἀκούσιον; ὁμοίως δὲ καὶ ἐπὶ τοῦ δικαιοῦσθαι· τὸ γὰρ δικαιοπραγεῖν πᾶν ἑκούσιον. ὥστ' εὔλογον ἀντικεῖσθαι ὁμοίως καθ' ἑκάτερον τό τ' ἀδικεῖσθαι καὶ τὸ δικαιοῦσθαι—ἢ ἑκούσιον ἢ ἀκούσιον εἶναι. ἄτοπον δ' ἂν δόξειε καὶ ἐπὶ τοῦ δικαιοῦσθαι, εἰ § 3 πᾶν ἑκούσιον· ἔνιοι γὰρ δικαιοῦνται οὐχ ἑκόντες. ἐπεὶ καὶ τόδε διαπορήσειεν ἄν τις, πότερον ὁ τὸ ἄδικον πεπονθὼς ἀδικεῖται πᾶς ἢ ὥσπερ καὶ ἐπὶ τοῦ πράττειν, καὶ ἐπὶ τοῦ πάσχειν ἐστίν; κατὰ συμβεβηκὸς γὰρ ἐνδέχεται ἐπ' ἀμφοτέρων μεταλαμβάνειν τῶν δικαίων, ὁμοίως δὲ δῆλον ὅτι καὶ ἐπὶ τῶν ἀδίκων· οὐ γὰρ ταὐτὸν τὸ τἄδικα πράττειν τῷ ἀδικεῖν οὐδὲ τὸ ἄδικα πάσχειν τῷ ἀδικεῖσθαι, ὁμοίως δὲ καὶ ἐπὶ τοῦ δικαιοπραγεῖν καὶ δικαιοῦσθαι·

---

2 δὲ] om. K^b.   ἀνθρωπικόν] ἀνθρώπινον H^aK^bQ *Bekker*.   4 ἱκανῶς] κανῶς pr. N^b.   5 ἀδικεῖν] τοῦ ἀδικεῖν H^aM^bQN^bO^bP^b.   εἰ] om. H^a. 6 ἀτόπως] τὸ πῶς K^b.   ἀτόπως. πῶς L^b.   ἀτόπως τὸ πῶς N^bO^b.   7 κατέκταν] κατεκνα N^b.   κατέκτα ceteri et *Bekker*.   8 οὐχ ἑκοῦσαν] codd. et *Bekker* θέλουσαν.   9 ἀληθῶς] ἀληθές M^bQ.   10 ἅπαν] πᾶν O^b.   11 πᾶν ante οὕτως] ἅπαν H^aL^bM^bQN^bP^b.   καί] om. M^bQ.   πᾶν ante ἑκούσιον] ἢ πᾶν K^bN^bP^b. πᾶν ἦν M^bQ.   12 ἢ τὸ—ἀκούσιον] om. K^b.   τὸ δ' ἀκούσιον (omissis ἢ τὸ μὲν ἑκούσιον) N^b.   13 δικαιοῦσθαι] διοῦσθαι pr. N^b.   14 καθ'] δὲ καθ' H^a.   δὴ καθ' M^bQ.   15 τὸ ante δικαιοῦσθαι] om. K^bP^b.   ἢ ἑκούσιον] ἢ ἅπαν ἑκούσιον M^b. εἰ ἅπαν ἑκούσιον Q.   17 πᾶν] ἅπαν H^aM^bQN^bO^b.   ἔνιοι] ἔνοι pr. N^b.   18 τόδε] τό γε N^bO^b.   21 ἐπ' ἀμφοτέρων μεταλαμβάνειν] μεταλαμβάνειν ἐπ' ἀμφοτέρων M^bQ.   23 πράττειν] om. P^b (add. marg. ποιεῖν.). τό] τῷ N^b.

which they do, not owing to ignorance, but in ignorance, owing to passion which is neither natural nor such as human beings are liable to, are not excusable.

It may perhaps be doubted whether we have been sufficiently explicit about ἀδικεῖσθαι and ἀδικεῖν: in the first place whether the matter is as Euripides has put it in his strange lines—

> *Al.* I killed my mother, that's the tale in brief.
> *Ph.* Were you both willing, or unwilling both?

In other words, is it really possible for a man ἑκόντα ἀδικεῖσθαι, or on the contrary is ἀδικεῖσθαι always ἀκούσιον as ὁ ἀδικεῖν is always ἑκούσιον? Is ἀδικεῖσθαι always ἀκούσιον or always ἑκούσιον, as ἀδικεῖν is always ἑκούσιον; or is it sometimes ἑκούσιον, sometimes ἀκούσιον? And so likewise in the case of δικαιοῦσθαι; δικαιοπραγεῖν being always ἑκούσιον. Thus we might fairly suppose that ἀδικεῖσθαι and δικαιοῦσθαι were similarly opposed to ἀδικεῖν and δικαιοπραγεῖν respectively, and so were either ἑκούσιον or ἀκούσιον. But again in the case of δικαιοῦσθαι, it would seem strange that it should always be ἑκούσιον; for some δικαιοῦνται οὐχ ἑκόντες. Indeed a further doubt may be raised whether in every case ὁ τὸ ἄδικον πεπονθὼς ἀδικεῖται, or, on the contrary, it is with πάσχειν as with πράττειν. In fact passively as well as actively actions may κατὰ συμβεβηκός partake of τὰ δίκαια, and plainly this also holds of τὰ ἄδικα: that is to say, τἄδικα πράττειν is not identical with ἀδικεῖν, nor ἄδικα πάσχειν with ἀδικεῖσθαι, and similarly this is true of δικαιοπραγεῖν and δικαιοῦσθαι; for a man cannot ἀδικεῖσθαι

ἀδύνατον γὰρ ἀδικεῖσθαι μὴ ἀδικοῦντος ἢ δικαιοῦσθαι
§ 4 μὴ δικαιοπραγοῦντος. εἰ δ' ἐστὶν ἁπλῶς τὸ ἀδικεῖν τὸ
βλάπτειν ἑκόντα τινά, τὸ δ' ἑκόντα εἰδότα καὶ ὃν καὶ ᾧ
καὶ ὥς, ὁ δ' ἀκρατὴς ἑκὼν βλάπτει αὐτὸς αὑτόν, ἑκών τ'
ἂν ἀδικοῖτο καὶ ἐνδέχοιτο αὐτὸν αὑτὸν ἀδικεῖν. (ἔστι 5
δὲ καὶ τοῦτο ἓν τῶν ἀπορουμένων, εἰ ἐνδέχεται αὐτὸν
§ 5 αὐτὸν ἀδικεῖν.) ἔτι ἑκὼν ἄν τις δι' ἀκρασίαν ὑπ' ἄλλου
βλάπτοιτο ἑκόντος, ὥστ' εἴη ἂν ἑκόντ' ἀδικεῖσθαι. ἢ οὐκ
ὀρθὸς ὁ διορισμός, ἀλλὰ προσθετέον τῷ βλάπτειν εἰδότα
§ 6 καὶ ὃν καὶ ᾧ καὶ ὡς τὸ παρὰ τὴν ἐκείνου βούλησιν; βλά- 10
πτεται μὲν οὖν τις ἑκὼν καὶ τἄδικα πάσχει, ἀδικεῖται δ'
οὐθεὶς ἑκών· οὐθεὶς γὰρ βούλεται, οὐδ' ὁ ἀκρατής, ἀλλὰ
παρὰ τὴν βούλησιν πράττει· οὔτε γὰρ βούλεται οὐθεὶς ὃ
μὴ οἴεται εἶναι σπουδαῖον, ὅ τε ἀκρατὴς ὃ οὐκ οἴεται δεῖν
§ 7 πράττειν πράττει. ὁ δὲ τὰ αὑτοῦ διδούς, ὥσπερ Ὅμηρός 15
φησι δοῦναι τὸν Γλαῦκον τῷ Διομήδει

χρύσεα χαλκείων, ἑκατόμβοι' ἐννεαβοίων,

οὐκ ἀδικεῖται· ἐπ' αὐτῷ γάρ ἐστι τὸ διδόναι, τὸ δ' ἀδικεῖσθαι οὐκ ἐπ' αὐτῷ, ἀλλὰ τὸν ἀδικοῦντα δεῖ ὑπάρχειν.
§ 8 περὶ μὲν οὖν τοῦ ἀδικεῖσθαι, ὅτι οὐχ ἑκούσιον, δῆλον. 20
ἔτι δ' ὧν προειλόμεθα δύ' ἔστιν εἰπεῖν, πότερόν ποτ'
ἀδικεῖ ὁ νείμας παρὰ τὴν ἀξίαν τὸ πλεῖον ἢ ὁ ἔχων, καὶ
§ 9 εἰ ἔστιν αὐτὸν αὑτὸν ἀδικεῖν· εἰ γὰρ ἐνδέχεται τὸ πρότερον
λεχθὲν καὶ ὁ διανέμων ἀδικεῖ ἀλλ' οὐχ ὁ ἔχων τὸ πλέον,

1 ἀδικοῦντος] ἀδικοῦντός τινος Hᵃ Mᵇ Q Oᵇ. δικαιοῦσθαι] δικαιοῦσθαι ἀδύνατον Pᵇ. 3 τὸ] τὸν Mᵇ Q. εἰδότα] εἰδεῖ Hᵃ. ᾧ] ὃ Hᵃ Kᵇ Mᵇ Q Nᵇ Oᵇ. 4 αὐτὸν] αὑτὸν Nᵇ. τ'] om. Mᵇ Q. 5 ἂν] αὖ Hᵃ. καὶ] κἂν Kᵇ. αὑτὸν] αὐτὸς Kᵇ Lᵇ Q. ἂν αὐτὸν Oᵇ. αὐτὸν] αὑτὸν Nᵇ. ἔστι—ἀδικεῖν] om. Mᵇ, 6 ἐν] om. Lᵇ. ἕν τι Hᵃ Nᵇ Oᵇ Bekker. αὐτὸν] αὑτὸς Lᵇ. 7 αὐτὸν ἀδι-κεῖν] αὐτὸν ἀδικεῖν Nᵇ. ἀδικεῖν αὐτὸν Oᵇ. 9 ὀρθὸς] ὀρθῶς Kᵇ. τῷ] τὸ Kᵇ Oᵇ Pᵇ. 10 καὶ ὃν] om. Kᵇ Lᵇ. ᾧ] ὃ Hᵃ Mᵇ Q et corr. Lᵇ. τὸ] Lᵇ. om. ceteri. 11 οὖν] οὔ Kᵇ. δ' οὐθεὶς] δ' οὐδὲ εἷς Kᵇ Pᵇ. 12 ἀκρατὴς] ἀκροατὴς Kᵇ. 13 γὰρ] om. Mᵇ Q. 14 εἶναι σπουδαῖον] σπουδαῖον εἶναι Oᵇ. τε] Kᵇ. δὲ ceteri. ὃ οὐκ] οὐχ ἃ Kᵇ Bekker. 15 αὑτοῦ] αὐτοῦ Hᵃ Nᵇ. 16 φησὶ] φυσὶ Q. 17 ἑκατόμβοι'] ἑκατομβί' ἃ Hᵃ. 18 ἐπ' αὐτῷ] ἐφ' αὑτῷ Oᵇ. 21 προειλόμεθα] προειλάμεθα Kᵇ. πότερόν ποτε] πότερόν τε Nᵇ. 22 τὸ πλεῖον] πλέον Kᵇ. τὸ πλέον Pᵇ. ἢ ὁ] om. Kᵇ. 23 αὐτὸν] αὑτὸν Nᵇ. πρότερον] πότερον Pᵇ. 24 ἀδικεῖ] ἀδικεῖν Q. ἔχων] ἑκὼν Kᵇ. πλέον] πλεῖον Lᵇ.

if there is not some one who ἀδικεῖ, nor δικαιοῦσθαι if there is not some one who δικαιοπραγεῖ. Now if τὸ ἀδικεῖν is simply τὸ βλάπτειν ἑκόντα τινά, where by ἑκόντα is meant εἰδότα καὶ ὃν καὶ ᾧ καὶ ὥς, and the incontinent man ἑκὼν βλάπτει αὑτόν, a man may ἑκὼν ἀδικεῖσθαι, and may ἀδικεῖν αὑτόν. (Whether a man can ἀδικεῖν αὑτόν, is another of the questions which we have to consider.) Again in consequence of ἀκρασία a man may ἑκών be harmed by another who is ἑκών, whence it will follow that a man may ἑκὼν ἀδικεῖσθαι. But is not this definition incorrect? and should we not add to the words βλάπτειν εἰδότα καὶ ὃν καὶ ᾧ καὶ ὥς the words παρὰ τὴν ἐκείνου βούλησιν? Thus a man may ἑκὼν βλάπτεσθαι and τἄδικα πάσχειν, but no one can ἑκὼν ἀδικεῖσθαι: for no one βούλεται βλάπτεσθαι, not even the incontinent man, so that the incontinent man's actions are contrary to his βούλησις, (for no one βούλεται what he does not think to be good, and the incontinent man does things which he does not think it right to do,) [and therefore, when the incontinent man under the influence of ἐπιθυμία does what he thinks wrong, the resistance of his βούλησις has ceased, and consequently he cannot be said ἀδικεῖσθαι.] Again one who gives what is his own, as Homer says Glaucus gave to Diomed 'gold for bronze, a hundred beeves' worth for the worth of nine', οὐκ ἀδικεῖται: for to give is in his power, but ἀδικεῖσθαι is not, as [in order that he may ἀδικεῖσθαι] there must be an ἀδικῶν. Thus it is clear that ἀδικεῖσθαι is not voluntary.

Furthermore of the questions which we undertook to answer two remain to be discussed: (1) is it one who distributes (or one who receives) more than the just proportion, who ἀδικεῖ? and (2) can a man ἀδικεῖν αὑτόν? [These questions appear to be connected:] for if the former of them is affirmed,—if it is the distributor, and not the recipient, of

εἴ τις πλέον ἑτέρῳ ἢ αὑτῷ νέμει εἰδὼς καὶ ἑκών, οὗτος αὐτὸς αὑτὸν ἀδικεῖ· ὅπερ δοκοῦσιν οἱ μέτριοι ποιεῖν· ὁ γὰρ ἐπιεικὴς ἐλαττωτικός ἐστιν. ἢ οὐδὲ τοῦτο ἁπλοῦν; ἑτέρου γὰρ ἀγαθοῦ, εἰ ἔτυχεν, ἐπλεονέκτει, οἷον δόξης ἢ τοῦ ἁπλῶς καλοῦ. ἔτι λύεται κατὰ τὸν διορισμὸν τοῦ 5 ἀδικεῖν· οὐθὲν γὰρ παρὰ τὴν αὑτοῦ πάσχει βούλησιν, ὥστε οὐκ ἀδικεῖται διά γε τοῦτο, ἀλλ' εἴπερ, βλάπτεται μόνον.

§ 10   φανερὸν δὲ ὅτι καὶ ὁ διανέμων ἀδικεῖ, ἀλλ' οὐχ ὁ τὸ πλέον ἔχων ἀεί· οὐ γὰρ ᾧ τὸ ἄδικον ὑπάρχει ἀδικεῖ, ἀλλ' ᾧ τὸ ἑκόντα τοῦτο ποιεῖν· τοῦτο δ' ὅθεν ἡ ἀρχὴ τῆς πρά- 10 ξεως, ἥ ἐστιν ἐν τῷ διανέμοντι ἀλλ' οὐκ ἐν τῷ λαμβάνοντι·

§ 11 [ἔτι] ἐπεὶ πολλαχῶς τὸ ποιεῖν λέγεται, καὶ ἔστιν ὡς τὰ ἄψυχα κτείνει καὶ ἡ χεὶρ καὶ ὁ οἰκέτης ἐπιτάξαντος οὐκ

§ 12 ἀδικεῖ μέν, ποιεῖ δὲ τὰ ἄδικα. ἔτι εἰ μὲν ἀγνοῶν ἔκρινεν, οὐκ ἀδικεῖ κατὰ τὸ νομικὸν δίκαιον οὐδ' ἄδικος ἡ κρίσις 15 ἐστίν, ἔστι δ' ὡς ἄδικος· ἕτερον γὰρ τὸ νομικὸν δίκαιον καὶ τὸ πρῶτον· εἰ δὲ γινώσκων ἔκρινεν ἀδίκως, πλεονεκτεῖ

§ 13 καὶ αὐτὸς ἢ χάριτος ἢ τιμωρίας. ὥσπερ οὖν κἂν εἴ τις μερίσαιτο τοῦ ἀδικήματος, καὶ ὁ διὰ ταῦτα κρίνας ἀδίκως πλέον ἔχει· καὶ γὰρ ἐπ' ἐκείνων ὁ τὸν ἀγρὸν κρίνας οὐκ 20 ἀγρὸν ἀλλ' ἀργύριον ἔλαβεν.

11   < πότερον δ' ἐνδέχεται ἑαυτὸν ἀδικεῖν ἢ οὔ, φανερὸν ἐκ τῶν εἰρημένων.

1 τις] τις δὲ L^bM^bQ. τις τὸ O^b. πλέον] πλεῖον O^b. πλέον δὲ (sed δὲ postea erasum est) P^b.   ἑτέρῳ ἢ αὑτῷ] αὑτοῦ ἑτέρῳ K^b.   οὗτος] om. K^bO^b. 2 αὐτὸς] om. N^b.   αὐτὸν] αὑτὸν N^b.   3 ἢ] ἢ N^b.   4 ἐπλεονέκτει] πλεονεκτεῖ K^bL^b.   5 τοῦ] τὸ Q.   λύεται] λύεται καὶ O^b (?) Bekker.   6 αὑτοῦ] αὐτοῦ K^bL^bO^bP^b.   αὐτὴν H^a.   7 διά] δὴ H^a.   8 δὲ ὅτι καὶ] διότι καὶ K^b.   δὲ καὶ ὅτι H^aM^bQN^bO^b Bekker.   9 ἔχων] om. H^a.   ἀεί] ἀδικεῖ K^b.   ὑπάρχει ἔχω ὑπάρχει K^b.   11 τῷ ante λαμβάνοντι] om. H^a.   12 ἐπεί] εἰ L^bN^bP^b. 13 κτείνει] κτεώνη H^a.   κτήνη P^b.   κτείνει δὲ L^b.   ὁ] om. O^b.   οὐκ ἀδικεῖ μέν] μὲν οὐκ ἀδικεῖ K^bN^bP^b.   15 οὐκ ἀδικεῖ κατὰ τὸ νομικὸν δίκαιον] κατὰ τὸ νομικὸν δίκαιον οὐκ ἀδικεῖ M^bQ.   νομικὸν] νόμιμον H^aM^bO^b.   νομικὸν καὶ N^b. 16 ἐστίν] om. O^b.   νομικὸν] νόμιμον M^bQ.   18 κἂν] καὶ K^b.   20 ἐκείνων ὁ] ἐκείνωι K^b.   ἐκείνω P^b.   9 §§ 14—16] vide supra, post 1 § 3.   9 § [17] vide supra, post 1 § 9.   cap. 10] vide infra, post 11 § 9.   22 ἑαυτὸν ἀδικεῖν] ἀδικεῖν ἑαυτὸν M^bQ.   ἑαυτὸν ἀδικεῖν ἢ οὔ, φανερὸν ἐκ τῶν εἰρημένων] φανερὸν ἐκ τῶν εἰρημένων ἀδικεῖν ἑαυτὸν ἢ οὔ. H^a.

τὸ πλέον, who ἀδικεῖ,—when a man knowingly and voluntarily distributes more to another than to himself, he ἀδικεῖ αὑτόν. (Modest men are thought to do this; thus the ἐπιεικής is one who does not insist upon his right.) But does not this statement require qualification? For (1) it may be that [by assigning more to another than to himself] the distributor obtained a larger share of some other good, such as reputation or τὸ ἁπλῶς καλόν; [in which case he οὐκ ἀδικεῖ αὑτόν] : (2) the inference may be met by an appeal to the definition of ἀδικεῖν; for the distributor suffers nothing contrary to his own βούλησις, and therefore οὐκ ἀδικεῖται in consequence, but at most βλάπτεται. [Hence if it is decided that ὁ νείμας παρὰ τὴν ἀξίαν τὸ πλεῖον, and not ὁ ἔχων, ἀδικεῖ, it does not necessarily follow that a man can ἀδικεῖν αὑτόν.]

That the distributor ἀδικεῖ, and that the recipient of τὸ πλέον does not do so in all cases, is clear: for it is not he who ἄδικον ποιεῖ, but he who ἑκὼν ποιεῖ τὸ ἄδικον, who ἀδικεῖ; that is to say, the one with whom the action originates, and the action originates not in the recipient but in the distributor: (for the word ποιεῖν is used in various senses, and there is a sense in which inanimate things are said to kill, and in which the hand or a slave acting under orders is said, not indeed ἀδικεῖν, but ποιεῖν τὰ ἄδικα.)

Again, though if the distributor gave his judgment ἀγνοῶν, he οὐκ ἀδικεῖ κατὰ τὸ νομικὸν δίκαιον, and his judgment is not ἄδικος, (except in a special sense, τὸ νομικὸν δίκαιον and τὸ πρῶτον δίκαιον being different things,) if he γινώσκων ἔκρινεν ἀδίκως, he πλεονεκτεῖ himself either in gratitude or in revenge; and one who for the sake of gratitude or revenge ἀδίκως κρίνει, is just as much a πλεονέκτης as if he were to share the ἀδίκημα with the recipient, in which last case indeed the distributor who wrongfully assigns a piece of land receives not land but money.

Whether it is possible for a man ἀδικεῖν ἑαυτόν or not, is clear from what has been said. For—Firstly, one class of

τὰ μὲν γάρ ἐστι τῶν δικαίων τὰ κατὰ πᾶσαν ἀρετὴν ὑπὸ τοῦ νόμου τεταγμένα, οἷον οὐ κελεύει ἀποκτιννύναι ἑαυτόν ὁ νόμος, ἃ δὲ μὴ κελεύει, ἀπαγορεύει· ἔτι ὅταν παρὰ τὸν νόμον βλάπτῃ (μὴ ἀντιβλάπτων) ἑκών, ἀδικεῖ, ἑκὼν δὲ ὁ εἰδὼς καὶ ὃν καὶ ᾧ· ὁ δὲ δι' ὀργὴν ἑαυτὸν σφάττων ἑκὼν τοῦτο δρᾷ παρὰ τὸν ὀρθὸν λόγον, ὃ οὐκ ἐᾷ ὁ νόμος· ἀδικεῖ ἄρα. ἀλλὰ τίνα; ἢ τὴν πόλιν, αὑτὸν δ' οὔ; ἑκὼν γὰρ πάσχει, ἀδικεῖται δ' οὐθεὶς ἑκών. διὸ καὶ ἡ πόλις ζημιοῖ, καί τις ἀτιμία πρόσεστι τῷ ἑαυτὸν διαφθείραντι ὡς τὴν πόλιν ἀδικοῦντι.

ἔτι καθ' ὃ ἄδικος ὁ μόνον ἀδικῶν καὶ μὴ ὅλως φαῦλος, οὐκ ἔστιν ἀδικῆσαι ἑαυτόν. (τοῦτο γὰρ ἄλλο ἐκείνου· ἔστι γάρ πως ὁ ἄδικος οὕτω πονηρὸς ὥσπερ ὁ δειλός, οὐχ ὡς ὅλην ἔχων τὴν πονηρίαν, ὥστ' οὐδὲ κατὰ ταύτην ἀδικεῖ.) ἅμα γὰρ τὸ αὐτὸ ἂν εἴη ἀφῃρῆσθαι καὶ προσκεῖσθαι τῷ αὐτῷ, τοῦτο δὲ ἀδύνατον· ἀλλ' ἀεὶ ἐν πλείοσιν ἀνάγκη εἶναι τὸ δίκαιον καὶ τὸ ἄδικον. ἔτι δὲ ἑκούσιόν τε καὶ ἐκ προαιρέσεως, καὶ πρότερον· (ὁ γὰρ διότι ἔπαθε καὶ τὸ αὐτὸ ἀντιποιῶν οὐ δοκεῖ ἀδικεῖν·) αὐτὸς δ' ἑαυτόν, τὰ αὐτὰ ἅμα καὶ πάσχει καὶ ποιεῖ. ἔτι εἴη ἂν ἑκόντα ἀδικεῖσθαι. πρὸς δὲ τούτοις ἄνευ τῶν κατὰ μέρος ἀδικημάτων οὐθεὶς ἀδικεῖ, μοιχεύει δ' οὐδεὶς τὴν ἑαυτοῦ οὐδὲ τοιχωρυχεῖ τὸν ἑαυτοῦ τοῖχον οὐδὲ κλέπτει τὰ ἑαυτοῦ.

1 τὰ ante κατά] om. O^b.   2 ἀποκτιννύναι ἑαυτόν] ἑαυτὸν ἀποκτιννύναι L^bO^b. ἑαυτὸν ἀποκτενεῖν H^aM^b.   ἑαυτὸν ἀποκτένειν Q.   ἀποκτενεῖν ἑαυτὸν N^b.   3 ἅ] ὁ P^b.   κελεύει] κελεύῃ N^b.   4 παρά] περί O^b.   μὴ ἀντιβλάπτων] om. P^b. 5 ᾧ] ὡς H^aM^bN^bP^b et corr. K^b.   ὀργήν] ὀργῇ P^b.   ἑαυτόν] αὐτόν M^b.   6 ὀρθόν] αὐτόν K^b.   λόγον] νόμον H^aM^bQN^bO^b.   7 αὑτὸν] αὐτὸν M^bN^b. 10 ἀδικοῦντι] ἀδικοῦντι ἢ αὐτόν M^bQ.   11 καθ' ὅ] καθ' ὅλου H^a.   μόνον] om. H^a.   ὅλως] ἁπλῶς K^bP^b.   ὅλοις H^a.   12 ἔστιν ἀδικῆσαι] ἀδικήσει M^bQ. ἑαυτόν] αὐτὸν H^aN^b.   13 πως] πος pr. N^b.   οὕτω] οὕτως P^b.   14 ταύτην] τὴν αὐτὴν pr. N^b.   15 ἀδικεῖ] ἀδικεῖ ἄν K^b.   τὸ αὐτὸ ἂν εἴη] L^b.   τῷ αὐτῷ ἂν εἴη H^aM^bQN^bO^b.   ἂν τῷ αὐτῷ εἴη K^bP^b Bekker.   16 τῷ αὐτῷ] τὸ αὐτὸ K^bN^bO^bP^b Bekker.   18 ὁ] καί M^bQ.   19 ἀδικεῖν—ἑκόντα] om. N^b.   δ' ἑαυτόν] δ' αὐτόν K^bP^b.   δὲ αὐτόν L^b.   20 τὰ αὐτά] ταῦτά P^b.   ταῦτα K^b. καὶ post ἅμα] om. L^bO^bP^b.   21 κατά] ἀνά M^bQ.   22 δ'] γὰρ M^bQ.   τὴν ἑαυτοῦ] τὴν ἑαυτοῦ γυναῖκα P^b.   23 τοιχωρυχεῖ] τυχωρυχεῖ N^b.   τοῖχον] οἶκον M^b.   ἑαυτοῦ] αὑτοῦ K^bP^b.

δίκαια includes those acts in accordance with any virtue which are prescribed by law: for example, the law does not allow a man to commit suicide, and what the law does not allow, it forbids; and when a man βλάπτῃ in contravention of the law (except in retaliation) voluntarily, he ἀδικεῖ, and one who knows the person and the instrument acts voluntarily; but he who stabs himself in a passion does it voluntarily in despite of right rule, and this the law does not permit: hence he ἀδικεῖ. But who is it whom he ἀδικεῖ? is it not the state rather than himself? for he suffers voluntarily, and no one ἀδικεῖται voluntarily. Hence it is the state which exacts the penalty, and hence a certain loss of civil rights attaches to one who commits suicide, because it is the state which he ἀδικεῖ.

Secondly, in the sense in which a man is ἄδικος who only ἀδικεῖ and is not universally bad, it is impossible for a man ἀδικῆσαι himself. (This case is distinct from the former; for the ἄδικος is vicious in the same sort of way as the coward, not as exhibiting vice in general: so that [I must further show that] a man οὐκ ἀδικεῖ αὑτόν in this sense.) For (1) if he could, the same thing might have been subtracted from and added to the same thing simultaneously, which is impossible; in fact τὸ δίκαιον and τὸ ἄδικον always of necessity imply more than one person. Again (2) τὸ ἀδικεῖν is voluntary or deliberate, and aggressive,—one who, having suffered, retaliates on the same scale on which he has suffered not being considered ἀδικεῖν,—whilst if a man harms himself, he suffers and does the same things at the same time. Again (3) if a man could ἀδικεῖν ἑαυτόν, it would be possible for him ἀδικεῖσθαι voluntarily. Furthermore (4) no one ἀδικεῖ without committing particular ἀδικήματα, and no one can commit adultery with his own wife, or burglary upon his own premises, or theft upon his own property.

ὅλως δὲ λύεται τὸ ἑαυτὸν ἀδικεῖν κατὰ τὸν διορισμὸν τὸν περὶ τοῦ ἑκουσίως ἀδικεῖσθαι.

§ 9 κατὰ μεταφορὰν δὲ καὶ ὁμοιότητα ἔστιν οὐκ αὐτῷ πρὸς αὑτὸν δίκαιον ἀλλὰ τῶν αὐτοῦ τισίν, οὐ πᾶν δὲ δίκαιον ἀλλὰ τὸ δεσποτικὸν ἢ τὸ οἰκονομικόν· ἐν τούτοις γὰρ τοῖς λόγοις διέστηκε τὸ λόγον ἔχον μέρος τῆς ψυχῆς πρὸς τὸ ἄλογον. εἰς ἃ δὴ βλέπουσι καὶ δοκεῖ εἶναι ἀδικία πρὸς αὑτόν, ὅτι [ἐν] τούτοις ἔστι πάσχειν τι παρὰ τὰς ἑαυτῶν ὀρέξεις· ὥσπερ οὖν ἄρχοντι καὶ ἀρχομένῳ εἶναι πρὸς ἄλληλα δίκαιόν τι καὶ τούτοις. >

6 § 3 < πῶς μὲν οὖν ἔχει τὸ ἀντιπεπονθὸς πρὸς τὸ δίκαιον, εἴρηται πρότερον· > περὶ δὲ ἐπιεικείας καὶ τοῦ ἐπιεικοῦς, πῶς ἔχει ἡ μὲν ἐπιείκεια πρὸς δικαιοσύνην τὸ δ' ἐπιεικὲς πρὸς τὸ δίκαιον, ἐχόμενόν ἐστιν εἰπεῖν· οὔτε γὰρ ὡς ταὐτὸν ἁπλῶς οὔθ' ὡς ἕτερον τῷ γένει φαίνεται σκοπουμένοις, καὶ ὁτὲ μὲν τὸ ἐπιεικὲς ἐπαινοῦμεν καὶ ἄνδρα τὸν τοιοῦτον, ὥστε καὶ ἐπὶ τὰ ἄλλα ἐπαινοῦντες μεταφέρομεν ἀντὶ τοῦ ἀγαθοῦ, τὸ ἐπιεικέστερον ὅτι βέλτιον δηλοῦντες· ὁτὲ δὲ τῷ λόγῳ ἀκολουθοῦσι φαίνεται ἄτοπον εἰ τὸ ἐπιεικὲς παρὰ τὸ δίκαιόν τι ὂν ἐπαινετόν ἐστιν· ἢ § 2 γὰρ τὸ δίκαιον οὐ σπουδαῖον ἢ τὸ ἐπιεικές, [οὐ δίκαιον,] εἰ ἄλλο· ἢ εἰ ἄμφω σπουδαῖα, ταὐτόν ἐστιν. ἡ μὲν οὖν ἀπορία σχεδὸν συμβαίνει διὰ ταῦτα περὶ τὸ ἐπιεικές, ἔχει δ' ἅπαντα τρόπον τινὰ ὀρθῶς καὶ οὐθὲν ὑπεναντίον ἑαυτοῖς· τό τε γὰρ ἐπιεικὲς δικαίου τινὸς ὂν βέλτιόν ἐστι δίκαιον, καὶ οὐχ ὡς ἄλλο τι γένος ὂν βέλτιόν ἐστι τοῦ δικαίου.

1 ἑαυτὸν] αὑτὸν K^bP^b. κατὰ] καὶ κατὰ K^b. 11 §§ 7, 8] vide supra, post § 18. 3 οὐκ αὑτῷ] οὐχ αὐτῶι K^bM^bQO^b. οὐκ αὐτοῦ L^b. οὐχ αὑτὸς H^a. 4 αὑτὸν] αὐτὸν H^aK^bN^b. τῶν αὐτοῦ] τὸν ἑαυτοῦ Q. δὲ] om. H^a. 6 μέρος τῆς ψυχῆς] τῆς ψυχῆς μέρος L^b. τῆς ψυχῆς (omisso μέρος) K^b. 7 καὶ] om. L^bO^b. αὑτὸν] αὐτὸν K^bM^bN^b. 8 παρὰ] περὶ L^b. 11 πῶς μὲν οὖν—πρότερον] 6 § 3 traieci. οὖν] suprascr. M^b. om. Q. 12 περὶ δὲ—ἕξις] cap. 10 traieci. ἐπιεικείας] ἐπιεικείας πρὸς δικαιοσύνην K^b. 16 ὁτὲ] οὔτε K^b. 20 ἐστιν· ἢ γὰρ] ἔστι γὰρ K^b. 21 ἐπιεικὲς οὐ] ἐπιεικὸς H^a. οὐ δίκαιον εἰ] om. N^b. 22 εἰ ἄλλο] εἶναι ἄλλο K^b. ἢ ἄλλο P^b. εἰ ante ἄμφω] om. H^a. ταὐτόν] om. K^b. 23 ἔχει] ἔχοι Q. 24 τρόπον τινά] τινα τρόπον P^b. 25 ὂν] om. N^b. 26 ὂν] om. K^b. ἐστι] om. O^b. τοῦ] om. Q.

And in general, the question 'Can a man ἀδικεῖν ἑαυτίν?' is resolved by our determination in regard to the question 'Can a man ἑκουσίως ἀδικεῖσθαι?'

Nevertheless κατὰ μεταφορὰν καὶ ὁμοιότητα there is a δίκαιον not between a man and himself, but between certain parts of him; yet not every δίκαιον, but only τὸ δεσποτικόν or τὸ οἰκονομικὸν δίκαιον: for in these discussions the rational and irrational parts of the ψυχή are distinguished. This distinction leads men to suppose that there is an ἀδικία towards oneself, because these parts may suffer something contrary to their respective inclinations, so that they may have a sort of δίκαιον with one another like that between ruler and subject.

How ἀντιπεπονθός is related to τὸ δίκαιον has been stated before: I have next to speak of ἐπιείκεια and τὸ ἐπιεικές, and to show how ἐπιείκεια is related to δικαιοσύνη and τὸ ἐπιεικές to τὸ δίκαιον: for on examination it appears that they are neither absolutely identical nor generically different; and though sometimes we praise τὸ ἐπιεικές and the ἐπιεικής, (so that we even apply the word eulogistically to other things in place of the word ἀγαθόν, meaning by ἐπιεικέστερον simply βέλτιον,) sometimes if we think about it, it seems strange that τὸ ἐπιεικές, being something other than τὸ δίκαιον, should be praised; for (1) if δίκαιον and ἐπιεικές are different, either δίκαιον or ἐπιεικές is not good, or (2) if both are good, they are identical.

These then are I think the considerations from which the difficulty in regard to τὸ ἐπιεικές arises: nevertheless all of them are in a manner right and not inconsistent: for τὸ ἐπιεικές is better than one sort of δίκαιον, being a δίκαιον itself; it is not as a different kind of thing that it is

ταὐτὸν ἄρα δίκαιον καὶ ἐπιεικές, καὶ ἀμφοῖν σπουδαίοιν
§ 3 ὄντοιν κρεῖττον τὸ ἐπιεικές. ποιεῖ δὲ τὴν ἀπορίαν ὅτι τὸ
ἐπιεικὲς δίκαιον μέν ἐστιν, οὐ τὸ κατὰ νόμον δέ, ἀλλ᾽
§ 4 ἐπανόρθωμα νομίμου δικαίου. αἴτιον δ᾽ ὅτι ὁ μὲν νόμος
καθόλου πᾶς, περὶ ἐνίων δ᾽ οὐχ οἷόν τε ὀρθῶς εἰπεῖν
καθόλου. ἐν οἷς οὖν ἀνάγκη μὲν εἰπεῖν καθόλου, μὴ
οἷόν τε δὲ ὀρθῶς, τὸ ὡς ἐπὶ τὸ πλέον λαμβάνει ὁ νόμος,
οὐκ ἀγνοῶν τὸ ἁμαρτανόμενον. καὶ ἔστιν οὐδὲν ἧττον
ὀρθῶς· τὸ γὰρ ἁμάρτημα οὐκ ἐν τῷ νόμῳ οὐδ᾽ ἐν τῷ
νομοθέτῃ ἀλλ᾽ ἐν τῇ φύσει τοῦ πράγματός ἐστιν· εὐθὺς
§ 5 γὰρ τοιαύτη ἡ τῶν πρακτῶν ὕλη ἐστίν. ὅταν οὖν λέγῃ
μὲν ὁ νόμος καθόλου, συμβῇ δ᾽ ἐπὶ τούτου παρὰ τὸ
καθόλου, τότε ὀρθῶς ἔχει, ᾗ παραλείπει ὁ νομοθέτης καὶ
ἥμαρτεν ἁπλῶς εἰπών, ἐπανορθοῦν τὸ ἐλλειφθέν, ὃ κἂν
ὁ νομοθέτης αὐτὸς ἂν εἶπεν ἐκεῖ παρών, καὶ εἰ ᾔδει,
§ 6 ἐνομοθέτησεν ἄν. διὸ δίκαιον μέν ἐστι, καὶ βέλτιόν τινος
δικαίου, οὐ τοῦ ἁπλῶς δὲ ἀλλὰ τοῦ διὰ τὸ ἁπλῶς ἁμαρτήματος. καὶ ἔστιν αὕτη ἡ φύσις ἡ τοῦ ἐπιεικοῦς,
ἐπανόρθωμα νόμου ᾗ ἐλλείπει διὰ τὸ καθόλου. τοῦτο
γὰρ αἴτιον καὶ τοῦ μὴ πάντα κατὰ νόμον εἶναι, ὅτι
περὶ ἐνίων ἀδύνατον θέσθαι νόμον, ὥστε ψηφίσματος δεῖ.
§ 7 τοῦ γὰρ ἀορίστου ἀόριστος καὶ ὁ κανών ἐστιν, ὥσπερ
καὶ τῆς Λεσβίας οἰκοδομῆς ὁ μολίβδινος κανών· πρὸς γὰρ

1 ταὐτὸν] τὸ αὐτὸ N^bO^b. ἀμφοῖν] γὰρ ἀμφοῖν H^aM^bQ. σπουδαίοιν ὄντοιν] σπουδαίων ὄντων K^b. 3 τὸ ante κατά om. H^aM^bQO^b. 4 νομίμου δικαίου] δικαίου νομίμου K^bL^bN^b. 5 δ᾽ post ἐνίων] om. N^b. ὀρθῶς εἰπεῖν] εἰπεῖν ὀρθῶς L^b. 6 ἐν οἷς οὖν ἀνάγκη μὲν] ἀνάγκη μὲν οὖν (omissis ἐν οἷς) M^bQ. 7 τὸ post ἐπί] om. L^b. πλέον] πλεῖον K^bO^bP^b. 9 ὀρθῶς] ὀρθὸν H^a. ὀρθός M^bQ. ἁμάρτημα] ἁμάρτημα μὲν H^a. τῷ νόμῳ] τοῖς νόμοις H^a. 10 ἐστιν post πράγματος] om. O^b. 11 τοιαύτη ἡ τῶν πρακτῶν ὕλη] ἡ τῶν πρακτῶν ὕλη τοιαύτη H^aM^bQN^b. πρακτῶν] πρακτέων K^b. πραγμάτων M^bQP^b. λέγῃ] λέγοι Q. 12 τούτου] τούτῳ L^bM^bQ. τούτοις N^bO^bP^b. παρά] om. M^bQ. 14 κἂν] καὶ M^bQ. 15 αὐτὸς] οὕτως N^bP^b. αὐτὸς οὕτως L^bO^b Bekker. ἄν] om. K^b. εἶπεν] K^b. εἴποι ceteri et Bekker. ἐκεῖ] om. K^b. ᾔδει] ἤδη H^aK^bO^b. 16 ἄν post ἐνομοθέτησεν] om. H^aK^bM^bQO^b. δίκαιον] καὶ δίκαιον O^b. 17 τὸ] τὰ H^a. τοῦ M^bQ. 19 νόμον] τοῦ νόμου N^b. 20 εἶναι] om. N^b. 21 ἐνίων τινων K^b. ἐνίων τινῶν P^b. ψηφίσματος] ψηφίσματα N^b. 23 Λεσβίας] Λεσβείας H^a. οἰκοδομῆς] οἰκοδομίας K^bP^b. μολίβδινος] μολύβινος L^bN^bP^b.

better than τὸ δίκαιον. Hence δίκαιον and ἐπιεικές are identical, and whereas both are good, τὸ ἐπιεικές is the better. The reason of the ἀπορία is that though τὸ ἐπιεικές is δίκαιον, it is not legal δίκαιον, but a rectification of it: and this distinction is due to the fact that law is always a general statement, whilst there are some cases for which it is not possible to provide in a statement which is general. Hence where it is necessary to speak in general terms, but impossible to do so correctly, the law considers the majority of cases, though it is not ignorant of the element of error. And it is not wrong in so doing: for the error is not in the law nor in the lawgiver but in the nature of the case, the matter of action being necessarily of this incalculable kind. Hence when the law speaks in general terms, and a case arises upon it which is not included in the general rule, it is right in such a case, where the lawgiver's provision is defective or erroneous in consequence of its generality, to rectify the defect by deciding as the lawgiver himself would do if he were with us, and as he would have done in legislating had he known the circumstances. Wherefore τὸ ἐπιεικές is δίκαιον, and better than one sort of δίκαιον, that is, not better than the general statement of δίκαιον but better than the erroneous decision to which its generality leads. Thus τὸ ἐπιεικές is a correction of law where it fails by reason of its generality. Indeed this is the reason why all things are not determined by law, viz. that there are some cases for which it is impossible to lay down laws, so that special ordinances become necessary: for where the thing to be measured is indefinite the rule is indefinite also, as for example the leaden rule which is used in Lesbian architecture:

τὸ σχῆμα τοῦ λίθου μετακινεῖται καὶ οὐ μένει ὁ κανών,
§ 8 καὶ τὸ ψήφισμα πρὸς τὰ πράγματα. τί μὲν οὖν ἐστὶ τὸ
ἐπιεικές, καὶ ὅτι δίκαιον, καὶ τίνος βέλτιον δικαίου, δῆλον.
φανερὸν δ' ἐκ τούτου καὶ ὁ ἐπιεικὴς τίς ἐστιν· ὁ γὰρ τῶν
τοιούτων προαιρετικὸς καὶ πρακτικός, καὶ ὁ μὴ ἀκριβο- 5
δίκαιος ἐπὶ τὸ χεῖρον ἀλλ' ἐλαττωτικός, καίπερ ἔχων τὸν
νόμον βοηθόν, ἐπιεικής ἐστι, καὶ ἡ ἕξις αὕτη ἐπιείκεια,
δικαιοσύνη τις οὖσα καὶ οὐχ ἑτέρα τις ἕξις.

11 § 10   περὶ μὲν οὖν δικαιοσύνης καὶ τῶν ἄλλων ἠθικῶν
ἀρετῶν διωρίσθω τὸν τρόπον τοῦτον.   10

3 ὅτι] τί τὸ HᵃMᵇQNᵇPᵇ.   4 ὁ ante γὰρ] ὃς Kᵇ.   τῶν] om. Nᵇ.   5 ὁ μὴ]
μὴ ὁ Hᵃ.   μὴ (omisso ὁ) MᵇQ.   6 καίπερ ἔχων] καὶ περιέχων Mᵇ.   τὸν]
καὶ τὸν Hᵃ.   11 §§ 1—6, 9] vide supra, post 9 § 13.   11 §§ 7, 8] vide supra,
post 5 § 18.   9 τῶν ἄλλων] τῶν ἄλλων τῶν HᵃKᵇNᵇOᵇPᵇ Bekker.   ἠθικῶν]
om. HᵃMᵇQ.

as the leaden rule is not rigid but adapts itself to the form of the stone, even so the special ordinance adapts itself to the circumstances of the case.

Thus we see what τὸ ἐπιεικές is, as well as that it is δίκαιον, and what sort of δίκαιον it is to which it is superior. And from this it is plain also what the ἐπιεικής is: one who deliberately chooses and does what is ἐπιεικές, one who does not stand upon his rights wrongfully but puts up with a smaller share though the law is on his side, is ἐπιεικής, and the ἕξις thus indicated is ἐπιείκεια, which is a sort of δικαιοσύνη, not a different ἕξις.

So much may be said by way of description of δικαιοσύνη and the rest of the moral virtues.

NOTES.

[In quoting the *N. E.*, the *E. E.*, and the *M. M.* I have given the chapters and sections of Bekker's Oxford Edition (1837): in quoting the *Politics* and the *Rhetoric* I have given the chapter, the page, and the line of Bekker's small Berlin Editions (1855 and 1843 respectively): with these exceptions all references are to the large Berlin Edition.]

1 § 1. περὶ δὲ δικαιοσύνης, κ.τ.λ.] In this sentence the questions to be considered in the first half of the book are concisely stated. Cf. 5 §§ 17—19, where the author recapitulates the results thus far attained, and declares that the questions proposed at the outset have been adequately answered.

§ 2. μέθοδον] The 'method' comprises the enumeration of the views entertained by the vulgar and by individuals in regard to the subject discussed, the criticism of those views, and the development of an original theory based upon the preliminary investigation. This process, "which, when performed between two disputants, Aristotle calls *dialectic debate*," is opposed to the strictly "didactic and demonstrative procedure: wherein the teacher lays down principles which he requires the learner to admit, and then deduces from them, by syllogisms constructed in regular form, consequences indisputably binding on all who have admitted the principles." Grote's *Aristotle* I. 67, 68: see also I. 300 sqq., 378 sqq. The method above described, for which we are prepared in *N. E.* I. 4 § 4, 8 § 6, pervades both the Nicomachean and the Eudemian treatise, though it may be thought perhaps that its steps are more precisely discriminated in the latter. Cf. *N. E.* VII. = *E. E.* VI. 1 § 5 δεῖ δ', ὥσπερ ἐπὶ τῶν ἄλλων, τιθέντας τὰ φαινόμενα καὶ πρῶτον διαπορήσαντας οὕτω δεικνύναι μάλιστα μὲν πάντα τὰ ἔνδοξα περὶ ταῦτα τὰ πάθη, εἰ δὲ μή, τὰ πλεῖστα καὶ κυριώτατα· ἐὰν γὰρ λύηταί τε τὰ δυσχερῆ καὶ καταλείπηται τὰ ἔνδοξα, δεδειγμένον ἂν εἴη ἱκανῶς.

§ 3. πρακτικοί] "Muretus vertit *propensi ad agendum*, cum reliqui vertant *apti* vel *idonei*." Zell. From a comparison of *E. E.* II. 1 § 23 and II. 5 § 1 it would appear that these two possible meanings are here to be combined. Cf. *Rhet.* I. 9. p. 30. 4. Hence the words καὶ ἀφ' ἧς δικαιοπραγοῦσι καὶ βούλονται τὰ δίκαια are to be regarded as an explanation of ἀφ' ἧς πρακτικοὶ τῶν δικαίων εἰσί. The definition of which these words form a part is only a rough, popular definition temporarily and provisionally accepted (διὸ καὶ ἡμῖν πρῶτον ὡς ἐν τύπῳ ὑποκείσθω ταῦτα). Cf. 5 § 17, where in recapitulating his results the author is careful to introduce the phrase κατὰ προαίρεσιν, by which his own definition is distinguished from the popular one of the present passage. Thus the use here of the word βούλονται ("cf. Plat. *Gorg.* 460 B,C," Fritzsche) instead of the Aristotelian προαιροῦνται is quite appropriate, not, as has been suggested, an Eudemian inaccuracy.

9 §§ 14—16.] On the position of these sections (and of 9 § 17 which I have introduced after § 9 of the present chapter) see Introduction, On dislocations in the text.

δοῦναι τῇ χειρὶ τὸ ἀργύριον] The remark in which these words occur applies to virtuous actions as well as to vicious ones. A virtuous action does not necessarily imply a virtuous ἕξις, any more than a vicious action a vicious ἕξις. The example alleged is a liberal action which does not necessarily proceed from ἐλευθερία. Williams translates "to actually deliver a bribe," supposing that vicious actions only are exemplified.

ὡδὶ ἔχοντας] Cf. *N. E.* II. 3 § 3. 'It is not easy, nor does it rest with ourselves at a given time to do a particular act in a given ἕξις, because time and practice are necessary to the attainment of the ἕξις in question, whether virtuous or vicious.' So Mich. Ephes. χρόνου γὰρ χρεία καὶ συνασκήσεως καὶ μαθήσεως πρὸς τὴν τῶν ἕξεων κτῆσιν.

9 § 15. οὐδὲν οἴονται σοφὸν εἶναι] For the phraseology cf. *Met.* I. 2. p. 982. a. 10, a place which also resembles the present passage in being part of a collection of ὑπολήψεις or popular notions.

ἀλλὰ πῶς πραττόμενα καὶ πῶς νεμόμενα] On the accentuation of the indefinite πώς when it is used emphatically see Schwegler on *Met.* III. 4 § 42.

τοῦτο δὲ πλέον ἔργον ἢ τὰ ὑγιεινὰ εἰδέναι] I. e. the knowledge of δίκαια is more difficult of attainment than that of νόμιμα, just as the knowledge of τὰ ἰατρικά is more difficult of attainment than that of (what Plato calls) τὰ πρὸ ἰατρικῆς. This is somewhat curtly expressed in the statement that 'to know δίκαια is more difficult than to know τὰ ὑγιεινά.' In other words, he who depends upon law for his conception of what is just, no more knows what is just than the apprentice knows surgery, if he understands the application of remedies, but does not know when they are to be applied. Zell appositely cites *M. M.* II. 3 § 5 sqq., q.v. See also *N. E.* X. 9 § 21 and Plat. *Phaedr.* 268 B, C. 269 A.

πῶς δεῖ νεῖμαι] Dependent upon εἰδέναι repeated from the preceding clause.

9 § 16. δι' αὐτὸ δὲ τοῦτο] Sc. ὅτι ἐφ' ἑαυτοῖς οἴονται εἶναι τὸ ἀδικεῖν, the fundamental error which lies at the root of all the misconceptions discussed in 9 §§ 14—16.

τοῦ δικαίου] The δίκαιος here spoken of is the man of universal justice: hence the notion, that τοῦ δικαίου ἐστὶν οὐθὲν ἧττον τὸ ἀδικεῖν, is tested in the case of ὁ ἀνδρεῖος as well as in that of ὁ δίκαιος, the man of particular justice.

οὐθὲν ἧττον τὸ ἀδικεῖν] Sc. ἢ τὸ δικαιοπραγεῖν. Mich. Ephes. and the Paraphrast however supply τοῦ ἀδίκου.

ἀλλὰ τὸ δειλαίνειν, κ.τ.λ.] For the form of the sentence cf. 9 § 15 supra, ἀλλ' οὐ ταῦτ' ἐστί, κ.τ.λ.

ἀλλὰ τὸ ὡδί] ὡδί = ἰατρικῶς, or as the Paraphrast puts it, ἕξιν ἰατρικὴν ἔχοντα: cf. *N. E.* II. 4 §§ 1, 2 ἀπορήσειε δ' ἄν τις, πῶς λέγομεν ὅτι δεῖ τὰ μὲν δίκαια πράττοντας δικαίους γίνεσθαι, τὰ δὲ σώφρονα σώφρονας· εἰ γὰρ πράττουσι τὰ δίκαια καὶ τὰ σώφρονα, ἤδη εἰσὶ δίκαιοι καὶ σώφρονες, ὥσπερ εἰ τὰ γραμματικὰ καὶ τὰ μουσικά, γραμματικοὶ καὶ μουσικοί. ἢ οὐδ' ἐπὶ τῶν τεχνῶν οὕτως ἔχει; ἐνδέχεται γὰρ γραμματικόν τι ποιῆσαι καὶ ἀπὸ τύχης καὶ ἄλλου ὑποθεμένου. τότε οὖν ἔσται γραμματικός, ἐὰν καὶ γραμματικόν τι ποιήσῃ καὶ γραμματικῶς· τοῦτο δ' ἐστὶ τὸ κατὰ τὴν ἐν αὐτῷ γραμματικήν.

1 § 4. οὐδὲ γὰρ τὸν αὐτόν, κ.τ.λ.] A reference to this doctrine seems appropriate, if not necessary, after the last of the sections which I have interpolated from ch. 9. This was felt by Mich. Ephes., who says in his comment upon 9 § 16 εἰ δὲ τὸ ἀπὸ ἕξεως ἀδίκου τὰ ἄδικα ποιεῖν τὸ ἀδικεῖν ἐστίν, οὐ μόνον οὐ ῥάδιον τῷ δικαίῳ ἀδικεῖν ἀλλὰ καὶ ἀδύνατον. ὡς γὰρ εἶπεν ἀρχόμενος τοῦ βιβλίου, αἱ μὲν ἐπιστῆμαι τῶν ἐναντίων εἰσὶν οὐκέτι δὲ καὶ αἱ ἕξεις. The passage before us may be paraphrased as follows: 'the δίκαιος cannot ἀδικεῖν, because he has not got the appropriate ἕξις: for although an ἐπιστήμη or a δύναμις (i.e. the δύναμις μετὰ λόγου of *Met.* IX. 2. p. 1046. *b.* 2) includes τὰ ἐναντία (and therefore, as we shall see, ἐναντίαι ἕξεις), a

given ἕξις does not enable its possessor to conform to the contrary ἕξις; for example, the healthy man cannot do what is characteristic of ill-health (ἀπὸ τῆς ὑγιείας οὐ πράττεται τὰ ἐναντία, ἀλλὰ τὰ ὑγιεινὰ μόνον).' That the knowledge of a thing includes the knowledge of its contrary is a Platonic maxim: cf. Plat. *Phaed.* 97 D ἐκ δὲ δὴ τοῦ λόγου τούτου οὐδὲν ἄλλο σκοπεῖν προσήκειν ἀνθρώπῳ καὶ περὶ αὑτοῦ καὶ περὶ τῶν ἄλλων, ἀλλ' ἢ τὸ ἄριστον καὶ τὸ βέλτιστον. ἀναγκαῖον δὲ εἶναι τὸν αὐτὸν τοῦτον καὶ τὸ χεῖρον εἰδέναι· τὴν αὐτὴν γὰρ εἶναι ἐπιστήμην περὶ αὐτῶν, and *Charm.* 166 E. The doctrine is referred to by Aristotle, *Anal. Pr.* I. p. 48. *b.* 4. 1. p. 50. *a.* 19. II. p. 69. *b.* 9. "The opinion that justice implies its contrary, as if it were an art," says Grant, "would be a consequence of the Socratic doctrine that justice is knowledge. Plato saw what this doctrine led to and drew out the paradoxical conclusion, *Repub.* p. 334 A. *Hipp. Min.* pp. 375, 6. The Aristotelian theory that justice is a moral state (ἕξις) sets the difficulty at rest."

δυνάμεων] With the Aristotelian use of this word cf. Plato's transitional employment of it in *Polit.* 304 D sqq.

ἕξις δ' ἡ ἐναντία τῶν ἐναντίων οὔ] Rassow (*Forschungen* p. 95) after Muretus reads ἕξις δ' ἡ αὐτή; Spengel (on *Rhet.* II. 19) ἕξις δ' ᾗ ἐναντία. I cannot see that any alteration is necessary. See Translation.

§ 5. πολλάκις μὲν οὖν, κ.τ.λ.] 'It follows from what has been said that, though one of two contrary ἕξεις does not give the power of doing acts characteristic of the other, the knowledge of one ἕξις includes the knowledge of the other. Furthermore, ἕξεις may be known from their ὑποκείμενα.' These statements are introduced as corollaries of the doctrine of § 4, whilst they materially promote the argument by justifying the joint and simultaneous consideration of δικαιοσύνη, ἀδικία, δίκαιον, ἄδικον.

ἀπὸ τῶν ὑποκειμένων] "As we might say 'from its facts,' the ὑποκείμενα being the singular instances in which a general notion is manifested. The meaning is, that τὰ δίκαια are to δικαιοσύνη as good symptoms are to good health." Grant. It would appear however from the statement subsequently made—that 'τὸ εὐεκτικόν is τὸ ποιητικὸν πυκνότητος ἐν σαρκί'—that τὰ ὑποκείμενα include not merely manifestations and symptoms of the ἕξις in question, but also its causes and conditions. In fact the ὑποκείμενα of ὑγίεια (to take a particular example) are τὰ ὑγιεινά in the various kindred senses of φυλακτικά, ποιητικά, σημαντικά, and δεκτικὰ τῆς ὑγιείας. For these senses of ὑγιεινά cf. *Met.* III. 2. p. 1003. *a.* 34. X. 3. p. 1061. *a.* 5.

Top. I. 15. p. 106. b. 35. The word ὑποκείμενα is similarly used to mean "res singulas notioni subjectas" (Bonitz) in *Met.* I. 2. p. 982. a. 23. In order to avoid including 'things which *produce* good condition' amongst the ὑποκείμενα of εὐεξία, Zell, after Muretus, takes εὐεκτικά to mean "corpora ipsa bene habita." See however the passage which Zell himself quotes for another purpose from *Top.* v. 7. p. 137. a. 3 οἷον ἐπεὶ ὁμοίως ἔχει ἰατρός τε πρὸς τὸ ποιητικὸς ὑγιείας εἶναι καὶ γυμναστής (not the athlete, but the trainer) πρὸς τὸ ποιητικὸς εὐεξίας, κ.τ.λ., whence it would appear that τὸ ποιητικὸν πυκνότητος ἐν σαρκί (and therefore τὸ εὐεκτικόν) is that which produces εὐεξία, not that which exhibits it.

ἐάν τε γὰρ ἡ εὐεξία, κ.τ.λ.] Cf. *Polit.* VIII. (V.) 8. p. 210. 3 εἴπερ ἔχομεν δι' ὧν φθείρονται αἱ πολιτεῖαι, ἔχομεν καὶ δι' ὧν σώζονται· τῶν γὰρ ἐναντίων τἀναντία ποιητικά, φθορὰ δὲ σωτηρίᾳ ἐναντίον. See also *Polit.* VIII. (V.) 11. p. 223. 17. Here as in other places τὲ γάρ means no more than γάρ or καὶ γάρ: see Shilleto on Demosth. *F. L.* 391 (critical note), and *Berlin Index* s. v. τέ. (Cf. x. 7 § 2, where the editors, not understanding this use of τὲ γάρ, have placed a comma, instead of a full stop, after ὁτιοῦν to the destruction of the argument. Rassow's *Forschungen* p. 134.) Of course εὐεξία must not be confounded with ὑγιεία: εὐεξία is "bona corporis habitudo," not "bona constitutio": see Zell.

§ 6. ὡς ἐπὶ τὸ πολύ] This qualifying phrase is introduced to meet such cases as that of φιλεῖν, which in the sense of τοῖς χείλεσιν ἀσπάζεσθαι has no correlative: cf. *Top.* I. 15. p. 106. b. 2, quoted by Mich. Ephes. on πολλάκις above.

εἰ τὸ δίκαιον, καὶ τὸ ἄδικον καὶ ἡ ἀδικία] So L^b: K^b P^b read εἰ τὸ ἄδικον καὶ ἡ ἀδικία: H^a M^b N^b O^b εἰ τὸ δίκαιον καὶ τὸ ἄδικον. This last reading is adopted by Bekker. But in § 5 it has been stated (1) that if we know one of two ἐναντίαι ἕξεις we can infer the other, and (2) that if we know τὰ ὑποκείμενα we can infer the corresponding ἕξις, and the example derived from γυμναστική (cf. 11 § 7) is framed accordingly. It would seem then that the statement of § 6 has reference to both pairs of correlatives, and therefore that we should prefer the reading of L^b, which unites that of K^b P^b on the one hand and that of the remaining MSS. on the other. For an application of the principle here laid down cf. *Polit.* VIII. (V.) 9. p. 214. 4 εἰ γὰρ μὴ ταὐτὸν τὸ δίκαιον κατὰ πάσας τὰς πολιτείας, ἀνάγκη καὶ τῆς δικαιοσύνης εἶναι διαφοράς.

§ 7. λανθάνει] The subject to λανθάνει is ἡ ὁμωνυμία ('the equivocation') supplied from τὴν ὁμωνυμίαν ('the equivocal uses'): cf. the words immediately following—καὶ οὐχ ὥσπερ ἐπὶ τῶν πόρρω δήλη μᾶλλον [sc. ἐστὶν ἡ ὁμωνυμία]. See also *Top.* VI. p. 139. *b.* 28 λανθανούσης τῆς ὁμωνυμίας. *Anal. Post.* II. p. 97. *b.* 30 αἱ ὁμωνυμίαι λανθάνουσι μᾶλλον. For διὰ τὸ σύνεγγυς εἶναι τὴν ὁμωνυμίαν cf. *Phys.* VII. 4. p. 249. *a.* 23 εἰσί τε τῶν ὁμωνυμιῶν αἱ μὲν πολὺ ἀπέχουσαι, αἱ δὲ ἔχουσαί τινα ὁμοιότητα, αἱ δ' ἐγγὺς ἢ γένει ἢ ἀναλογίᾳ, διὸ οὐ δοκοῦσιν ὁμωνυμίαι εἶναι οὖσαι. For the words καὶ οὐχ ὥσπερ, κ.τ.λ., constructed independently of the preceding clause with a finite verb of their own, viz. ἐστί understood, cf. Plat. *Epist.* VII. 333A ἕτοιμον γὰρ εἶναι τούτων γενομένων πολὺ μᾶλλον δουλώσασθαι Καρχηδονίους τῆς ἐπὶ Γέλωνος αὐτοῖς γενομένης δουλείας, ἀλλ' οὐχ ὥσπερ νῦν τοὐναντίον ὁ πατὴρ αὐτοῦ φόρον ἐτάξατο φέρειν τοῖς βαρβάροις, and other places quoted by Heindorf on *Gorg.* 522 A, and in the Index of the Berlin Aristotle. The words δήλη μᾶλλον, which Spengel would transpose, seem to me to be rightly rendered by Grant "comparatively plain."

κλείς] Cf. *de spiritu* p. 484. *b.* 21 ἔτι δὲ παρὰ ταῦτ' ἐπὶ συναφῆς καὶ συγκλείσεως χάριν, οἷον ἡ κλείς· ὅθεν ἴσως καὶ τοὔνομα.

§ 8. καὶ ὁ ἄνισος] These words, which after Trendelenburg I have bracketed, but which Bekker retains, cannot be said to destroy the sense, as they might be taken as an explanation of ὁ πλεονέκτης. But they are certainly awkward, especially as the same idea is introduced with a justificatory explanation in § 11. See Trendelenburg's *Historische Beiträge zur Philosophie* II. 354. I conceive that the scribe, not seeing that the word πλεονέκτης suggested ἴσος as its correlative, bridged the apparent gap by anticipating § 11.

§ 9. περὶ ὅσα εὐτυχία καὶ ἀτυχία] I. e. τὰ ἐκτὸς ἀγαθά: cf. *Polit.* IV. (VII.) I. p. 95. 16 ἐπεὶ καὶ τὴν εὐτυχίαν τῆς εὐδαιμονίας διὰ ταῦτ' ἀναγκαῖον ἑτέραν εἶναι· τῶν μὲν γὰρ ἐκτὸς ἀγαθῶν τῆς ψυχῆς αἴτιον ταὐτόματον καὶ ἡ τύχη, δίκαιος δ' οὐδεὶς οὐδὲ σώφρων ἀπὸ τύχης οὐδὲ διὰ τὴν τύχην ἐστίν.

ἃ ἐστὶ μὲν ἁπλῶς ἀεὶ ἀγαθά, τινὶ δ' οὐκ ἀεί] *N. E.* I. 3 § 3 τοιαύτην δέ τινα πλάνην ἔχει καὶ τἀγαθὰ διὰ τὸ πολλοῖς συμβαίνειν βλάβας ἀπ' αὐτῶν· ἤδη γάρ τινες ἀπώλοντο διὰ πλοῦτον, ἕτεροι δὲ δι' ἀνδρείαν. Cf. Plat. *Men.* 88 A sqq. The ἁπλῶς ἀγαθά are ἀγαθά to the σπουδαῖος, *N. E.* III. 4 § 4 εἰ δὲ δὴ ταῦτα μὴ ἀρέσκει, ἆρα φατέον ἁπλῶς μὲν καὶ κατ' ἀλήθειαν βουλητὸν εἶναι τἀγαθὸν ἑκάστῳ δὲ τὸ φαινόμενον; τῷ μὲν οὖν σπουδαίῳ τὸ κατ' ἀλήθειαν εἶναι τῷ δὲ φαύλῳ τὸ τυχόν, ὥσπερ καὶ ἐπὶ τῶν σωμάτων τοῖς μὲν εὖ διακειμένοις ὑγιεινά ἐστι τὰ κατ' ἀλήθειαν τοιαῦτα ὄντα, τοῖς δ' ἐπινόσοις ἕτερα. *Polit.* IV. (VII.) 13. p. 117. 12 καὶ γὰρ τοῦτο διώρισται κατὰ τοὺς ἠθικοὺς λόγους, ὅτι τοιοῦτός ἐστιν ὁ σπουδαῖος, ᾧ διὰ τὴν ἀρετὴν ἀγαθά ἐστι τὰ ἁπλῶς ἀγαθά. *M. M.* II. 3 §§ 7, 8 ὡς δ' αὔτως ὁ ἄδικος ὅτι μὲν οὖν ἁπλῶς καὶ ἡ τυραννὶς ἀγαθὸν καὶ ἡ ἀρχὴ καὶ ἡ ἐξουσία, οἶδεν· ἀλλ' εἰ αὐτῷ ἀγαθὸν ἢ μή, ἢ πότε, ἢ πῶς διακειμένῳ, οὐκέτι οἶδεν. τοῦτο δ' ἐστὶ μάλιστα τῆς φρονήσεως, ὥστε τῷ ἀδίκῳ οὐ παρακολουθεῖ ἡ φρόνησις. αἱρεῖται γὰρ τἀγαθά, ὑπὲρ ὧν ἀδικεῖ, τὰ ἁπλῶς ἀγαθά, οὐ τὰ αὐτῷ ἀγαθά. ὁ γὰρ πλοῦτος καὶ ἡ ἀρχὴ ἁπλῶς μὲν ἀγαθόν, αὐτῷ μέντοι ἴσως οὐκ ἀγαθόν· εὐπορήσας γὰρ καὶ ἄρξας πολλὰ κακὰ αὐτὸς ἑαυτῷ ποιήσει καὶ τοῖς φίλοις· οὐ γὰρ δυνήσεται ἀρχῇ ὀρθῶς χρήσασθαι. See also *E. E.* III. 1 § 7. *Polit.* IV. (VII.) 1. p. 94. 29.

9 § 17. ἔστι δὲ τὰ δίκαια, κ.τ.λ.] See Introduction, On dislocations in the text. 'Particular justice subsists among those who are liable, but not certain, to misuse the goods of fortune'; i.e. among ordinary mortals, not on the one hand amongst the gods, nor on the other hand amongst the θηριώδεις of *N. E.* VII. 5. So *Polit.* I. 2. p. 3. 16 καὶ ὁ ἄπολις διὰ φύσιν καὶ οὐ διὰ τύχην ἤτοι φαῦλός ἐστιν ἢ κρείττων ἢ ἄνθρωπος. p. 4. 8 ὁ δὲ μὴ δυνάμενος κοινωνεῖν, ἢ μηθὲν δεόμενος δι' αὐτάρκειαν, οὐθὲν μέρος πόλεως, ὥστε ἢ θηρίον ἢ θεός.

ὑπερβολὴν καὶ ἔλλειψιν] If the words ἐν τούτοις omitted by K[b] L[b] are retained, either the clause must be construed as though it were ἐν οἷς δ' ἔχουσι (sc. τὰ ἁπλῶς ἀγαθά) ὑπερβολὴν καὶ ἔλλειψιν, or ἐν τούτοις must be taken here and in the preceding clause in different senses. For the subaudition of the relative οἵ from the preceding οἷς see Madvig's *Greek Syntax* § 104. For the sentiment cf. *Polit.* IV. (VII.) 1. p. 94. 29 τὰ μὲν γὰρ ἐκτὸς ἔχει πέρας ὥσπερ ὄργανόν τι· πᾶν (πέρας Bernays) δὲ τὸ χρήσιμόν ἐστιν· ὧν (ὥστε Bernays) τὴν ὑπερβολὴν ἢ βλάπτειν ἀναγκαῖον ἢ μηθὲν ὄφελος εἶναι αὐτῶν τοῖς ἔχουσιν.

διὰ τοῦτ' ἀνθρώπινόν ἐστιν] At present ἐστίν has no evident subject. Should we read διό instead of διά? Susemihl (Bursian's *Jahresbericht* 1876, p. 278) points out that this alteration was suggested by Zwinger.

1 § 10. ὁ δ' ἄδικος οὐκ ἀεί, κ.τ.λ.] Cf. 3 §§ 15, 16. *Polit.* VIII. (V.) 2. p. 196. 19.

§ 11. καὶ παράνομος—ἀδικίας] Bekker rejects this sentence. I have contented myself with bracketing the words ἡ παρανομία ἤτοι ἢ ἀνισότης, which are obviously interpolated. So Fritzsche. Bekker is mistaken in saying that after κοινόν H[a] and N[b] give τὸ γὰρ ἄνισον ἔχει τὸ πλέον καὶ τὸ ἔλαττον.

§ 12. ἦν] The reference is to § 8.

πάντα τὰ νόμιμά ἐστί πως δίκαια] Even οἱ κατὰ τὰς παρεκβεβηκυίας πολιτείας νόμοι, which are ἁπλῶς οὐ δίκαιοι (*Polit.* III. 11. p. 78. 7), are πως δίκαιοι.

§ 13. ἢ τοῦ κοινῇ συμφέροντος, κ.τ.λ.] Spengel proposes to omit either ἢ τοῖς ἀρίστοις or κατ' ἀρετὴν ἢ. Rassow is certainly right in preferring to omit ἢ τοῖς ἀρίστοις, and probably right in reading ἢ κατ' ἀρετήν; vide Crit. comment. The laws which aim at τοῦ κοινῇ συμφέροντος πᾶσιν are those of the ὀρθαὶ πολιτεῖαι, in which the government is administered by the one, the few, or the many, with a view to the common good: the laws which aim at τοῦ τοῖς κυρίοις συμφέροντος are those of the παρεκβάσεις, in which the governing class regards only its own interest. *Polit.* III. 7. p. 69. 22 ἐπεὶ δὲ πολιτεία μὲν καὶ πολίτευμα σημαίνει ταὐτόν, πολίτευμα δ' ἐστὶ τὸ κύριον τῶν πόλεων, ἀνάγκη δ' εἶναι κύριον ἢ ἕνα ἢ ὀλίγους ἢ τοὺς πολλούς, ὅταν μὲν ὁ εἷς ἢ οἱ ὀλίγοι ἢ οἱ πολλοὶ πρὸς τὸ κοινὸν συμφέρον ἄρχωσι, ταύτας μὲν ὀρθὰς ἀναγκαῖον εἶναι τὰς πολιτείας, τὰς δὲ πρὸς τὸ ἴδιον ἢ τοῦ ἑνὸς ἢ τῶν ὀλίγων ἢ τοῦ πλήθους παρεκβάσεις. The words ἢ κατ' ἀρετὴν ἢ κατ' ἄλλον τινὰ τρόπον τοιοῦτον indicate the different principles which in different states determine the possession of political power. *Polit.* VI. (IV.) 8. p. 159. 15 δοκεῖ δὲ ἀριστοκρατία μὲν εἶναι μάλιστα τὸ τὰς τιμὰς νενεμῆσθαι κατ' ἀρετήν· ἀριστοκρατίας μὲν γὰρ ὅρος ἀρετή, ὀλιγαρχίας δὲ πλοῦτος, δήμου δ' ἐλευθερία. For the general sentiment cf. § 17 and VIII. 9 § 4. 10 § 2. See Rassow's *Forschungen* pp. 76, 77, whence this note is in the main derived.

ὥστε ἕνα μὲν τρόπον δίκαια, κ.τ.λ.] 'So that in one sense we call that just which produces and preserves happiness and its parts. But the law also prescribes the doing of acts characteristic of the several virtues': cf. 2 §§ 10, 11 where νόμιμα which promote virtue through education are distinguished from νόμιμα which enforce the different virtues.

§ 14. τὰ κατὰ τὰς ἄλλας ἀρετάς] The article, which Rassow (*Forschungen* p. 60) restores on the authority of L[b], though perhaps not indispensable, is certainly an improvement.

§ 15. ἐν δὲ δικαιοσύνῃ, κ.τ.λ.] Theogn. 147. Fritzsche quotes *Polit.* III. 13. p. 80. 13 κοινωνικὴν γὰρ ἀρετὴν εἶναί φαμεν τὴν δικαιοσύνην, ᾗ πάσας ἀναγκαῖον ἀκολουθεῖν τὰς ἄλλας.

τελεία δ' ἐστίν, κ.τ.λ.] Bekker after the MSS. reads καὶ τελεία μάλιστα ἀρετή, ὅτι τῆς τελείας ἀρετῆς χρῆσίς ἐστιν. τελεία δ' ἐστίν, ὅτι ὁ ἔχων, κ.τ.λ. But from the opening words of this §, as well as from the argument generally, it is clear that the phrase πρὸς ἕτερον does not explain τελεία, but differentiates δικαιοσύνη from τελεία ἀρετή ἁπλῶς. This being so, it follows that the words ὅτι τῆς τελείας ἀρετῆς χρῆσίς ἐστιν do not justify the statement καὶ τελεία μάλιστα ἀρετή, and that the words ὅτι ὁ ἔχων αὐτήν, κ.τ.λ. do not justify the statement τελεία δ' ἐστίν. Trendelenburg (*Beiträge* II. 356) substitutes ὅτι τελεία τῆς ἀρετῆς χρῆσίς ἐστιν for ὅτι τῆς τελείας ἀρετῆς χρῆσίς ἐστίν, whilst Ueberweg (*Grundriss* I. 189) inserts τελεία after χρῆσίς ἐστι, supposing the word to have been dropped in consequence of its occurrence at the beginning of the next sentence. I presume that they agree in understanding ἡ χρῆσις with τελεία δ' ἐστίν, otherwise they have not met the difficulty raised at the outset of this note. Now this subaudition appears to me excessively awkward, especially as αὐτήν seems to indicate that ἡ δικαιοσύνη is the subject of τελεία δ' ἐστίν. I conjecture therefore that either τελεία in τελεία δ' ἐστίν, ὅτι, κ.τ.λ. has taken the place of κρατίστη, or that καὶ τελεία μάλιστα and τελεία δ' ἐστίν have been transposed. In either case the sentences succeeding the proverbial hexameter amplify and explain the statements already made, that justice is ἀρετὴ τελεία, and that it is κρατίστη τῶν ἀρετῶν. On the whole I am in favour of the second of the above alternatives, and have altered the text accordingly. The sentence τελεία δ' ἐστὶν ἀρετὴ ὅτι τῆς τελείας ἀρετῆς χρῆσίς ἐστιν is thus a justification of the statement that αὕτη ἡ δικαιοσύνη ἀρετή ἐστι τελεία, whilst the sentence καὶ τελεία μάλιστα ὅτι ὁ ἔχων αὐτήν, κ.τ.λ. repeats in a more definite form the substance of the sentence καὶ διὰ τοῦτο πολλάκις, κ.τ.λ. In other words, this sort of justice is (1) τῆς τελείας ἀρετῆς χρῆσις, (2) πρὸς ἕτερον, and therefore not only (1) τελεία, but also (2) τελεία μάλιστα. The statement in 2 § 10, that ἡ κατὰ τὴν ὅλην ἀρετὴν τεταγμένη δικαιοσύνη is τῆς ὅλης ἀρετῆς χρῆσις πρὸς ἄλλον, shows clearly what is meant by τελεία ἀρετή. Cf. *Rhet.* I. 9. p. 29. 30 ἀνάγκη δὲ μεγίστας εἶναι ἀρετὰς τὰς τοῖς ἄλλοις χρησιμωτάτας, εἴπερ ἐστὶν ἡ ἀρετὴ δύναμις εὐεργετική. διὰ τοῦτο τοὺς δικαίους καὶ ἀνδρείους μάλιστα τιμῶσιν· ἡ μὲν γὰρ ἐν πολέμῳ ἡ δὲ καὶ ἐν εἰρήνῃ χρήσιμος ἄλλοις. The phrase ὅτι τῆς τελείας ἀρετῆς χρῆσίς ἐστιν [sc. ἡ δικαιοσύνη] is strange, since χρῆσις is almost equivalent to ἐνέργεια (*Berlin Index*, s. v.), and a ἕξις can hardly be identified with an ἐνέργεια; but cf. 2 § 10, quoted above. Apparently in this place δικαιοσύνη is the practice of the virtue, not the virtue itself. Aristotle would hardly have expressed himself so loosely. For the sentiment cf. *Polit.* IV. (VII.) 2. p. 97. 9 ἐφ' ἑκάστης γὰρ ἀρετῆς οὐκ εἶναι πράξεις μᾶλλον τοῖς ἰδιώταις ἢ τοῖς τὰ κοινὰ πράττουσι καὶ πολιτευομένοις.

§ 16. ἀρχὴ ἄνδρα δείξει] The editors quote Soph. *Antig.* 175.

§ 17. ἀλλότριον ἀγαθόν] Plat. *Rep.* 343 C.

ἢ κοινωνῷ] Bekker is mistaken in saying that H^a N^b read κοινῷ. On the strength of Bekker's statement Michelet admits this reading into his text, commenting thus : "ἢ ἄρχοντι ἢ κοινῷ referendum est ad duplex civitatum genus, quod Aristoteles *Polit.* III. 7 exponit...Κοινωνῷ non esset diversum ab ἄρχοντι, cum ii, penes quos summa imperii est, participes sint civitatis (κοινωνοῦσι τῆς πόλεως). A nobis stat Michael Ephesius." The alteration is unnecessary. The words ἢ ἄρχοντι ἢ κοινωνῷ may be paraphrased : 'either that of the governing class in the case of a παρεκβεβηκυῖα πολιτεία, or that of his fellow-citizens in the case of a πολιτεία ὀρθή.' See note on § 13. Michelet's reference to the Latin translation of Mich. Ephes. ("si populus administret, reipublicae") is not justified by the Greek original of the commentary.

§ 18. ὁ καὶ πρὸς αὑτὸν καὶ πρὸς τοὺς φίλους] The first καί means 'even' i. e. 'not merely towards his neighbour but'; not 'both,' because friends are looked upon as part of the man himself (πρὸς δὲ τὸν φίλον ἔχειν ὥσπερ πρὸς ἑαυτόν, ἔστι γὰρ ὁ φίλος ἄλλος αὐτός IX. 4 § 5), and therefore cannot be identified with the ἕτερος. See Rassow's *Forschungen* p. 61. Nötel (*Quaest. Aristot. Spec.* p. 10) would omit the first καί and the second πρός.

ἀλλ' ὁ πρὸς ἕτερον] So Rassow l. c. with the countenance of H^a N^b O^b. Bekker with the remaining MSS. omits the article.

§ 19. ὅλη ἀρετή] This seems to be an Eudemian phrase: cf. *E. E.* II. 1 § 14 ἡ τούτου ἀρετὴ οὐκ ἔστι μόριον τῆς ὅλης ἀρετῆς.

§ 20. ἔστι μὲν γάρ, κ.τ.λ.] Cf. *de anima* II. 12. p. 424. a. 25. III. 2. p. 425. b. 25. p. 427. a. 7. *de somniis* I. p. 459. a. 15. *E. N.* VI. 8 § 1 (all quoted by Trendelenburg, *Beiträge* II. 356), as well as the references in the *Berlin Index*, s. v. εἶναι p. 221. a. 50. Trendelenburg is most certainly right in taking ἁπλῶς, not (as Bekker takes it) with ἀρετή, but with τοιάδε ἕξις : " Inwiefern sich jene Gesinnung und Fertigkeit (ἕξις), welche dem Gesetz überhaupt angemessen ist, auf einen Andern bezieht, ist sie Gerechtigkeit; inwiefern sie eine solche Gesinnung und Fertigkeit schlechthin ist, Tugend. Das ἁπλῶς steht dem πρὸς ἕτερον entgegen, wie p. 1129. b. 26 αὕτη μὲν οὖν ἡ δικαιοσύνη ἀρετὴ μέν ἐστι τελεία, ἀλλ' οὐχ ἁπλῶς ἀλλὰ πρὸς ἕτερον. Stände ἁπλῶς nicht dabei, so läge in τοιάδε ἕξις möglicher Weise πρὸς ἕτερον mit."

2 § 1. τὴν ἐν μέρει ἀρετῆς δικαιοσύνην—ἀδικίας τῆς κατὰ μέρος] For

the equivalence of ἐν μέρει and κατὰ μέρος see Waitz *Organ*. I. 375, and Eucken *über den Sprachgebrauch des A.* II. p. 24 sq.

§§ 2—5. Nötel, supposing these §§ to contain three distinct arguments,—the second (§ 4) and the third (§ 5) being introduced by the word ἔτι,—remarks that the third argument (§ 5) is identical with the first (§§ 2, 3): "Si quid uideo aliud nihil his uerbis (ἔτι περὶ μὲν τἆλλα, κ.τ.λ.) efficitur, nisi lucri cupiditatis non proprium esse nomen, sed idem, quod ipsius est improbitatis universae. Quid uero? Nonne id iam prima argumentatione satis atque abunde dictum est? Aliam uero sententiam ex istis uerbis equidem elicere non possum. Atque si ipsa uocabula diligentius inspicimus, uidemus exempla, quae hoc loco usurpantur, iam omnia in eis, quae praecedunt, exstare." *Quaest. Aristot. Spec.* p. 11. He proposes to meet the difficulty by excising the third argument (§ 5). I think that this measure is unnecessary. The author wishes to establish two propositions: (1) that there is such a thing as partial or particular injustice, (2) that its motive is gain. The first of these propositions is proved in § 2, and affirmed in § 3. The ἔτι at the beginning of § 4 introduces the second of the two propositions, which is proved in § 4, and affirmed in the words δῆλον ἄρα ὅτι διὰ τὸ κερδαίνειν. Finally the argument of § 2 is restated in § 5, with the substitution of the emphatic words εἰ δ' ἐκέρδανεν for ὅταν δὲ πλεονεκτῇ, so as to mark both points simultaneously. If this interpretation is the true one, it is clearly unnecessary to read with Spengel (*Aristot. Stud.* I. 40) δῆλον γὰρ ὅτι in place of δῆλον ἄρα ὅτι.

§ 6. συνώνυμος] Both ἡ ὅλη ἀδικία and ἡ ἐν μέρει ἀδικία are πονηρία πρὸς ἕτερον; hence the word ἀδικία is used, in reference to the ἕξεις in question, συνωνύμως, not ὁμωνύμως. See Trendelenburg's *Elem. Log. Aristot.* p. 116.

§ 7. παρὰ τὴν ὅλην ἀρετήν] So the MSS.: but cf. § 6 ὥστε φανερὸν ὅτι ἔστι τις ἀδικία παρὰ τὴν ὅλην ἄλλη ἐν μέρει, and § 10 ἡ μὲν οὖν κατὰ τὴν ὅλην ἀρετὴν τεταγμένη δικαιοσύνη καὶ ἀδικία; whence it would appear that the phrases admissible are (1) παρὰ τὴν ὅλην δικαιοσύνην, and (2) παρὰ τὴν κατὰ τὴν ὅλην ἀρετὴν τεταγμένην. Hence I should like with Spengel (who also suspects ἀρετῆς in 2 § 1) to expunge ἀρετήν.

§ 9. ἐπεὶ δὲ τὸ ἄνισον καὶ τὸ πλέον οὐ ταὐτὸν ἀλλ' ἕτερον ὡς μέρος πρὸς ὅλον (τὸ μὲν γὰρ πλέον ἅπαν ἄνισον, τὸ δ' ἄνισον οὐ πᾶν πλέον), καὶ τὸ ἄδικον καὶ ἡ ἀδικία οὐ ταὐτὰ ἀλλ' ἕτερα ἐκείνων, τὰ μὲν ὡς μέρη τὰ δ' ὡς ὅλα· μέρος γὰρ αὕτη ἡ ἀδικία τῆς ὅλης ἀδικίας, ὁμοίως δὲ καὶ ἡ δικαιοσύνη τῆς δικαιοσύνης. ὥστε καὶ περὶ τῆς ἐν μέρει δικαιοσύνης καὶ περὶ τῆς ἐν μέρει ἀδικίας λεκτέον, κ.τ.λ. So reads Bekker. In a paper in the *Journal of Philology* 1872, IV. 318, I proposed with Spengel to omit the parenthetical sentence τὸ μὲν γὰρ πλέον ἅπαν ἄνισον, τὸ δ' ἄνισον οὐ πᾶν πλέον, understanding after ταὐτόν, τῷ παρανόμῳ, and after ἕτερον, τοῦ παρανόμου. This mode of treating the passage seemed at least better than that adopted by Mich. Ephes., whose note runs thus: ἐξ ἀναλόγου τινὸς δείκνυσι τὴν διαφορὰν τῆς τε μερικῆς ἀδικίας καὶ τῆς ὅλης ἀδικίας καὶ τῆς μερικῆς δικαιοσύνης καὶ τῆς ὅλης, δυνάμει λέγων, ὡς τὸ πλέον πρὸς τὸ ἄνισον οὕτως ἡ μερικὴ δικαιοσύνη πρὸς τὴν ὅλην δικαιοσύνην. On further consideration however I have come to the conclusion that Trendelenburg is certainly right in accepting the correction of Muretus—ἐπεὶ δὲ τὸ ἄνισον καὶ τὸ παράνομον οὐ ταὐτὸν ἀλλ' ἕτερον ὡς μέρος πρὸς ὅλον· τὸ μὲν γὰρ ἄνισον ἅπαν παράνομον, τὸ δὲ παράνομον οὐχ ἅπαν ἄνισον· καὶ τὸ ἄδικον, κ.τ.λ. Indeed it would seem that this reading, which gives a perfect sense, has just as much support in the MSS. as the nonsense which has been preferred to it. If I am not mistaken P[b] has retained intact or almost intact a double reading from which the other MSS. have variously diverged. The text in this MS. is as follows ἐπεὶ δὲ τὸ ἄνισον καὶ τὸ παράνομον [πλέον] οὐ ταὐτὸν ἀλλ' ἕτερον ὡς μέρος πρὸς ὅλον· τὸ μὲν γὰρ ἄνισον ἅπαν παράνομον τὸ δὲ παράνομον οὐχ ἅπαν ἄνισον· [τὸ μὲν γὰρ πλέον ἅπαν ἄνισον τὸ δ' ἄνισον οὐ πᾶν πλέον·] καὶ τὸ ἄδικον, κ.τ.λ. The words which I have enclosed in brackets are clearly second readings. Now K[b] retains both readings in the first clause, but in the parenthetical sentence which follows exhibits only the second of the two readings. On the other hand M[b] giving only the second reading, and O[b] hesitating between the first and second readings in the first clause, agree in retaining the double reading in the second clause, but differ in the words by which the two readings are connected. L[b] and N[b] however consistently prefer the second reading in both clauses, and this consistency has secured to their text a preference to which it was not entitled by its merits. The inferior MSS. which I have had an opportunity of consulting exhibit similar varieties of text. Thus Par. 1853, 2023, Ambros. H. 113, and the New College MS., have the first reading in the first clause, the double reading in the second: Par. 1856, 2024, have the first reading in the first clause, the second in the second; the translatio vetus has with unimportant deviations the second reading in the first clause, both readings in the second: Par. 1417, 1855, Ambros. B. 95, G. 86, have the second reading in both clauses: finally whereas Par. 1852 has the first reading in the first clause, and the second in the second, and Ambros. A 62 has the second reading in both clauses, these two MSS. agree in the absurd confusion τὸ μὲν γὰρ ἄνισον ἅπαν ἄνισον. I conceive then that all our MSS. are based upon a MS. which had the double reading, and I have no hesitation in preferring in both clauses the first reading to the second, since (1) the distinction between the two kinds of justice depends, not upon the distinction between ἄνισον and πλέον, but upon that between παράνομον and ἄνισον in which πλέον is included, and (2) Bekker's reading is after all inconsistent with itself, as τὸ ἄνισον and τὸ πλέον are related to one another, not ὡς μέρος πρὸς ὅλον, but ὡς ὅλον πρὸς μέρος. In the foregoing statement of the readings it has not been mentioned that, instead of ὡς μέρος πρὸς ὅλον, K^b gives ὡς μέρος καὶ πρὸς ὅλον. As καὶ is manifestly superfluous, it would seem that here again we have a double reading. If so, all the extant MSS. are derived from one in which the text ran thus: ἐπεὶ δὲ τὸ ἄνισον καὶ τὸ παράνομον [πλέον] οὐ ταὐτὸν ἀλλ' ἕτερον ὡς μέρος καὶ [πρὸς] ὅλον· τὸ μὲν γὰρ ἄνισον ἅπαν παράνομον τὸ δὲ παράνομον οὐκ ἅπαν ἄνισον· [τὸ μὲν γὰρ πλέον ἅπαν ἄνισον τὸ δ' ἄνισον οὐ πᾶν πλέον] καὶ τὸ ἄδικον, κ.τ.λ.

ὥστε] I have removed the full stop which Bekker places after δικαιοσύνης, as ὥστε clearly introduces the apodosis of the sentences which precede.

§ 10. διοριστέον] Rassow (*Forschungen*, p. 93) conjectures ἀφοριστέον.

σχεδὸν γάρ, κ.τ.λ.] Universal δίκαια and ἄδικα, being respectively τὰ νόμιμα and τὰ παράνομα, may be ascertained by a reference to the particular virtues and vices: for, as we have seen in 1 §§ 13, 14, law is concerned (1) with the direct encouragement of the particular virtues which together make up universal virtue, and the direct discouragement of the particular vices which together make up universal vice, and (2) with the indirect encouragement of the particular virtues, and the indirect discouragement of the particular vices, by means of educational enactments.

§ 11. περὶ παιδείαν τὴν πρὸς τὸ κοινόν] The education which fits a man to perform his duties as citizen of a particular state.

περὶ δὲ τῆς καθ' ἕκαστον, κ.τ.λ.] 'Whether it is the business of πολιτική or of some other science to provide that education which makes the individual a good *man*, must be determined hereafter.' That there is a difference between the education which produces a good *citizen*, and that which produces a good *man*, follows from the doctrine, enunciated here in anticipation of *Polit*. III. 4. p. 63. 5 sqq., that the virtue of the good man and the virtue of the perfect citizen are not in every case (παντί) identical. In *Polit*. III. 6. p. 67. 21 Aristotle says more precisely that in some states the two sorts of virtue are distinct, i.e. the virtue of the perfect citizen is not coincident with that of the good man, but that in others the virtue of the good man is identical with that of a citizen who engages in politics, and takes part or may take part alone or in conjunction with others in the administration of public affairs: cf. *Polit*. IV. (VII.) 14. p. 119. 22. From *Polit*. VI. (IV.) 7. p. 157. 32 we learn further that it is only in the ἀριστοκρατία (here expressly identified with Aristotle's perfect polity) that this identity is possible; ἐν μόνῃ γὰρ ἁπλῶς ὁ αὐτὸς ἀνὴρ καὶ πολίτης ἀγαθός ἐστιν· οἱ δ' ἐν ταῖς ἄλλαις ἀγαθοὶ πρὸς τὴν πολιτείαν εἰσὶ τὴν αὑτῶν: cf. III. 18. p. 93. 11. The preliminary question—πότερον ἑτέραν ἢ τὴν αὐτὴν ἀρετὴν θετέον καθ' ἣν ἀνὴρ ἀγαθός ἐστι καὶ πολίτης σπουδαῖος;—having been answered in this sense, it follows that in general παιδεία should be πρὸς τὴν πολιτείαν 'adapted to the particular constitution' (*Polit*. I. 13. p. 22. 17. V. (VIII.) 1. p. 130. 2 sqq. VIII. (V.) 9. p. 215. 29), but that in the ἀρίστη πόλις, where the virtue of the perfect citizen is identical with that of the good man, the legislator will endeavour to make his fellow citizens good *men* (*Polit*. IV. (VII.) 14. p. 119. 22. cf. III. 18. p. 93. 11). In any case the state should superintend education, instead of leaving it to the discretion of parents (*Polit*. V. (VIII.) 1. p. 130. 10. *N. E.* X. 9 §§ 13, 14). I cannot think that Grant's note upon the present passage accurately represents Aristotle's views. For the phrase ἀνδρὶ ἀγαθῷ εἶναι see Trendelenburg on *de Anim*. III. 4. p. 29. b. 10. With the emphatic παντί 'in all cases' compare τινός 'in some cases' in *Polit*. III. 4. p. 64. 11 ἀλλ' ἆρα ἔσται τινὸς ἡ αὐτὴ ἀρετὴ πολίτου τε σπουδαίου καὶ ἀνδρὸς σπουδαίου;

§ 12. τῆς δὲ κατὰ μέρος δικαιοσύνης, κ.τ.λ.] This classification may be represented thus

```
                          τὸ κατὰ μέρος δίκαιον
          ┌──────────────────────┴──────────────────────┐
  τὸ ἐν ταῖς διανομαῖς         τὸ ἐν τοῖς συναλλάγμασι διορθωτικόν
                       ┌──────────────────┴──────────────────┐
              τὸ ἐν τοῖς ἑκουσίοις              τὸ ἐν τοῖς ἀκουσίοις
              συναλλάγμασι διορθωτικόν          συναλλάγμασι διορθωτικόν
                                        ┌───────────────┴───────────────┐
                              τὸ δ. τὸ ἐν τοῖς ἀκουσίοις    τὸ δ. τὸ ἐν τοῖς ἀκουσίοις
                              σ. ὅσα λαθραῖά ἐστιν          σ. ὅσα βίαιά ἐστιν
```

Here τὸ ἐν ταῖς διανομαῖς or τὸ διανεμητικὸν δίκαιον (4 § 2) is that δίκαιον which is exhibited in the distribution of public position, property, and advantages. In general the author assumes the χρήματα distributed, as well as the τιμαί, to belong to the state (§ 12 and 4 § 2), but it is obvious that his remarks apply also to smaller κοινωνίαι such as companies of merchants or manufacturers. For the political application of the conception of τὸ διανεμητικὸν δίκαιον see especially *Polit.* III. 9 and VIII. (v.) 1, where τὸ ὀλιγαρχικὸν δίκαιον and τὸ δημοκρατικὸν δίκαιον are investigated. In these passages we are told that τὸ δίκαιον is τὸ κατ' ἀναλογίαν ἴσον (p. 193. 30) and again that τὸ ἁπλῶς δίκαιον is τὸ κατ' ἀξίαν (p. 195. 15), but that oligarchs and democrats differ in their interpretation of the fundamental formula, the former laying claim to an universal superiority in virtue of their superior wealth, and the latter asserting universal equality in virtue of equality of birth: cf. infra 3 § 7, which agrees exactly with the above-mentioned passages. This is not inconsistent with *Polit.* VII. (VI.) 2. p. 179. 11 καὶ γὰρ τὸ δίκαιον τὸ δημοτικὸν τὸ ἴσον ἔχειν ἐστὶ κατ' ἀριθμὸν ἀλλὰ μὴ κατ' ἀξίαν, since the democratic interpretation converts τὸ κατ' ἀξίαν ἴσον (proportionate equality) into τὸ κατ' ἀριθμόν (numerical equality). With τὸ ἴσον τὸ ἀντιπεπονθός, which, we are told in *Polit.* II. 2. p. 24. 11, σώζει τὰς πόλεις, we are not yet concerned.

τὸ ἐν τοῖς συναλλάγμασι δ.] I. e. the justice which rectifies unjust divisions both voluntary and involuntary. Thus voluntary transactions do *not* "come under the head of corrective justice" (Grant Edit. 2); it is the *rectification* of wrong arising out of such transactions with which this sort of justice is concerned, cf. *Journal of Philology* 1872, IV. 311. In his edition of 1874 Grant accepts this interpretation.

§ 13. λαθραῖα—βίαια] Cf. Plat. *Laws* IX. 864 C.

δουλαπατία δολοφονία] Mich. Ephes. appears to have read δουλαπατία δουλοφονία, as he remarks—ὁμοίως καὶ ὁ δοῦλον ἀπατήσας καὶ φονεύσας ἀντάλλαγμα δίδωσιν.

βίαια] Of course αἰκία, κ.τ.λ. are called βίαια from the point of view of the sufferer, not in the sense in which the word is used in *N. E.* III. 1.

πήρωσις] Cf. Plat. *Laws* 874 E.

3 § 2. τὸ πλέον καὶ τὸ ἔλαττον] 'Excess' and 'defect' the two elements of which τὸ ἄνισον consists.

§ 3. τὸ δίκαιον ἴσον] *Polit.* III. 12. p. 78. 16 δοκεῖ δὲ πᾶσιν ἴσον τι τὸ δίκαιον εἶναι, καὶ μέχρι γέ τινος ὁμολογοῦσι τοῖς κατὰ φιλοσοφίαν λόγοις ἐν οἷς διώρισται περὶ τῶν ἠθικῶν· τί γὰρ καὶ τισὶ τὸ δίκαιον, καὶ δεῖν τοῖς ἴσοις ἴσον εἶναι φασίν. ποίων δ' ἰσότης ἐστὶ καὶ ποίων ἀνισότης, δεῖ μὴ λανθάνειν: cf. also *Polit.* III. 9. p. 71. 25, quoted by Grant as "a passage from which it is not improbable that the present chapter may be partly taken, though an interpolated reference (καθάπερ εἴρηται πρότερον ἐν τοῖς ἠθικοῖς) gives the passage in the Politics a fallacious appearance of having been written later, and of having accepted conclusions from the present book. Far rather it is likely that the conception of 'distributive justice' having been received as a conception from Plato, and farther worked out by Aristotle in his *Politics*, only became stereotyped into a phrase in the after-growth of his system, at the end of his own life, or in the exposition of his views made by Eudemus." I cannot assent to this theory. Books VIII. and IX. afford evidence that the investigation of justice contained in the original fifth book resembled that contained in the extant Eudemian paraphrase. Why then may we not suppose that the passage in the Politics quotes, not indeed from the Eudemian book, but from a Nicomachean equivalent, and that in the passage before us Eudemus draws upon his ordinary sources of information? Grant also condemns the words ὥσπερ ἐν τοῖς ἠθικοῖς εἴρηται πρότερον in *Polit.* II. 2. p. 24. 12, and tries to explain away ἐν οἷς διώρισται περὶ τῶν ἠθικῶν in *Polit.* III. 12. p. 78. 17 (quoted above).

§ 4. ἀνάγκη τοίνυν, κ.τ.λ.] 'The just, as has been shewn, is (1) μέσον, (2) ἴσον; it is also (3) πρός τι 'relative.' Inasmuch as it is μέσον, it implies certain extremes between which it lies; inasmuch as it is ἴσον, it implies, as has been said, two things; inasmuch as it is δίκαιον, it implies certain persons. Hence the just implies at least four terms, two persons and two things.' "A confusion is made" says Grant with reason, "by the introduction of the idea of μέσον with regard to justice, which at the present part of the argument was not required." Though irrelevant, the reference to τὸ μέσον is not, I think, an interpolation; cf. *M. M.* I. 34 § 7 τὸ δέ γε ἴσον ἐν ἐλαχίστοις δυσὶν ἐγγίνεται· τὸ ἄρα πρὸς ἕτερον ἴσον εἶναι δίκαιόν ἐστι, καὶ δίκαιος ὁ τοιοῦτος ἂν εἴη. ἐπεὶ οὖν ἡ δικαιοσύνη ἐν δικαίῳ καὶ ἐν ἴσῳ καὶ ἐν μεσότητι, τὸ μὲν δίκαιον ἔν τισι λέγεται δίκαιον, τὸ δ' ἴσον τισὶν ἴσον, τὸ δὲ μέσον τισὶ μέσον, ὥσθ' ἡ δικαιοσύνη καὶ τὸ δίκαιον ἔσται καὶ πρός τινας καὶ ἔν τισιν. This passage seems to me to prove the substantial integrity of §§ 3, 4. In both places (1) τὸ ἴσον is said to imply two terms, (2) the irrelevant reference to τὸ μέσον is introduced, and (3) the four terms of the ἀναλογία are obtained by the consideration of δίκαιον, firstly as ἴσον, and secondly as δίκαιον. But whereas in v. 3 § 4 as read by Bekker, [καὶ πρός τι] καὶ τισίν, we have an abrupt and premature anticipation of the after statement ᾗ δὲ δίκαιον, τισίν, in the corresponding sentence of *M. M.* I. 34 § 7 we have the preliminary proposition τὸ ἄρα πρὸς ἕτερον ἴσον εἶναι δίκαιόν ἐστι. Hence with L[b] I retain καὶ πρός τι as the equivalent of πρὸς ἕτερον in the *M. M.*, and omit καὶ τισίν as a gloss anticipatory of ᾗ δὲ δίκαιον, τισίν. (Cf. Plat. *Phileb.* 51 C and D, where πρός τι and πρὸς ἕτερον are used indifferently: ταῦτα γὰρ οὐκ εἶναι πρός τι καλὰ λέγω, καθάπερ ἄλλα, ἀλλ' ἀεὶ καλὰ καθ' αὑτὰ πεφυκέναι......λέγω δὴ [τὰς] τῶν φθογγῶν τὰς λείας καὶ λαμπράς, τὰς ἕν τι καθαρὸν ἱείσας μέλος, οὐ πρὸς ἕτερον καλὰς ἀλλ' αὐτὰς καθ' αὑτὰς εἶναι.) This course is countenanced by the V. A., which, at the end of § 4, where we read ᾗ δὲ δίκαιον, τισίν, has 'secundum autem quod iustum aliquibus et ad aliquos: ad alios enim est,' i.e. ᾗ δὲ δίκαιον, τισὶ καὶ πρός τινας· πρὸς ἑτέρους γάρ ἐστιν; and perhaps by Mich. Ephes., who writes ᾗ δὲ δίκαιον τισὶ καὶ πρός τινας. τὸ δὲ τισὶ καὶ πρός τινας ἐκ παραλλήλου κεῖται ταὐτὸν σημαῖνον· πρὸς ἄλλους γὰρ τὸ δίκαιον καὶ ἡ δικαιοσύνη, ὡς εἴρηται, δύναται. Whether the words added by the V. A. belong to the text or not, I am sure that they represent the argument. Recent editors have attempted in spite of *M. M.* I. 34 § 7 to connect ᾗ μὲν μέσον, τινῶν with the main argument, and with a view to this have allowed themselves considerable licence of conjectural emendation. Thus Spengel (*Aristotelische Studien* I. 42) reads ἀνάγκη τοίνυν τὸ δίκαιον μέσον τε καὶ ἴσον (ὂν) εἶναι (τινῶν) καὶ τισίν, καὶ ᾗ μὲν μέσον, τινῶν, ᾗ δ' ἴσον, τισίν. ἀνάγκη ἄρα τὸ δίκαιον ἐν ἐλαχίστοις εἶναι τέτταρσιν· οἷς τε γὰρ δίκαιον τυγχάνει ὄν, δύο ἐστί, καὶ ἐν οἷς: and Münscher ἀνάγκη τοίνυν τὸ δίκαιον μέσον τε καὶ ἴσον ὂν εἶναι καὶ ἐν τισὶ καὶ τισίν· ἀνάγκη ἄρα τὸ δίκαιον ἐν ἐλαχίστοις εἶναι τέτταρσιν· οἷς τε γὰρ δίκαιον τυγχάνει ὄν, δύο ἐστί, καὶ ἐν οἷς τὰ πράγματα δύο. καὶ αὕτη ἔσται ἡ ἰσότης, οἷς καὶ ἐν οἷς.

§ 5. οἷς καὶ ἐν οἷς] I conceive that throughout the passage οἷς means the *persons*, ἐν οἷς the *things* concerned. Cf. *Polit.* III. 9. p. 71. 25 οἷον δοκεῖ ἴσον τὸ δίκαιον εἶναι, καὶ ἔστιν, ἀλλ' οὐ πᾶσιν ἀλλὰ τοῖς ἴσοις. καὶ τὸ ἄνισον δοκεῖ δίκαιον εἶναι· καὶ γὰρ ἔστιν, ἀλλ' οὐ πᾶσιν ἀλλὰ τοῖς ἀνίσοις. οἱ δὲ τοῦτ' ἀφαιροῦσι, τὸ οἷς, καὶ κρίνουσι κακῶς....ὥστ' ἐπεὶ τὸ δίκαιον τισίν, καὶ διῄρηται τὸν αὐτὸν τρόπον ἐπί τε τῶν πραγμάτων καὶ οἷς, καθάπερ εἴρηται πρότερον ἐν τοῖς ἠθικοῖς, τὴν μὲν τοῦ πράγματος ἰσότητα ὁμολογοῦσι, τὴν δὲ οἷς ἀμφισβητοῦσι. (Grant assumes that the writer of this book borrows from the *Politics*. See note on 3 § 3.) Hence in καὶ ἐν οἷς τὰ πράγματα δύο, I have bracketed τὰ πράγματα. That ἐν οἷς τὰ πράγματα does not stand for ἐν οἷς τὰ πράγματά ἐστι, "two shares at least into which the matter of the action will be divided" (Williams), was understood by Mich. Ephes., who comments thus: τὴν δὲ λέξιν τὴν καὶ ἐν οἷς τὰ πράγματα, δύο ὑπερβατῶς ἀναγνωστέον, καὶ τὰ πράγματα ἐν οἷς, δύο. In § 6 I omit the words τὰ ἐν οἷς which appear in all the MSS. except K^b, and in Bekker's text, in order that here, as in the sentences before and after, the persons may take precedence of the things distributed. The MS. followed by the V. A. added τὰ οἷς after οὕτω κἀκεῖνα in place of ἔχει. (In *M. M.* I. 34 § 7 ἔν τισι and τισίν appear to have been transposed. Read τὸ μὲν δίκαιον τισὶ λέγεται δίκαιον, τὸ δ' ἴσον ἔν τισιν ἴσον.)

§ 6. καὶ ἡ αὐτὴ ἔσται ἰσότης, οἷς καὶ ἐν οἷς] I. e. where the persons are equal, the things are equal. The author takes first the case which is represented by the formula $\frac{A}{B} = \frac{C}{D} = 1$, because he has not yet explained that εἰ μὴ ἴσοι, οὐκ ἴσα ἕξουσιν.

εἰ γὰρ μὴ ἴσοι, κ.τ.λ.] Cf. Plat. *Laws* 757, together with Isocrat. *Areop.* § 21. Plutarch *Symp.* VIII. p. 729 B, C. Xen. *Cyrop.* II. 2. 17. (quoted by Stallbaum in his commentary): also *Gorg.* 508 A. In the face of the quotations from Plato it is unnecessary to suppose with Grant that this "is taken from the saying in Aristotle's *Polit.* III. ix. 4. Cf. *Ib.* III. ix. 15": though, as might have been expected, the sentiment recurs again and again in that treatise; cf. II. 5. p. 28. 25. II. 7. p. 38. 15. p. 39. 25. III. 9. p. 71. 25. III. 12. p. 78. 18. III. 16. p. 89. 28. IV. (VII.) 3. p. 100. 7. VIII. (V.) 2. p. 196. 12. VIII. (V.) 3. p. 199. 14. See also Bacon's *Advancement of Learning* II. (III. 348, Spedding's edition) "Is not the rule, 'Si inaequalibus aequalia addas, omnia erunt inaequalia, an axiom as well of justice as of the mathematics?"

§ 7. ἔτι ἐκ τοῦ κατ' ἀξίαν] The statement made in the last § is now extended to the more general case represented by $\frac{A}{B} = \frac{C}{D}$, when A is not necessarily equal to B, τοῦτο being equivalent to ὅτι ὡς ἐκεῖνα ἔχει, οὕτω κἀκεῖνα ἔχει. Here τὸ κατ' ἀξίαν includes τὸ κατ' ἀριθμόν, as in *Polit.* VIII. (V.) 1. p. 195. 14 ὁμολογοῦντες δὲ τὸ ἁπλῶς εἶναι δίκαιον τὸ κατ' ἀξίαν, διαφέρονται, καθάπερ ἐλέχθη πρότερον, οἱ μὲν ὅτι, ἐὰν κατά τι ἴσοι ὦσιν, ὅλως ἴσοι νομίζουσιν εἶναι, οἱ δ' ὅτι, ἐὰν κατά τι ἄνισοι, πάντων ἀνίσων ἀξιοῦσιν ἑαυτούς. But in general the phrase κατ' ἀξίαν is used in a narrower sense, so as to exclude the case in which the persons are assumed to be equal, this case being said to be determined κατ' ἀριθμόν: cf. *Polit.* VII. (VI.) 2. p. 179.

11 καὶ γὰρ τὸ δίκαιον τὸ δημοτικὸν τὸ ἴσον ἔχειν ἐστὶ κατ' ἀριθμὸν ἀλλὰ μὴ κατ' ἀξίαν. VII. (VI). 6. p. 188. 3 τὰς μὲν οὖν δημοκρατίας ὅλως ἡ πολυανθρωπία σώζει· τοῦτο γὰρ ἀντίκειται πρὸς τὸ δίκαιον τὸ κατὰ τὴν ἀξίαν. VIII. (V.) 10. p. 217. 24 κατ' ἀξίαν γάρ ἐστιν, ἢ κατ' ἰδίαν ἀρετὴν ἢ κατὰ γένους, ἢ κατ' εὐεργεσίας, ἢ κατὰ ταῦτά τε καὶ δύναμιν.

τὴν μέντοι ἀξίαν, κ.τ.λ.] Cf. *Polit.* III. 9. p. 72. 4. VIII. (V.) 1. p. 193. 31. VIII. (V.) 1. p. 195. 14 (see preceding note). In democracy freedom is the ἀξία, and as freedom does not admit of degrees, all men are equal and τὸ κατ' ἀξίαν ἴσον is resolved into τὸ κατ' ἀριθμὸν ἴσον: in oligarchy either wealth or birth, and in aristocracy excellence, is the ἀξία, and as men possess these qualifications in different degrees, τὸ κατ' ἀξίαν ἴσον, in the narrower sense in which it excludes τὸ κατ' ἀριθμόν (or τὸ κατὰ ποσόν *N. E.* VIII. 7 § 3) ἴσον, constitutes δίκαιον in these polities.

οἱ δ' εὐγένειαν] *Polit.* VI. (IV.) 8. p. 159. 25 ἐπεὶ δὲ τρία ἐστὶ τὰ ἀμφισβητοῦντα τῆς ἰσότητος τῆς πολιτείας, ἐλευθερία πλοῦτος ἀρετή (τὸ γὰρ τέταρτον, ὃ καλοῦσιν εὐγένειαν, ἀκολουθεῖ τοῖς δυσίν· ἡ γὰρ εὐγένειά ἐστιν ἀρχαῖος πλοῦτος καὶ ἀρετή), φανερόν, κ.τ.λ. VIII. (V.) 1. p. 194. 14 εὐγενεῖς γὰρ εἶναι δοκοῦσιν οἷς ὑπάρχει προγόνων ἀρετὴ καὶ πλοῦτος. Thus the εὐγενής is one whose ancestors have been distinguished either by merit or by wealth (which implies merit of some sort in its possessor); but as Aristotle had not much faith in the γενναιότης of εὐγενεῖς (*Rhet.* II. 15), i.e. in their preserving the virtues of their ancestors, we may infer that he had no particular respect for oligarchy founded on birth.

§ 8. Euclid. *Elem.* V. Def. 3 λόγος ἐστὶ δύο μεγεθῶν ὁμογενῶν ἡ κατὰ πηλικότητα πρὸς ἄλληλα ποιὰ σχέσις. Def. 6 τὰ δὲ τὸν αὐτὸν ἔχοντα λόγον μεγέθη, ἀνάλογον καλείσθω. Def. 8 ἀναλογία δέ ἐστιν ἡ τῶν λόγων ταυτότης. Def. 9 ἀναλογία δὲ ἐν τρισὶν ὅροις ἐλαχίστοις ἐστίν. It will be observed (1) that the author's definition of ἀναλογία is equivalent to Euclid's def. 8, which, with def. 6, modern mathematicians agree in condemning: (2) that the definition is here regarded as an arithmetical, not as a geometrical, definition of proportion: (3) that in this definition he anticipates Barrow's remark that ἰσότης would be an improvement upon ὁμοιότης or ταυτότης: (4) that he differs from Euclid in accounting a continued proportion a proportion of four terms at least: and (5) that the phraseology of this § and § 4 confirms the text of Euclid V. def. 9, in which Peyrard and Camerer would substitute ἐλαχίστη for ἐλαχίστοις; cf. also Nicom. Gerasen. II. 21 § 3.

μοναδικοῦ ἀριθμοῦ] "Eiusmodi numeris (sc. Pythagoreorum) Aristoteles opponit τοὺς μοναδικοὺς ἀριθμούς, i. e. eos numeros, quibus non certae quaedam res (cf. *N*. 5. 1092. *b*. 19), sed ipsae unitates, abstractae ab omni rerum qualitate et varietate, individuae (cf. 8. 1083. *b*. 17) neque inter se distinctae (cf. 7. 1082. *b*. 16) numerentur. Ac talem quidem numerum quum investiget scientia arithmetica, eundem numerum ἀριθμητικόν et μοναδικόν appellat." Bonitz on *Met*. XII. 6. 1080. *b*. 19; cf. Plat. *Phileb*. 56 D, where arithmeticians who deal with μονάδας ἀνίσους such as two armies, two oxen, &c., are distinguished from arithmeticians who deal with μονάδες which are all alike.

§ 9. διῃρημένη—συνεχής] These two kinds of proportion are called by Nicom. Gerasenus II. 21 §§ 5, 6 συνημμένη and διεζευγμένη respectively. Throughout §§ 9, 11, 12, where I have given ordinal numbers, most of the editors write cardinals (α, β, γ, δ). In order to avoid the arithmetical absurdity (1 : 2 = 3 : 4) thus produced, I proposed in the *Journal of Philology* 1872, IV. 310 to write (with Fritzsche) A, B, Γ, Δ: but on further consideration I am convinced that πρώτου, δευτέρου, κ.τ.λ. should be substituted. The otherwise strange phrases ὁ α ὅρος, τοῦ α ὅρου in §§ 11, 12 suggest this alteration, and it is confirmed by several MSS., H[a] and K[b] throughout §§ 9, 11, 12, and P[b] and N[b] in §§ 9, 12, writing ordinals in full, whilst P[b] pr. man. gives sometimes ordinals in full, sometimes α β γ δ with superposed marks which may perhaps represent the terminations of ordinals, cf. Bast *Comment. Palaeogr*. p. 850. Michael Ephesius and Averroes seem to have had ordinals. But in § 9 there is a further difficulty. What is the meaning of the phrases ἡ τοῦ πρώτου, τὴν τοῦ δευτέρου, κ.τ.λ.? Can they mean 'the line which we take for our first term,' 'the line which we take for our second term'? Mich. Ephes. comments as follows—τὸ δὲ τῆς λέξεως τῆς οἷον ὡς ἡ τοῦ πρώτου πρὸς τὴν τοῦ δευτέρου τοιοῦτόν ἐστιν, ὡς ἡ τοῦ πρώτου ὅρου σχέσις τοῦ ὀκτὼ πρὸς τὸν δεύτερον τὸν δ (qu. τὴν τοῦ δευτέρου τοῦ δ̄), οὕτως ἡ τοῦ δευτέρου τοῦ δ̄ πρὸς τὴν τοῦ τρίτου τοῦ β̄. But is not this a misuse of the word σχέσις? Cf. Eucl. *El*. v. def. 3, quoted above. At any rate we may safely reject the alternative suggestion of Grant that στιγμή is to be supplied, as well as his theory that the proportionals are algebraical quantities.

§ 10. διῄρηνται γὰρ ὁμοίως, οἷς τε καὶ ἅ] *Polit*. III. 9. p. 71. 31 διῄρηται τὸν αὐτὸν τρόπον ἐπί τε τῶν πραγμάτων καὶ οἷς.

§ 11. ἐναλλάξ] Euclid *Elem*. v. def. 13 ἐναλλὰξ λόγος ἐστὶ λῆψις τοῦ ἡγουμένου πρὸς τὸ ἡγούμενον, καὶ τοῦ ἑπομένου πρὸς τὸ ἑπόμενον. Cf. v. prop. 16.

§ 12. ἡ ἄρα τοῦ πρώτου ὅρου, κ.τ.λ.] I.e. (to take a simple case) let A and B be the wealth of two citizens in a plutocracy, and let C and D be the shares which are justly assigned to them in a distribution of property won in war. Thus $A : B$ represents their relation before the distribution, $A + C : B + D$ their relation after it. The distribution being ex hypothesi a just one and their position relatively to one another consequently remaining unaltered,

$$\frac{A+C}{B+D} = \frac{A}{B}.$$

Hence as here A, B, C, D, are said to be in geometrical ἀναλογία, i.e. proportion, geometrical ἀναλογία is the rule of distributive justice.

σύζευξις] = Euclid's σύνθεσις: σύνθεσις λόγου ἐστὶ λῆψις τοῦ ἡγουμένου μετὰ τοῦ ἑπομένου ὡς ἑνὸς πρὸς αὐτὸ τὸ ἑπόμενον. v. def. 15. Cf. v. prop. 17, 18.

§ 14. ὁ μὲν γὰρ ἀδικῶν πλέον ἔχει, κ.τ.λ.] In this case, as will be seen hereafter, corrective justice steps in to restore the balance.

§ 15. ἐν ἀγαθοῦ γὰρ λόγῳ, κ.τ.λ.] Cf. 1 § 10.

4 § 1. τὸ δὲ λοιπὸν ἓν τὸ διορθωτικόν] Vide supra 2 §§ 12, 13. Corrective justice is the justice which rectifies wrong arising out of a συνάλλαγμα, whether the person wronged was or was not in the first instance a voluntary agent. Thus to take an example of a 'voluntary' transaction: A borrows money from B (who is here ἑκών) and does not fulfil his engagement to repay the loan at a certain time; corrective justice takes from A the proper amount and restores it to B. Again in an 'involuntary' transaction, e.g. when A slanders B (who is here ἄκων), corrective justice secures to the injured person compensation for the loss which he has sustained. Although in his note upon 2 §§ 12, 13 Grant appears to accept this interpretation, his note upon the present passage stands as it did in his second edition. "The term 'corrective justice' is itself an unfortunate name, because it appears only to lay down principles for restitution, and therefore implies wrong. Thus it has a tendency to confine the view to 'involuntary transactions,' instead of stating what must be the principle of the just in all the dealings between man and man." Apparently Grant forgets that it is the original transaction which

is said to be either voluntary or involuntary, and that it is the rectification of wrong arising out of the original transaction with which corrective justice is concerned. Again in his next note Grant remarks that "τὸ διορθωτικὸν δίκαιον implies not merely 'regulative,' but strictly 'remedial justice.'" I do not think that it means regulative justice at all. Mich. Ephes. appears to have read τὸ δὲ λοιπὸν εἶδος in place of τὸ δὲ λοιπὸν ἕν.

§ 2. τὸ μὲν γὰρ διανεμητικόν, κ.τ.λ.] Grant supposes this remark to be founded upon *Polit.* III. 9. p. 74. 3.

§ 3. '*A* and *B* being equal in the eye of the law, διορθωτικὸν δίκαιον is the arithmetical mean between *A*'s position unjustly augmented and *B*'s position unjustly impaired.'

καὶ χρῆται ὡς ἴσοις] These words (if they are not interpolated) are parenthetical, εἰ ὁ μὲν ἀδικεῖ, κ.τ.λ. being necessarily connected with πρὸς τοῦ βλάβους τὴν διαφορὰν μόνον βλέπει.

ἀδικεῖ—ἀδικεῖται—ἔβλαψεν—βέβλαπται] The tenses are thoroughly appropriate. When *A* has done a wrong to *B*, *A* is said ἀδικεῖν and *B* is said ἀδικεῖσθαι until compensation is made. Thus ἀδικεῖν expresses the resultant state rather than the commission of wrong. The aorist ἔβλαψε is appropriate to the doer of harm, because the question asked in his case is '*did* he *inflict* harm?' and the perfect βέβλαπται to the sufferer of harm because the question in his case is '*has* he *sustained* harm?'

§ 4. καὶ γὰρ ὅταν, κ.τ.λ.] "Die Ausdehnung des Ausgleichs von dem engern Kreise des Verkehrs auf den Umfang der correctiven Gerechtigkeit überhaupt, ist in dem καὶ γάρ angedeutet; denn dieses steht auch sonst für καὶ γάρ καί." Trendelenburg *Beiträge* III. 426. See my note on § 5.

ἀλλὰ πειρᾶται τῇ ζημίᾳ, κ.τ.λ.] I.e. πειρᾶται τῇ ζημίᾳ ἰσάζειν τὸ κέρδος ἀφαιρῶν αὐτοῦ. 'He endeavours to equalize the unjustly augmented advantages of the one (τὸ κέρδος) and the unjustly impaired advantages of the other (τὴν ζημίαν) by taking from the former and giving to the latter.' [So Münscher *Quaest. Crit.* p. 70.] Mich. Ephes. wrongly takes ζημία to mean the penalty by the imposition of which the δικαστής restores equality.

§ 5. λέγεται γάρ, κ.τ.λ.] 'Strictly speaking these words κέρδος and ζημία apply only to cases in which the one seeks the restitution of property wrongfully appropriated by the other: but they may be used in an extended sense; for example, the satisfaction which *A* derives from striking *B* may be regarded as a κέρδος, and the injury which *B* suffers may be regarded as a ζημία. Originally however, as we are told in § 13, these words applied to neither of these cases, but only to the profit and loss of commerce and of other transactions not interfered with by law.' Thus § 13 is not (as is commonly supposed) a repetition of § 5 : vide infra.

§ 6. ἀλλ' ὅταν γε μετρηθῇ, κ.τ.λ.] 'But the words ζημία and κέρδος are not applicable until the wrong done and suffered comes to be estimated by the δικαστής.' So I understand these words, not at all agreeing with Trendelenburg, *Beiträge* III. 426, 427 "Wenn nun das Leiden abgeschätzt worden, dann wird das κέρδος des Schlagenden zur ζημία und der Nachtheil des Geschlagenen zu einem κέρδος, wodurch die Gleichheit hergestellt wird"; and not altogether agreeing with Rassow, *Forschungen* p. 122 "Nach meiner Ansicht ist zu übersetzen: aber erst dann nennt man das eine ζημία, das andere κέρδος, wenn das Erlittene gemessen ist. Es macht z. B. einen Unterschied, ob eine Misshandlung durch Beleidigung provocirt worden ist oder nicht, oder, um ein von Aristoteles unten (5 § 4) gebrauchtes Beispiel zu benutzen, es kann darauf Rücksicht zu nehmen sein, dass der Gemisshandelte eine obrigkeitliche Person ist."

§ 7. καὶ ζητοῦσι, κ.τ.λ.] *Polit.* III. 16. p. 90. 28 ὥστε δῆλον ὅτι τὸ δίκαιον ζητοῦντες τὸ μέσον ζητοῦσιν · ὁ γὰρ νόμος τὸ μέσον. Fritzsche compares *Polit.* VI. (IV.) 12. p. 167. 3 διαιτητὴς δ' ὁ μέσος, and Thuc. IV. 83 ἑτοῖμος ὢν Βρασίδᾳ μέσῳ δικαστῇ ἐπιτρέπειν.

μεσιδίους] The phrase ἄρχοντι μεσιδίῳ is to be found in *Polit.* VIII. (V.) 6. p. 206. 13, but the commentators know of no instance in which the word is equivalent to δικαστής. " Camerarius commonefacit nos verbi μεσιδιωθῆναι." Zell.

§ 8. δίχα διαιρεθῇ] δίχα διαιρεῖν is 'to divide into two *equal* parts,' " cf. Eucl. *Elem.* I. 10. I. 9. III. 30." Trendelenburg *Beiträge* III. 428.

§ 9. The restoration of the true sequence of thought in this § is due to Rassow, *Forschungen* p. 30.

ὅτι δίχα ἐστίν] *Theolog. Arith.* p. 12 (Ast's edition) ἀπὸ δὲ τῆς εἰς δύο τομῆς [sc. καλεῖται ἡ δυάς] Δίκη τε, οἱονεὶ δίχη, καὶ Ἶσις, κ.τ.λ. τῆς μείζονος καὶ ἐλάττονος] Sc. γραμμῆς. Cf. τῆς ἡμισείας, § 8.

§ 10. <τοῦ> ἀφ' οὗ] Bekker, who reads ἀφ' οὗ with the MSS., is mistaken in saying that O^b has τὸ ἀφ' οὗ. " Articulus (τό) est procul dubio omittendus aut refingendus in τοῦ" (Zell). It is clearly necessary to insert τοῦ.

§ 12. αἱ ἐφ' ὧν AA BB ΓΓ, κ.τ.λ.] I.e. the lines designated AA, BB, ΓΓ. "Statt einfach den Buchstaben hinzuzufügen ἔστω A, wird sehr oft gesagt ἔστω τὸ ἐφ' οὗ (ᾧ) A 'das, woran A,' wobei der Artikel τό auch sehr oft fehlt." Eucken *über den Sprachgebrauch des A.* 11. 53. Cf. Waitz *Organ.* 1. 398. But what are we to say to τὸ ἐφ' ὧν ΓΔ, which is found in all the MSS. except O[b], and retained by all the editors? Plainly we require either τὸ ἐφ' οὗ ΓΔ, or τὸ ἐφ' ᾧ ΓΔ, or simply τὸ ΓΔ. I prefer τὸ ἐφ' ᾧ ΓΔ as nearest to τὸ ἐφ' ὧν ΓΔ, and I am confirmed in my choice by finding that O[b] has this reading. The genitive and the dative appear to be used indifferently in such phrases. It will be observed that the whole lines are described as ἡ AA, κ.τ.λ., and the segments of them as τὸ AE, κ.τ.λ. Thus ἡ AA is what Euclid would call ἡ AA γραμμή, τὸ AE what he would call τὸ AE τμῆμα. In the following figure ΓΔ = ΓΖ = AE. It is strange that this is not expressly stated in the text.

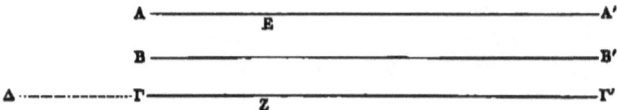

ἔστι δὲ καὶ ἐπὶ τῶν ἄλλων, κ.τ.λ.—τοιοῦτον] This sentence appears again in the next chapter § 9. In the passage before us it has no meaning whatever, so far as I can see. Mich. Ephes. (if the Aldine text and the Parisian version are to be trusted) placed it here; but his explanation is derived from ch. 5.

§ 13. ἐλήλυθε δέ, κ.τ.λ.] I have already pointed out that this § is not a mere repetition of § 5. The author now remarks that the terms profit and loss do not originally belong to corrective justice, or to any form of it, but to commerce. That this is his meaning is clear from the words ἐν ὅσοις ἄλλοις ἄδειαν ἔδωκεν ὁ νόμος. Similarly § 14 is a justification of the use of the phrase ἔχειν τὰ αὑτῶν in the concluding sentence of § 8. Properly speaking, this phrase is used of one who has neither increased nor diminished his means: but (like ζημία and κέρδος) it is sometimes used in matters of corrective justice, ὅταν λάβωσι τὸ ἴσον, i.e. when property wrongfully appropriated by another has been restored, or when satisfaction has been made for injury to person or to honour. Thus §§ 13, 14 contain purely philological remarks upon the phraseology of the subject, conveniently introduced at the end of this chapter before another matter is opened. Cf. the remark about the word δικαίωμα at the end of ch. 7.

§ 14. αὐτὰ δι' αὑτῶν γένηται] The editors all read δι' αὑτῶν, and most take these words in connection with αὐτά. "Nemo interpretum haec verba intellexit," says Michelet. " Felicianus vertit : *sed sua cuique per se ipsa evaserint;* Argyropylus : *sed sua per se ipsa sunt facta;* Lambinus : *sed paria paribus respondent.* Cum § 13 dixisset, nomina κέρδος et ζημία orta esse ex contractibus voluntariis, iam § 14 proponit, ea nomina translata esse ad obligationes ex delicto, ita ut in iis solis usurpentur. Verte : *ubi vero neque plus neque minus habent, praeterquam quae per se ipsos facta sint,* etc." Rassow (*Forschungen* p. 94) proposes to insert τά before δι' αὑτῶν, and to translate " das, was man durch seine eigene Arbeit besass." Grant would construe " 'but result in being themselves by means of reciprocity,' i.e. by mutual giving and taking, ἑαυτῶν being equivalent to ἀλλήλων." Finally, as I learn from a note to Williams' translation, Professor Chandler reads δι' αὑτῶν, and translates "But when, by buying and selling (δι' αὑτῶν), men have got neither more nor less than they had at first, but exactly the same." Agreeing with Professor Chandler in his rendering of πλέον, ἔλαττον, and αὐτά (sc. τὰ ἐξ ἀρχῆς), I take δι' αὑτῶν γένηται to mean 'comes into their possession.' If we can say δι' αὑτῶν εἶναι 'to be in their possession' (*Polit.* VII. (VI.) 4. p. 182. 28. VIII. (V.) 1. p. 194. 23. 6. p. 206. 2, (see Eucken *über den Sprachgebrauch des A.* II. 38,) surely δι' αὑτῶν γίγνεσθαι must also be admissible. The sentence thus means, as it ought to do, 'But when people *get* what is their own, they are said to *have* what is their own.' Cf. *Polit.* VIII. (V.) 7. p. 208. 26 μόνον γὰρ μόνιμον τὸ κατ' ἀξίαν ἴσον καὶ τὸ ἔχειν τὰ αὑτῶν. Otherwise I had thought of ὅταν δὲ μήτε πλέον μήτ' ἔλαττον ἀλλ' αὐτὰ ἃ δεῖ αὐτῶν γένηται, comparing for the supposed corruption 5 § 12, where K[b] has οὐ διάγειν for οὐ δεῖ ἄγειν, and for the genitive with γίγνεσθαι Lys. 16, 34 ἐγένετο ὁ Εὐμάρης οὗτος Νικοκλέους (Kühner's *Gr. Gr.* II. 316) and Plat. *Phileb.* 27 C. With Rassow I have placed a colon instead of a full stop after νόμος, and instead of a colon, a full stop after κερδαίνειν.

τῶν παρὰ τὸ ἑκούσιον] This is not inconsistent with 2 § 13 and 4 § 1, because, whether the original transaction was ἀκούσιον or ἑκούσιον, the *result* must have been παρὰ τὸ ἑκούσιον in regard to the person injured, else there would be nothing to rectify.

5. 'The Pythagoreans resolved justice into τὸ ἀντιπεπονθός (re-

taliation). This definition does not adequately represent either distributive or corrective justice; but the just in commerce may be defined as τὸ ἀντιπεπονθός, if by τὸ ἀντιπεπονθός is understood, not ἀντιπεπονθὸς κατ' ἰσότητα (retaliation), but ἀντιπεπονθὸς κατ' ἀναλογίαν (reciprocal proportion), the formula being $A : B :: D : C$, which proportion is attained by cross-conjunction (ἡ κατὰ διάμετρον σύζευξις).'

The following extract from Grant's commentary will serve to recal the usual interpretation of this chapter:

"'Now the joining of the diagonal of a square gives us proportionate return.' The joining of the diagonal gives each producer some of the other's work, and thus an exchange is made, but the respective value of the commodities must be first adjusted, else there can be no fair exchange. What, then, is the law of value? It is enunciated a little later (§ 10). δεῖ τοίνυν—τροφήν. 'As an architect (or a farmer it may be) is to a shoemaker, so many shoes must there be to a house or to corn.' That is, the value of the product is determined by the quality of the labour spent upon it. The sort of comparison here made between the quality of farmer and shoemaker seems connected with a Greek notion of personal dignity and a dislike of βαναυσία."

In my opinion ch. 5 should be read in close connection with ch. 2—4, the passage as a whole being an attempt at once to connect and to distinguish three kinds of particular justice. In order to connect these three kinds of particular justice, the author regards them each as ἀνάλογόν τι: in order to distinguish them, he represents each by a special and appropriate kind of ἀναλογία, the word ἀναλογία being employed in the larger of the two senses recognized by the Greek mathematicians, and therefore including arithmetical proportion which is, strictly speaking, a μεσότης. Cf. Nesselmann *die Algebra der Griechen* pp. 210—212, where it is shown from Nicomachus Gerasenus and Iamblichus, that, though properly ἀναλογία meant geometrical proportion (all other proportions being μεσότητες), ἀναλογία and μεσότης are frequently used synonymously for any kind of proportion. I shall henceforth use the word proportion as an equivalent for ἀναλογία in its extended meaning.

Premising that in the earlier part of ch. 3 particular justice has been made to consist in τὸ ἴσον, and that it has been afterwards explained that the ἰσότης spoken of is ἰσότης λόγων, or ἀναλογία, § 8, 'between the persons and the things, according to some standard' (πρός τι), §§ 5, 6, I proceed to state as briefly as possible the substance of the investigation of distributive, corrective, and commercial justice. In the course of my summary, it will, I hope, appear, that the purpose of the author is merely to translate into the language of proportion the following proposition: 'Particular justice is attained in distribution, correction, and barter, when the parties are, after the transaction, in the same position relatively to one another, as they were before it.' What constitutes identity of relative positions, the author does not ask. The investigation is in fact introduced in order to justify the statement made in 3 § 8, ἔστιν ἄρα τὸ δίκαιον ἀι ἀλογόν τι, just as the list of virtues is introduced in II. 7 to justify the definition of virtue. But though the author's principal aim is to show that the just in distribution, in correction, and in commerce is ἀνάλογόν τι, he thinks it worth while to enter into detail and to distinguish them, because Plato had taken one kind of proportion, ἡ ἰσότης ἡ γεωμετρική, as the rule of justice (*Gorg.* 508 A, *Laws* 757 A, B: cf. Plutarch *Symp.* VIII. 2 § 2), whilst the Pythagoreans had endeavoured to reduce all justice to retaliation, τὸ ἀντιπεπονθός, a phrase which may be interpreted by reference to proportion.

1. The first of the three kinds of particular justice, distributive justice, in the distribution of property or honour secures to the individual a share proportioned to his desert. Desert is differently estimated in different cases: for example, in a democracy freedom constitutes desert, in an oligarchy wealth or birth, in an aristocracy ἀρετή.

Thus distributive justice assigns to the persons concerned shares such that the position of the persons relatively to one another is not altered by the distribution, but it does not determine what constitutes alteration of relative position.

Let A, B, C, D be proportionals, so that $A : B :: C : D$. Hence alternando $A : C :: B : D$, and componendo A taken together with $C : B$ taken together with $D :: A : B$, which last proportion exactly represents distributive justice as above described. Or, as the author expresses it, distributive justice consists in the conjunction or composition of A and C, B and D, A, B, C, D being proportionals (ἡ ἄρα τοῦ πρώτου ὅρου τῷ τρίτῳ καὶ ἡ τοῦ δευτέρου τῷ τετάρτῳ σύζευξις τὸ ἐν διανομῇ δίκαιόν ἐστι 3 § 12), since by such conjunction the position of the two parties, relatively to one another, is not altered, whether, as in democracy, A and B are equal, and therefore C and D, or, as in oligarchy and aristocracy, a difference is assumed between the persons, which therefore necessitates a difference in the shares assigned to them. Distributive justice then may be represented by the formula

$$A + C : B + D :: A : B.$$

But mathematically when A taken together with C is to B taken together with D as A is to B, A, B, C, D are said to be in geometrical proportion. Hence distributive justice is a geometrical proportion.

At this point I would call attention to 3 §§ 11, 12 : ὥστε καὶ τὸ ὅλον πρὸς τὸ ὅλον· ὅπερ ἡ νομὴ συνδυάζει· κἂν οὕτως συντεθῇ, δικαίως συνδυάζει. ἡ ἄρα τοῦ πρώτου ὅρου τῷ τρίτῳ καὶ ἡ τοῦ δευτέρου τῷ τετάρτῳ σύζευξις τὸ ἐν διανομῇ δίκαιόν ἐστι· καὶ μέσον τὸ δίκαιον τοῦτ' ἐστὶ τοῦ παρὰ τὸ ἀνάλογον. Here σύζευξις seems to mean what in the language of proportion is called σύνθεσις (cf. Eucl. v. Def. 15), our 'componendo;' the more familiar word being employed in preference to the technical one, because, according to strict usage, σύνθεσις can hardly be applied to the union of persons and things.

2. Corrective justice, the function of which is to remove inequality after it has arisen, deprives the gainer of his unjust gain, and restores to the loser his unjust loss, the words 'gain' and 'loss' being used in an extended sense. The author does not limit this kind of justice to the correction of ἀκούσια συναλλάγματα, but says expressly, 2 §§ 12, 13, 4 § 1, that it is also concerned with ἑκούσια συναλλάγματα (πρᾶσις, ὠνή, κ.τ.λ.), i.e. with the correction of voluntary transactions in which the balance has been disturbed. Cases of such disturbance will hereafter present themselves.

Now when one man has appropriated what belongs to another, the latter has as much less, as the former has more, than his just right. Hence the former is in excess of the latter by twice the amount by which the former is in excess, or the latter in defect, of his just right. Manifestly justice is attained when the unjust gain of the one is taken from him and restored to the other.

But what we have called the just right of both is an arithmetical mean between the excessive position of the one and the defective position of the other. Corrective justice is therefore represented by an arithmetical proportion in which the positions of the two parties, after the wrong and before the correction of it, are the extremes. Of course, as the author points out in 5 § 4, it may be necessary, in estimating the loss of the injured person, to take into account his superior position. It is not necessary to take into account the wrong done to the state, because we are now considering injustice of the particular kind, which consists in unfairness,—not universal injustice, which consists in the violation of law.

3. At the beginning of ch. 5 the author criticizes the Pythagorean theory that justice consists in τὸ ἀντιπεπονθός, i.e. τὸ ἀντιπεπονθὸς

τὸ κατ' ἰσότητα, or retaliation, and objects that it does not apply either to distributive, or to corrective, justice. In commercial transactions however τὸ ἀντιπεπονθός is the bond of society: but the ἀντιπεπονθός which regulates commercial transactions is, not τὸ ἀντιπεπονθὸς τὸ κατ' ἰσότητα (retaliation), but τὸ ἀντιπεπονθὸς τὸ κατ' ἀναλογίαν (reciprocal proportion). Now ἡ κατ' ἀναλογίαν ἀντίδοσις is secured by ἡ κατὰ διάμετρον σύζευξις, i.e. the conjunction of A and D, B and C. For example, let A be a builder, B a shoemaker, C a house, and D a shoe. If A and B agree that a house and a shoe are of equal value, barter may take place without altering the position of A and B relatively to one another: or in the symbolism of ch. 3,

$$A + D : B + C :: A : B,$$
whence $$A : B :: D : C.$$

But as barter does not take place between persons of the same trade, the transaction will be in general more complicated, C and D not being of equal value. In general then B will give to A x shoes in return for his house. Hence commercial justice is represented in general by the proportion

$$A + xD : B + C :: A : B,$$
whence as before
$$A : B :: xD : C.$$

Now when $A : B :: xD : C$, A and C, B and xD, are said to be reciprocally proportional (ἀντιπεπονθέναι). Hence commercial justice is represented by reciprocal proportion, τὸ ἀντιπεπονθὸς τὸ κατ' ἀναλογίαν.

It will be observed (1) that in this explanation of ch. 5 I have followed exactly the method of interpretation adopted in ch. 3; (2) that according to my view the author not only limits the application of τὸ ἀντιπεπονθός to commercial transactions, but also gives a new meaning to the phrase by the addition of the words τὸ κατ' ἀναλογίαν; (3) that I conceive the author to say no more than that 'A and B exchange on equal terms if xD is equivalent to C, x having been determined by the higgling of the market.'

Thus, as I understand the author, he justifies in ch. 3—5 the assertion made in 3 § 8, that τὸ δίκαιον τὸ ἐν μέρει is ἀνάλογόν τι, and assigns kinds of proportion to the several kinds of particular justice. In so doing he shows controversially (1) that the γεωμετρικὴ ἰσότης of Plato does not include all the varieties of particular justice, and (2) that the Pythagorean theory of τὸ ἀντιπεπονθός (retaliation) is applicable only to commercial transactions, and to them only if by τὸ ἀντιπεπονθός is meant τὸ ἀντιπεπονθὸς τὸ κατ' ἀναλογίαν (reciprocal proportion). On the other hand he has not attempted any investigation of the laws of value, and is wholly innocent of the theory "that the value of the product is determined by the quality of the labour spent upon it." Economically, he contents himself with the statements that barter presumes mutual demand, and that the terms of the barter must be settled before, not after, the needs of the two parties are satisfied.

Before proceeding to comment upon the chapter in detail, it will be convenient to notice some other passages in which τὸ ἀντιπεπονθός plays a part.

(1) While in barter A and B exchange on equal terms wares, C and xD, which are equal in value, when proportion is used to express the claims of the superior and the inferior in friendship, A and B, and therefore C and D, would seem to be unequal; but friendship is reduced to a simple case of barter on equal terms, if we assume that the inferior is entitled to the greater amount of assistance, the superior to the greater amount of respect. Thus unequal friends barter assistance and respect, precisely as the shoemaker and the weaver barter wares. *N. E.* IX. 1 § 1. VIII. 7 § 2. 8 § 1. 11 §§ 1 sqq. 14 § 2. Cf. Plat. *Euthyphr.* 15 A.

(2) It follows that a good man will not be on terms of friendship with a superior, unless the superior in rank is also superior in merit, because otherwise the inferior will not feel for the superior that love and regard by which alone he can requite superior services. *N. E.* VIII. 6 § 6.

(3) As however friendship in general assumes equality of persons, quantitative equality (τὸ κατὰ ποσόν) is the primary rule of friendly intercourse, i.e. the *same* service which A at one time renders to B, B at another time renders to A, proportionate equality (τὸ κατ' ἀξίαν, cf. *Polit.* v. 1. p. 195. 8) being of secondary importance. In justice, on the contrary, proportionate equality ranks first, quantitative equality second. *N. E.* VIII. 7 § 3. (Geometrical proportion is said to be κατὰ ποιότητα, arithmetical proportion κατὰ ποσότητα, cf. Nicomach. Gerasen. II. 21 § 5. *Polit.* VIII. (V.) 3. p. 198. 3.) Thus arithmetical proportion takes precedence of reciprocal proportion as the rule of friendship, because friends are in general equals and exchange actually equal services: if however the friends are unequal, the rule of friendship is proportionate, qualitative, equality, i.e. that kind of geometrical proportion which is called reciprocal.

(4) Manifestly in barter $\frac{A}{B} = \frac{xD}{C} = 1$,

the formula $A : B :: xD : C$ being preferred to $A : B :: C : xD$ only because the former proportion represents the relations of A and B after the exchange, the latter their relations before it. Now from these two proportions which represent the relations of A and B before and after the exchange, we obtain the proportion

$$A : B :: B : A.$$

Accordingly the author of the *Magna Moralia*, I. 34 § 11, substitutes for the Eudemian theory the simple statement that just exchange takes place 'when the farmer is to the builder, as the builder is to the farmer', i.e. when the offers of the two have been equated by the ordinary process of higgling.

(5) Finally in *Polit.* II. 2. p. 24. 10 we are told that the members of the social union are diverse, διόπερ τὸ ἴσον τὸ ἀντιπεπονθὸς σώζει τὰς πόλεις, ὥσπερ ἐν τοῖς ἠθικοῖς εἴρηται πρότερον: i.e. the citizen, as we shall see in 6 § 7, renders τιμὴ καὶ γέρας to the magistrate in return for his services.

§ 1. δοκεῖ δέ τισι, κ.τ.λ.] For the Pythagorean doctrine see *M. M.* I. 34 §§ 13—15, and Alexand. on *Metaph.* I. 5. p. 985. *b.* 26 (quoted by Zeller, I. 360) τῆς μὲν γὰρ δικαιοσύνης ἴδιον ὑπολαμβάνοντες εἶναι τὸ ἀντιπεπονθός τε καὶ ἴσον, ἐν τοῖς ἀριθμοῖς τοῦτο εὑρίσκοντες ὄν, διὰ τοῦτο καὶ τὸν ἰσάκις ἴσον ἀριθμὸν πρῶτον ἔλεγον εἶναι δικαιοσύνην·......τοῦτον δὲ οἱ μὲν τὸν τέσσαρα ἔλεγον,...οἱ δὲ τὸν ἐννέα. See also *Theolog. Arith.* p. 28 (Ast), where the Pythagorean definition of justice is said to be δύναμις ἀποδόσεως τοῦ ἴσου καὶ τοῦ προσήκοντος, ἐμπεριεχομένη ἀριθμοῦ τετραγώνου περισσοῦ μεσότητι. In spite of Alexander l.c. the ἀντιπεπονθός of the Pythagoreans seems to have been, not reciprocal proportion, but, as our author expressly states, simple retaliation.

The wording of this opening sentence is rather strange, ὡρίζοντο γὰρ ἁπλῶς, κ.τ.λ. being wholly superfluous. Is it possible that the words καὶ τὸ ἀντιπεπονθὸς εἶναι ἁπλῶς δίκαιον are interpolated, and that the text should stand thus—δοκεῖ δέ τισιν ὥσπερ οἱ Πυθαγορεῖοι ἔφασαν· ὡρίζοντο γὰρ ἁπλῶς, κ.τ.λ.? I omit ἄλλῳ, (which Bekker inserts at the end of the sentence on the authority of K^b P^b only,) because it is grammatically impossible to combine it with ἀντιπεπονθός. Grant, who translates "retaliation on one's neighbour," seems to forget that ἀντιπεπονθός expresses the notion of retaliation, not actively, but passively. I suspect that ἄλλῳ is a corruption of ἄλλως prefixed to one of the double readings which in the following sentence are preserved by P^b, and therefore may have occurred in the common progenitor of P^b and K^b.

§ 3. *καίτοι—γένοιτο*] "Zwingerus hunc § transposuit post vocabula ἀντιπεπονθὸς ἄλλῳ methodo, ut dicit, iubente, etsi contra omnium codicum auctoritatem." (Zell.) This change seems to me wholly unnecessary.

τά τ' ἔρεξε] *τά κ' ἔρεξε*, the reading of the MSS., can hardly be right. The line is quoted also by Seneca, *de morte Claud.* 14.

§ 4. *πολλαχοῦ γὰρ διαφωνεῖ*] The inapplicability of this theory to cases of distributive justice is assumed as obvious. There is more to be said for its applicability to corrective justice, and therefore the author is careful to show that even here the Pythagorean principle is inadequate.

§ 5. *ἔτι τὸ ἑκούσιον, κ.τ.λ.*] I.e. the principle of retaliation ignores the important distinction between wrongs done voluntarily and wrongs done involuntarily, of which more hereafter.

§ 6. *ἐν μὲν ταῖς κοινωνίαις, κ.τ.λ.*] "Interdum oppositio per part. μέν indicata et inchoata non accurate continuatur, cuius usus exempla attulit Waitz *ad Anal. Prior.* II. 61. *a.* 19." *Berlin Index,* s. v. μέν.

κατ' ἀναλογίαν καὶ μὴ κατ' ἰσότητα] I.e. the ἀντιπεπονθός which regulates commercial transactions is not, as the Pythagoreans think, τὸ ἀντιπεπονθὸς τὸ κατ' ἰσότητα, 'retaliation,' but τὸ ἀντιπεπονθὸς τὸ κατ' ἀναλογίαν, 'reciprocal proportion.' For, as will appear presently, commercial justice is represented by the formula $A : B :: D : C$; and when $A : B :: D : C$, A and C, B and D, are said by the Greek geometricians ἀντιπεπονθέναι 'to be reciprocally proportional.' Vide Euclid VI. 15 ἔστω ἴσα τρίγωνα τὰ ΑΒΓ, ΑΔΕ, μίαν μιᾷ ἴσην ἔχοντα γωνίαν τὴν ὑπὸ ΒΑΓ τῇ ὑπὸ ΔΑΕ· λέγω ὅτι τῶν ΑΒΓ, ΑΔΕ τριγώνων ἀντιπεπόνθασιν αἱ πλευραὶ αἱ περὶ τὰς ἴσας γωνίας, τουτέστιν ὅτι ἐστὶν ὡς ἡ ΓΑ πρὸς τὴν ΑΔ οὕτως ἡ ΕΑ πρὸς τὴν ΑΒ. See also Simson's Def. 2 of Bk. VI. "Two magnitudes are said to be reciprocally proportional to two others, when one of the first is to one of the other magnitudes as the remaining one of the last two is to the remaining one of the first." Cf. Aristot. *Mech.* 3. p. 850. *a.* 39. ὃ οὖν τὸ κινούμενον βάρος πρὸς τὸ κινοῦν, τὸ μῆκος πρὸς τὸ μῆκος ἀντιπέπονθεν.

Grant objects that this passage is inconsistent with *Polit.* II. 2. p. 24. 11. "For while *Pol.* II. ii. 4 says that 'equal retaliation preserves the State,' *Eth. Nic.* v. v. 6. says that 'Retaliation is a bond of union provided that it be on principles *not of equality*, but of proportion.' In fact the remarks on Retaliation in the *Ethics* have all the appearance of being a development and improvement of those in the *Politics*." Vol. I. p. 51. The inconsistency is merely apparent. Grant forgets that ἀντιπεπονθὸς κατ' ἀναλογίαν καὶ μὴ κατ' ἰσότητα is an ἴσον just as much as ἀντιπεπονθὸς κατ' ἰσότητα, since every ἀναλογία is an ἰσότης λόγων. In fact τὸ ἴσον τὸ ἀντιπεπονθός in *Polit.* II. 2 is identical with ἀντιπεπονθὸς κατ' ἀναλογίαν here: cf. § 8 ἐὰν οὖν πρῶτον ᾖ, κ.τ.λ. It will be observed that in the place in the *Politics* the statement τὸ ἴσον τὸ ἀντιπεπονθὸς σώζει τὰς πόλεις rests upon the statement that the πόλις, being an organised unity, has diverse reciprocating elements, just as in the present passage the doctrine of τὸ ἀντιπεπονθὸς τὸ κατ' ἀναλογίαν rests upon the diversity of reciprocating professions, § 9, and as in VIII. 7 §§ 2, 3 τὸ κατ' ἀξίαν is introduced to regulate friendship between persons in diverse positions. Moreover in *Polit.* II. 2. p. 24. 17 an example is introduced which at once reminds us of the chapter before us. So far from seeing any inconsistency, I should rather infer from the passage in the *Politics* (as from that in VIII.), that the lost Nicomachean discussion of τὸ ἀντιπεπονθός corresponded in the main with that which has been preserved in this Eudemian book.

ἢ γὰρ τὸ κακῶς, κ.τ.λ.] 'If the citizens are so completely subjected to one or more individuals that they cannot requite any evil which is done to them, they are rather slaves than citizens: if they do not requite good, there is no reciprocity to bind the citizens together.'

§ 7. διὸ καὶ Χαρίτων, κ.τ.λ.] 'Hence it is (i.e. because the stability of the state depends upon τὸ ἀντιποιεῖν ἀνάλογον) that men set up a shrine of the Χάριτες in some frequented place.' For ἐμποδών cf. IV. 7 § 16 περὶ τὰ μὴ λίαν ἐμποδὼν καὶ φανερά, but the word does not seem very appropriate. Should we read ἐν πόλεσιν? According to the commentators a temple to the Graces was frequently to be found in the ἀγορά of a Greek town. For the Χάριτες as patronesses and personifications of εὐεργεσία and εὐεργεσίας ἀπόδοσις cf. Philodem. περὶ εὐσεβείας: τὸν Δία νόμον φησὶν εἶναι καὶ τὰς Χάριτας τὰς ἡμετέρας καταρχὰς καὶ τὰς ἀνταποδόσεις τῶν εὐεργεσιῶν. Gomperz *Herkulanische Studien* II. 81.

ἀνθυπηρετῆσαί τε γάρ, κ.τ.λ.] Mich. Ephes. tries to show that these lessons are implied in the conventional attitude of the Χάριτες.

§ 8. ἡ κατὰ διάμετρον σύζευξις] This phrase is understood by

NOTES. 95

the older commentators and by Grant to mean the junction of the diagonals *AD*, *BC* in the square *ABDC*, by Williams to mean the junction of one diagonal of a parallelogram, the sides of which are the lines *A*, *B*, *D*, *C*.

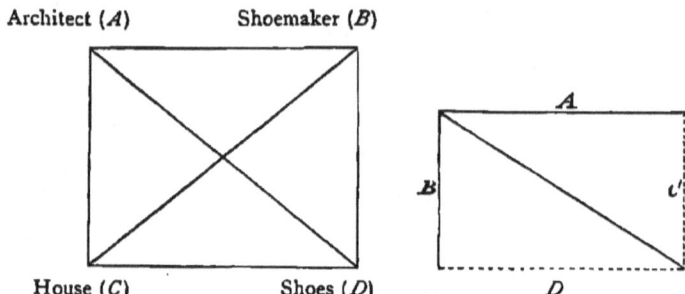

But (1) ἐφ' ᾧ A, κ.τ.λ. are lines, not, as in Grant's figure, points: for if we take points for our proportionals, what is the use of introducing the notion of proportion at all? (2) in Williams' figure, which avoids the former objection, *D* and *C* are made equal to *A* and *B*, i.e. the shoes and the house to the architect and the shoemaker respectively, whereas it is clear that the shoes should be equal to the house, the architect to the shoemaker; (3) the junction of the diagonal is called in Greek ἐπίζευξις, not σύζευξις; vide Euclid passim: (4) the editors fail to show why 'the junction of the diagonal' is mentioned, whereas the author says expressly that ἡ κατὰ διάμετρον σύζευξις produces τὴν ἀντίδοσιν τὴν κατ' ἀναλογίαν, and implies that ἡ κατὰ διάμετρον σύζευξις and the proportion *A* : *B* :: *D* : *C* are both of them ways of representing the operation of barter; compare § 8 with § 12.

Now it seems reasonable to assume that σύζευξις is used here in the same sense as in 3 § 12, and that if σύζευξις in the last-named passage means the 'composition' of *A* and *C*, *B* and *D*, ἡ κατὰ διάμετρον σύζευξις, 'cross-conjunction,' means the 'composition' of *A* and *D*, *B* and *C*.

'Cross-conjunction' then will give us the proportion

$$A + D : B + C :: A : B,$$

whence *A* : *B* :: *D* : *C* as in § 12.

This interpretation is confirmed by *E. E.* VII. 10 §§ 9, 10, where we are told that in an unequal friendship the ὑπερέχων conceives his claims to be represented by the formula ὡς αὐτὸς πρὸς τὸν ἐλάττω οὕτω τὸ παρὰ τοῦ ἐλάττονος γινόμενον πρὸς τὸ παρ' αὐτοῦ, but that the ὑπερεχόμενος τοὐναντίον στρέφει τὸ ἀνάλογον καὶ κατὰ διάμετρον συζεύγνυσιν. That is to say, if A and B are the persons, C and D their claims, A, the superior in rank, thinking himself entitled to superior advantages, argues that $\frac{A+C}{B+D} = \frac{A}{B}$, or $\frac{A}{B} = \frac{C}{D}$: on the other hand B, the inferior, holding that 'noblesse oblige,' maintains that $\frac{A+D}{B+C} = \frac{A}{B}$, or $\frac{A}{B} = \frac{D}{C}$. These opposing views are reconciled here in the same way as in the *Nic. Eth.* (see above, introductory note upon this chapter): i.e. the ὑπερεχόμενος is held to be entitled to superior service, the ὑπερέχων to superior respect; and consequently κέρδος and τιμή must be bartered against one another, just as the house and the shoes are bartered in commerce. In this way equality is effected.

ἐφ' ᾧ Α] See note on 4 § 12. Here, and again in § 12, the terms of the proportion are specified, but the example is not worked out; may we infer that the treatise was supplemented by extempore additions? Cf. *Anal. Prior.* I. 46. p. 52. *a*. 16.

τοῦ αὐτοῦ] Bekker reads τὸ αὐτοῦ, taking no notice of the reading of the MSS.

ἐὰν οὖν πρῶτον, κ.τ.λ.] 'If the article offered by the shoemaker is equal in value to the article offered by the builder, and then the exchange is effected, the demands of commercial justice will be satisfied. Otherwise the transaction is not equal and does not hold, because the article offered by the one may be, and in this case is, more valuable than the article offered by the other.' For example (1) a husbandman goes into the market with a bushel of corn and a shoemaker with a pair of shoes. If the husbandman and the shoemaker agree that the bushel of corn is κατ' ἀναλογίαν equal to the pair of shoes (ἐὰν οὖν πρῶτον ᾖ τὸ κατὰ τὴν ἀναλογίαν ἴσον), in other words that the bushel of corn is equal in value to the pair of shoes, and then the articles are exchanged (εἶτα τὸ ἀντιπεπονθὸς γένηται), the justice of commerce is satisfied. But if (2) a builder offers a house whilst the shoemaker offers only one pair of shoes, the market-value of the house being more than one pair of shoes, an exchange on this basis will not be equal and permanent. Hence the shoemaker must offer several pairs of shoes, the number of pairs being determined by the higgling of the market.

οὐδὲ συμμένει] 'The settlement is not a final one': for one of the two parties will be obliged to have recourse to corrective justice in order to obtain his rights.

§ 9. ἐπὶ τῶν ἄλλων τεχνῶν] See note on 4 § 12. 'The statement already made in regard to the arts of the builder and the shoemaker holds generally of all the arts.' (The remark is hardly necessary, but cf. *Polit.* 1. 9. p. 13. 22 τὸν αὐτὸν δὲ τρόπον ἔχει καὶ περὶ τῶν ἄλλων κτημάτων. III. 11. p. 76. 20 ὁμοίως δὲ τοῦτο καὶ περὶ τὰς ἄλλας ἐμπειρίας καὶ τέχνας.) 'They would fall into disuse if there were no exchange, and in order that an exchange may take place, some method of equalizing unequal wares is required, exchange being between members of different trades or professions, whose wares are necessarily unlike.'

ἀνῃροῦντο γὰρ ἄν, κ.τ.λ.] This sentence is written and punctuated by the editors thus: ἀνῃροῦντο γὰρ ἄν, εἰ μὴ ἐποίει τὸ ποιοῦν καὶ ὅσον καὶ οἷον, καὶ τὸ πάσχον ἔπασχε τοῦτο καὶ τοσοῦτον καὶ τοιοῦτον, and is understood to mean "for they would have been destroyed if there had not been the producer producing so much, and of a certain kind, and the consumer (τὸ πάσχον) consuming just the same quantity and quality" (Grant). Accepting this interpretation I formerly suggested (*Journal of Philology* 1872, IV. 318), the insertion of ὃ before ἐποίει, a conjecture which Rassow had anticipated. But on further consideration I find myself wholly unable to harmonize the sentence, as it is ordinarily punctuated and interpreted, with the main argument. It is true that "the arts would perish if there were no demand for their products:" but how does this tend to prove the necessity and importance of the principle of *proportionate* exchange? Moreover the terms ποιοῦν and πάσχον (which as Grant himself says "may probably have some reference to the ἀντιπεπονθός") imply that the reciprocity of the transaction is what we are here concerned with. The sense required is then 'for the arts would fall into disuse if the article manufactured by A and received in exchange by B were not somehow equated with the article manufactured by B and received in exchange by A.' Cf. § 10 τοῦτο δ', εἰ μὴ ἴσα εἴη πως; οὐκ ἔσται. This meaning I try to get by changing the punctuation, and making τοῦτο the subject, instead of the object, of ἔπασχε: ἀνῃροῦντο γὰρ ἄν, εἰ μὴ ἐποίει τὸ ποιοῦν, καὶ ὅσον καὶ οἷον καὶ τὸ πάσχον (subaud. πάσχει), ἔπασχε τοῦτο (i.e. τὸ ποιοῦν) καὶ τοσοῦτον καὶ τοιοῦτον· οὐ γάρ, κ.τ.λ. 'for the arts would perish, if the producer did not produce, and did not in return for his produce receive from the recipient of it an exact equivalent, quantity and quality being taken into account; [an equivalent, not an article precisely similar,] because two of a trade have no occasion to exchange their wares.' Rassow, understanding the drift of the passage as I do, and admitting that it would be clearer if for ἔπασχε we had ἀντεποίει or ἀνταπεδίδου, nevertheless thinks the insertion of ὅ the only change which is necessary: "Man muss nur bedenken, dass, wie es bei dem ἀντιπεπονθός nöthig ist, beide Theile geben und empfangen, dass also das ποιοῦν auch ein πάσχον und das πάσχον auch ein ποιοῦν ist." *Forschungen* p. 18. I should have thought that he would have found further change necessary, either (with Trendelenburg) the omission of τὸ before πάσχον, or the omission of τὸ πάσχον, or the substitution of ἐποίει for ἔπασχε. I do not of course pretend that the text naturally and properly bears the meaning which I have endeavoured to extract from it; but rather suspect that there is a lacuna after ἐποίει, and that the sentence ought to run in some such way as this: ἀνῃροῦντο γὰρ ἄν, εἰ μὴ ἐποίει <τὸ πάσχον ὅσον καὶ οἷον ποιεῖ> τὸ ποιοῦν, καὶ ὅσον καὶ οἷον καὶ τὸ πάσχον, ἔπασχε τοῦτο καὶ τοσοῦτον καὶ τοιοῦτον.

§ 10. διὸ πάντα συμβλητά, κ.τ.λ.] From this point the chapter abounds in repetitions. Nötel (*Quaest. Aristot. Spec.* p. 28) would condemn §§ 11, 12. Rassow again finds in §§ 10—16 three distinct statements of the same matter; the first being contained in § 10 διὸ πάντα συμβλητὰ—οὐκ ἔσται, the second in §§ 11—14 δεῖ ἄρα ἑνί τινι— μένειν μᾶλλον, and the third in §§ 14—16 διὸ δεῖ πάντα—πέντε κλῖναι. The difficulty is also discussed by Imelmann, *Observat. Crit.* p. 35 sqq. Certainly the chapter would gain in perspicuity if §§ 11— 16 were rejected. The remarks upon currency, both as to thought and as to expression, recal Plat. *Rep.* II. 371 B. *Laws* XI. 918 B. *Polit.* 289 E.

§ 11. ἢ οὐκ ἔσται ἀλλαγή] These words apply to the former of the two cases mentioned (εἰ μηθὲν δέοιντο); ἢ οὐχ ἡ αὐτή to the latter (ἢ μὴ ὁμοίως).

ὅτι οὐ φύσει, κ.τ.λ.] Cf. *Polit.* I. 9. p. 14. 28 sqq.

§ 12. εἰς σχῆμα δ' ἀναλογίας, κ.τ.λ.] I have materially altered the punctuation of this sentence which is usually printed thus: εἰς σχῆμα δ' ἀναλογίας οὐ δεῖ ἄγειν, ὅταν ἀλλάξωνται· εἰ δὲ μή, ἀμφοτέρας ἕξει τὰς ὑπεροχὰς τὸ ἕτερον ἄκρον. ἀλλ' ὅταν ἔχωσι τὰ αὑτῶν, οὕτως ἴσοι καὶ κοινωνοί, ὅτι αὕτη ἡ ἰσότης δύναται ἐπ' αὐτῶν γίνεσθαι. γεωργὸς A, κ.τ.λ. As I understand this difficult passage, it is a warning that the terms of the bargain must be determined by the ordinary process of higgling, before the exchange takes place, that is, during the continuance of the mutual demand, cf. § 11: e.g. *A* must arrange with *B*, before the transfer is effected, how many pairs of shoes the latter is to give him in return for a house. If *A* accepts one pair of shoes on account, trusting that B will subsequently make up to him the market value of the house, and B takes advantage of A's negligence, it is no longer an affair of commercial justice, but of corrective justice, which, as has been pointed out in 2 §§ 12, 13 and in 4 § 1, plays a part in the rectification of voluntary transactions such as πρᾶσις, ὠνή, δανεισμός, ἐγγύη, χρῆσις, παρακαταθήκη, μίσθωσις, as well as in the rectification of involuntary transactions such as κλοπή, μοιχεία, κ.τ.λ. In the case supposed A has now got one pair of shoes only, whilst B has got a house worth x pairs of shoes, and $x - 1$ pairs of shoes into the bargain. Hence A has $x - 1$ pairs of shoes less than his just right, B has $x - 1$ pairs of shoes more than his just right. Thus B has the advantage of A to the extent of $2(x-1)$ pairs of shoes: in the language of our author 'B has both superiorities.' If then the time for arranging the terms of the bargain is allowed to pass by, the two parties to the transaction are to be regarded as two extremes, one of which exceeds the mean by as much as the mean exceeds the other: the reciprocal proportion of commercial justice must therefore be supplemented by the arithmetical proportion of corrective justice. The words τὸ ἕτερον ἄκρον point unmistakeably to this interpretation, since A and B cannot possibly be regarded as extremes in the proportion $A : B :: D : C$. For ὅταν ἔχωσι τὰ αὐτῶν the commentators refer to 4 §§ 8, 14, forgetting that, whereas by corrective justice each recovers his own, commercial justice is attained when each surrenders his own (cf. § 8 δεῖ......αὐτὸν ἐκείνῳ μεταδιδόναι τοῦ αὐτοῦ). It seems to me clear that in the present passage these words are antithetical to ὅταν ἀλλάξωνται, and mean 'before they have delivered up their respective wares.' H. Richards anticipates me in referring to 4 §§ 10—12 for the explanation of ἀμφοτέρας τὰς ὑπεροχάς and τὸ ἕτερον ἄκρον (*Journal of Philology* 1872, IV. 150), but interprets otherwise.

§ 13. οὐκ ἀλλάττονται, ὥσπερ, κ.τ.λ.] Bekker reads ἐξαγωγῆς with K^b, and places a comma after οἴνου. We must then construe: 'whereas when B wants what A has, wine for example, they exchange; that is, A gives it to him in return for the privilege of exporting corn.' But (1) the separation of the words οἷον οἴνου from διδόντες, κ.τ.λ., which this reading involves, is surely an unnecessary complication of a sentence already harsh enough; and (2) I conceive that the weight, as well as the bulk, of the MS. authority is against ἐξαγωγῆς. For ὥσπερ with ἀλλάττονται understood from οὐκ ἀλλάττονται in the main sentence, 'as they do when,' 'whereas they do exchange when,' see

Berlin Index. In the present instance the construction is all the harsher because διδόντες belongs grammatically to both the parties concerned, whereas in sense it refers only to one of them. For αὐτός used to distinguish the person chiefly thought of from the other person concerned (τις), cf. 8 § 3 ὥσπερ εἴ τις λαβὼν τὴν χεῖρα αὐτοῦ, κ.τ.λ. The same illustration of exchange occurs in *Polit.* I. 9. p. 14. 3 οἷον οἶνον πρὸς σῖτον διδόντες καὶ λαμβάνοντες. ἐξαγωγή is commonly translated here 'an export': but the passages referred to in the *Berlin Index* seem to show that it is 'the privilege of exporting.' Cf. Theophr. περὶ ἀλαζονείας.

§ 14. μηδὲν δεῖται] Apparently the subject of δεῖται is τις supplied from δέηταί τις.

δεῖ, κ.τ.λ.] Rassow's conjecture, ἀεὶ γὰρ τούτο φέροντι ἔσται λαβεῖν, is tempting.

§ 15. οἰκία, κ.τ.λ.] 'The house A and the bed Γ are, τῇ ἀληθείᾳ, incommensurable; but their values may be compared πρὸς τὴν χρείαν, and expressed in minas. Now if the house is worth 5 minas and the bed 1, 5 beds = 1 house: and in primitive times, before currency was invented, the terms of the contract were formulated in this way.'

§ 16. ἢ κλῖναι] Rassow (*Forschungen* p. 94) conjectures ἢ κλίνας: "denn das unpersönliche διαφέρει hat entweder einen indirecten Fragesatz oder Infinitive nach sich." I have allowed the text to stand, thinking that διαφέρει is used personally, its subject being the whole phrase ἢ κλῖναι, κ.τ.λ., and that in that phrase a participle, not an infinitive, is suppressed.

§§ 17—19. In these sections the investigation of the questions proposed in 1 § 1 is concluded, and its results are summarized. It remains in the second half of the book to distinguish particular kinds of δίκαιον and ἄδικον, to investigate δίκαιον and ἄδικον as exhibited by individuals, to discuss certain supplementary ἀπορίαι, and to determine the relations subsisting between justice and ἐπιείκεια.

ἡ δὲ δικαιοσύνη, κ.τ.λ.] With Rassow I have inserted τίς after μεσότης (K^b L^b P^b), and δὲ after αὐτόν (K^b L^b O^b P^b), and substituted ἄλλαις for πρότερον (K^b L^b P^b). For the form of the sentence cf. 10 §§ 3, 6.

ὅτι μέσου ἐστίν] The original theory of ἀρετή as a μεσότης is here virtually admitted to be a failure so far as justice is concerned. Nevertheless in the *E. E.* II. 3 § 4 κέρδος, ζημία, and δίκαιον stand side by side with ἀσωτία, ἀνελευθερία, ἐλευθεριότης.

καὶ ὥσπερ, κ.τ.λ.] See Introduction, On dislocations in the text.

§ 18. τοῦ ἴσου τοῦ κατ' ἀναλογίαν] This genitive is not anacoluthic, as it belongs to the main sentence, and is regularly governed by διανεμητικός.

ἡ δ' ἀδικία τοὐναντίον, κ.τ.λ.] I. e. ἡ δ' ἀδικία τοὐναντίον [ἐστὶ καθ' ἣν ὁ ἄδικος λέγεται πρακτικὸς κατὰ προαίρεσιν] τοῦ ἀδίκου.

ἐπὶ δὲ τῶν ἄλλων, κ.τ.λ.] 'The statement made in the preceding sentence, that ἐφ᾽ αὑτοῦ the unjust man assigns an unduly large share of what is advantageous and an unduly small share of what is harmful, from the nature of the case does not apply ἐπὶ τῶν ἄλλων, i.e. when he does not himself take a share in the distribution.'

11 §§ 7, 8. See Introduction, On dislocations in the text. In § 7 I have bracketed καὶ ὥσπερ—γυμναστικῇ (vide supra, 5 § 17), and added ἐν οἷς δ' ἀδικία—ἀδικία from 6 § 4. If I am right in making the second of these alterations, perhaps I ought to go a step further and write γὰρ for δ'. The sense of the passage is as follows: 'ἀδικεῖσθαι and ἀδικεῖν are both bad, because, as has been shown, they are deviations from the mean; but ἀδικεῖν is the worse of the two, since it implies κακία, κακία which is either τελεία καὶ ἁπλῶς (if the act is ἐκ προαιρέσεως), or nearly so (if the act, though not ἐκ προαιρέσεως, is ἑκούσιον). Of course ἀδικεῖσθαι may be κατὰ συμβεβηκός the greater evil, because of its possible results.' Cf. *E. E.* II. 10 §§ 18, 19 for the distinction between προαιρετόν and ἑκούσιον, of which we shall hear more in the sequel. For the doctrine that it is worse ἀδικεῖν ἢ ἀδικεῖσθαι, see Plat. *Gorg.* 469 C, 508 B.

6 §§ 1—3. See Introduction, On dislocations in the text.

6 § 4.] 'Hitherto we have been considering τὸ ἁπλῶς δίκαιον, i.e. that which is characteristic of the virtue called δικαιοσύνη, irrespective of the κοινωνίαι in which it is exhibited. Our statements are therefore true καθόλου,—of a trading company or a household as well as of a πόλις—though our illustrations have been drawn for the most part from the political κοινωνία. We must now say something of δίκαιον as it presents itself in different κοινωνίαι: and of these species of δίκαιον, τὸ πολιτικὸν δίκαιον, i.e. the δίκαιον of a community of free and equal citizens, is the most perfect representation of τὸ ἁπλῶς δίκαιον [and moreover concerns us most nearly, as this treatise is preparatory to a treatise on politics]. Other species of δίκαιον are τὸ δεσποτικόν, τὸ πατρικόν, and τὸ οἰκονομικόν, which differ from τὸ

πολιτικὸν δίκαιον in so far as (1) master and slave, (2) father and son, (3) husband and wife are not ἐλεύθεροι καὶ ἴσοι ἢ κατ' ἀναλογίαν ἢ κατ' ἀριθμόν possessing definite rights secured to them by law. Of the three relations the last exhibits the nearest approach to τὸ πολιτικὸν δίκαιον.'

It will be seen that in dealing with the three imperfect or καθ' ὁμοιότητα δίκαια Eudemus takes a purely legal view, recognizing no rights except those which are embodied in law, and no law except written law. Hence it has been supposed by some that the three καθ' ὁμοιότητα δίκαια are not included in τὸ ἁπλῶς δίκαιον, and consequently that τὸ ἁπλῶς δίκαιον is identical with τὸ πολιτικὸν δίκαιον. This is surely a mistake. In so far as there is a δίκαιον between father and son, the statements made about τὸ ἁπλῶς δίκαιον are true of it; τὸ ἀντιπεπονθός at any rate is very fully realized in this relation, since father and son, like unequal friends (*N. E.* IX. 1 § 1), or magistrate and citizen (*Polit.* II. 2. p. 24. 13), barter protection and honour. Hence ὅταν γονεῦσι μὲν τέκνα ἀπονέμῃ ἃ δεῖ τοῖς γεννήσασι, γονεῖς δὲ υἱέσιν ἃ δεῖ τοῖς τέκνοις, μόνιμος ἡ τῶν τοιούτων καὶ ἐπιεικὴς ἔσται φιλία (VIII. 7 § 2). Moreover there are other relations in which δίκαιον is more perfectly realized than in the more or less one-sided relations of the household. Thus a trading company and an ἔρανος are κοινωνίαι governed by law, and consequently have their respective δίκαια, which are not identical with τὸ πολιτικὸν δίκαιον: cf. omnino *N. E.* VIII. 9 §§ 4—6. I cannot therefore assent to the statement of Rassow that τὸ ἁπλῶς δίκαιον and τὸ πολιτικὸν δίκαιον are different expressions for the same thing (*Forschungen* p. 123). Again I cannot allow that there is any force in the criticism of Trendelenburg: "according to the traditional arrangement of the text the words δεῖ δὲ μὴ λανθάνειν, κ.τ.λ. are preceded by two chapters and a half in which the distributive and corrective justice of the state are discussed at length: the warning that we must not overlook τὸ πολιτικὸν δίκαιον is therefore in this place unmeaning" (*Beiträge* III. 418). It is quite true that in the preceding chapters τὸ ἁπλῶς δίκαιον has been constantly regarded in its political form, because reference to some particular kind of δίκαιον was necessary, and political δίκαιον afforded the most convenient examples. But nothing has been said which is not capable of application to other forms of δίκαιον. Now, however, we may proceed to distinguish the several species of τὸ ἁπλῶς δίκαιον, and to contrast the most important species, viz. πολιτικὸν δίκαιον, with the δίκαια of the household.

ἢ κατ' ἀναλογίαν ἢ κατ' ἀριθμόν] Equality may be either actual or proportionate. Thus it may be assumed that all free men are κατ' ἀριθμὸν ἴσοι, and therefore that in distributions of conquests and of offices all should share alike. Again in an aristocracy, (and in βασιλεία, the limiting case of ἀριστοκρατία, where the claims of a single person are in virtue of his superior merit superior to those of all the rest put together,) τὸ κατ' ἀναλογίαν ἴσον is the principle assumed, regard being had to differences in merit. (See note on 3 § 7.) But when the citizens are not ἴσοι either κατ' ἀναλογίαν or κατ' ἀριθμόν, as in a δεσποτεία, there cannot be said to be πολιτικὸν δίκαιον: still even in this case there is a sort of δίκαιον καθ' ὁμοιότητα, an undefined δίκαιον like that which is exhibited in the relation of master and slave.

The chief passages in the *Politics* which bear upon the subject of these §§ are the following:

III. 9. p. 71. 21. It is generally assumed that τὸ δίκαιον consists in τὸ ἴσον, but τὸ ἴσον is differently interpreted. Hence the distinction between τὸ ὀλιγαρχικὸν δίκαιον and τὸ δημοκρατικόν.

III. 12. p. 78. 15. What constitutes a claim to political privileges? There is something to be said for all the kinds of excellence which are exhibited in the sphere of the state.

III. 17. p. 91. 31. Different sorts of πολιτικὸν δίκαιον are recognized, which are φύσει. There is however no δίκαιον κατὰ φύσιν in τυραννίς and the other παρεκβάσεις, because these are παρὰ φύσιν.

VII. (VI.) 2. p. 179. 11 and p. 180. 21. τὸ δημοτικὸν (or δημοκρατικόν) δίκαιον consists in τὸ ἴσον ἔχειν κατ' ἀριθμόν.

VIII. (VI.) 3. p. 181. 9. An ὀλιγαρχικὸν δίκαιον is recognized.

VIII. (V.) 9. p. 214. 4. τὸ δίκαιον is not the same in all polities. There are therefore different sorts of δικαιοσύνη, and the would-be politician must possess that sort which is appropriate to the constitution of the state.

For the words κοινωνῶν βίου cf. *Polit.* III. 3. p. 62. 23. III. 4. p. 63. 9: for πρὸς τὸ εἶναι αὐτάρκειαν cf. *Polit.* III. 1. p. 60. 26. VI. 8. p. 189. 29: and for the marked distinction here made between ἡ τῶν ἐλευθέρων καὶ ἴσων ἀρχή and ἡ δεσποτική cf. *Polit.* I. 7. p. 10. 3. IV. (VII.) 14. p. 119. 16. p. 121. 15.

ἐν οἷς—πᾶσιν ἀδικία] Zell rejects these words. Münscher, with whom I so far agree, thinks that they are wrongly given in this place. See Introduction, On dislocations in the text. I take the sentence ἔστι γὰρ δίκαιον, κ.τ.λ. to be a justification of the preceding remarks about πολιτικὸν δίκαιον: 'for there is δίκαιον where there is law, and law exists where ἀδικία is recognized, δίκη, the administration of law, being the discrimination of the just and the unjust, where by the unjust is meant the distribution to oneself of too large a share of what is ἁπλῶς good, and too small a share of what is ἁπλῶς evil.' Thus there is a δίκαιον πολιτικόν in a democracy, because all the members of a democracy are subject to law based upon a certain theory of right and wrong. But between a tyrant, properly so called, and his subjects there is no δίκαιον πολιτικόν, because there is no law to determine their mutual rights and relations, and where there is no law there is no polity: cf. *Polit.* VI. (IV.) 4. p. 154. 28 ὅπου γὰρ μὴ νόμοι ἄρχουσιν, οὐκ ἔστι πολιτεία. δεῖ γὰρ τὸν μὲν νόμον ἄρχειν πάντων, τῶν δὲ καθ' ἕκαστα τὰς ἀρχὰς καὶ τὴν πολιτείαν κρίνειν. For the argument as a whole cf. *Polit.* I. 2. p. 4. 19 ἡ δὲ δικαιοσύνη πολιτικόν· ἡ γὰρ δίκη πολιτικῆς κοινωνίας τάξις ἐστίν· ἡ δὲ δίκη τοῦ δικαίου κρίσις.

I have written πρὸς αὐτούς for πρὸς αὑτούς in the first clause of this sentence.

§ 5. διό, κ.τ.λ.] This question πότερον συμφέρει μᾶλλον ὑπὸ τοῦ ἀρίστου ἀνδρὸς βασιλεύεσθαι ἢ ὑπὸ τῶν ἀρίστων νόμων is discussed by Plato in the *Politicus* 293 E sqq. and in the *Laws* IX. 874 E—875 D, and by Aristotle in the *Politics* III. 15. p. 87. 3—17 and III. 16. p. 90. 1—32. p. 91. 8—18. See also *Polit.* III. 11. p. 77. 31.

For the phraseology cf. omnino *Polit.* III. 10. p. 75. 1 (where however emendation is necessary) and III. 16. p. 90. 1 τὸν ἄρα νόμον ἄρχειν αἱρετώτερον μᾶλλον ἢ τῶν πολιτῶν ἕνα τινά. These passages would seem to countenance the reading of M^bQ, ἀλλὰ τὸν νόμον, which is preferred by Susemihl (Bursian's *Jahresbericht* 1874—75, p. 368); but the change is not necessary, as λόγον may mean the formula contained in the law; cf. *Polit.* III. 15. p. 87. 12 ἀλλὰ μὴν κἀκεῖνον δεῖ ὑπάρχειν τὸν λόγον τὸν καθόλου τοῖς ἄρχουσιν. Plat. *Polit.* 294 C παρὰ τὸν λόγον ὃν αὐτὸς [i. e. ὁ νόμος] ἐπέταξεν. Grant in his note on § 4 renders τὸν λόγον "the impersonal reason;" this can hardly be right.

ὅτι ἑαυτῷ τοῦτο ποιεῖ] 'Because a man rules in his own interest:' cf. *Polit.* III. 7. p. 70. 11 ἡ μὲν γὰρ τυραννίς ἐστι μοναρχία πρὸς τὸ συμφέρον τὸ τοῦ μοναρχοῦντος.

ὁ ἄρχων] 'The magistrate who executes the law.' There is a certain awkwardness in the close proximity of ὁ ἄρχων (meaning no more than the executive magistrate) and ἄρχειν (in the sense of κύριον εἶναι); but cf. *Polit.* VI. (IV.) 4. p. 154. 28, quoted above on § 4. I have marked οὐ γὰρ νέμει—πρότερον as a parenthesis, thinking with Grant that μισθὸς ἄρα τις, κ.τ.λ. is the apodosis of ἐπεὶ δ' οὐθὲν αὐτῷ πλέον εἶναι δοκεῖ (cf. Bonitz *Aristot. Stud.* I. II. 28): 'The administrator is the guardian of what is just, and therefore of what is equal: and, seeing that it is assumed that in the distribution he takes no more than his due, compensation for his services must be given him in the shape of honour and dignity, otherwise he becomes a tyrant.'

§ 6. ἐπεὶ δ' οὐθέν, κ.τ.λ.] "But since he does not seem to gain at all." Grant. Rather, I think, 'but since *it is assumed* that he does not profit in the distribution.'

διὸ ἑτέρῳ πονεῖ] The modern editors except Cardwell and Michelet read ποιεῖ, and Bekker takes no notice of the reading πονεῖ which is to be found in every one of the MSS. which I have consulted. It may perhaps be thought at first sight that ἑαυτῷ τοῦτο ποιεῖ in the preceding § justifies διὸ ἑτέρῳ ποιεῖ: but a little consideration will show that though the two datives are in themselves precisely similar, τοῦτο ποιεῖ, which represents ἄρχει, is no justification of ποιεῖ in § 6 in the sense of "acts," for so it is understood by Grant, Williams, &c. On the other hand nothing could be more suitable than πονεῖ, and in *Polit.* II. 5. p. 28. 24 (αὐτῶν δ' αὑτοῖς διαπονούντων τὰ περὶ τὰς κτήσεις πλείους ἂν παρέχοι δυσκολίας) we have authority for the conjunction with it of a dative of the person interested.

§ 7. μισθὸς ἄρα τις δοτέος] *Polit.* VIII. (v.) 8. p. 213. 11 τοῦ δὲ ἀκερδῶς ἄρχειν τιμὰς εἶναι δεῖ νενομοθετημένας τοῖς εὐδοκιμοῦσιν. Plat. *Rep.* I. 345 E, 347 A. Here, as in unequal friendships, the assistance rendered by the superior and the honour or respect which compensates it are equated by means of τὸ ἀντιπεπονθός. Cf. *Polit.* II. 2. p. 24. 11 and *N. E.* VIII. IX. *ut supra.*

§§ 8, 9. 'There are in the household δίκαια which are analogous to the above-mentioned δίκαια of the state. Of these domestic δίκαια that which appears in the relation of husband and wife corresponds more nearly than τὸ δεσποτικόν and τὸ πατρικόν to the πολιτικὸν δίκαιον of § 4, and is the true οἰκονομικὸν δίκαιον.'

δεσποτικὸν δίκαιον, the δίκαιον which appears in the relationship of master and slave, and πατρικὸν δίκαιον, that which appears in the relationship of father and son, correspond rather to the δίκαιόν τι καὶ καθ' ὁμοιότητα of a tyranny, because here too ἀδικία is impossible on the part of the superior, and therefore law has no place. Cf. *Polit.* I. 12. p. 19. 16 ἐπεὶ δὲ τρία μέρη τῆς οἰκονομικῆς ἦν, ἓν μὲν δεσποτική, περὶ ἧς εἴρηται πρότερον, ἐν δὲ πατρική, τρίτον δὲ γαμική· καὶ γὰρ γυναικὸς ἄρχειν καὶ τέκνων, ὡς ἐλευθέρων μὲν ἀμφοῖν, οὐ τὸν αὐτὸν δὲ τρόπον τῆς ἀρχῆς, ἀλλὰ γυναικὸς μὲν πολιτικῶς τέκνων δὲ βασιλικῶς. (See the whole of this chapter.)

κτῆμα] 'slave.' Cf. *Polit.* I. 4. p. 6. 7.

ἕως ἂν ᾖ πηλίκον καὶ χωρισθῇ.] With K^bP^bN^bO^b, the V.A., Münscher, and the *Berlin Index*, I have omitted μή (which in all the editions stands before χωρισθῇ), translating ἕως 'until' instead of 'whilst.' Cf. *M. M.* I. 34 § 18 ὥσπερ γὰρ μέρος τί ἐστι τοῦ πατρὸς ὁ υἱός, πλὴν ὅταν ἤδη λάβῃ τὴν τοῦ ἀνδρὸς τάξιν καὶ χωρισθῇ [ὑπ'] αὐτοῦ.

§ 9. ἦν] 'are, as we said before:' sc. § 4.

οἰκονομικόν] In *Polit.* III. 6. p. 68. 25 however οἰκονομική as an epithet of ἀρχή is used comprehensively to include all three relations.

7 § 1. οἷον τὸ μνᾶς λυτροῦσθαι.] The editors point out that this passage is inconsistent with Herodot. VI. 79 ἄποινα δέ ἐστι Πελοποννησίοισι δύο μνέαι τεταγμέναι κατ' ἄνδρα αἰχμάλωτον ἐκτίνειν, and V. 77 χρόνῳ δὲ ἔλυσάν σφεας διμνέως ἀποτιμησάμενοι. But, as Blakesley remarks, the prisoners in the latter case being the Chalcidian Hippobotae, two minae "may be considered as the ransom of a man-at-arms, not of an inferior soldier." One mina then may have been the ransom of men of the lowest rank.

ἢ τὸ αἶγα, κ.τ.λ.] On the strength of Herodot. II. 42 ὅσοι μὲν δὴ Διὸς Θηβαιέος ἵδρυνται ἱρὸν ἢ νομοῦ τοῦ Θηβαίου εἰσί, οὗτοι μέν νυν πάντες οἴων ἀπεχόμενοι αἶγας θύουσι Muretus proposed to read αἶγα Διὶ θύειν ἀλλὰ μὴ πρόβατα. Cf. *N. E.* IX 2 § 6. *de Mirabilibus* 844. *a.* 35. (In Athen. IV. 138 *f* θύουσι δ' ἐν ταῖς κοπίσιν αἶγας ἄλλο δ' οὐδὲν ἱερεῖον Zeus is not the divinity honoured.) But the addition of Διί does not explain the awkward antithesis of the singular αἶγα and the plural δύο πρόβατα. Is it possible that ἀλλὰ μή is a corruption of μίαν ἤ?

τὸ θύειν Βρασίδᾳ.] The editors quote Thuc. V. 11.

§§ 2, 3. 'Some think that all δίκαια are determined by convention, because τὸ μὲν φύσει ἀκίνητον, τὰ δὲ δίκαια κινούμενα ὁρῶσιν. (This last statement, that τὰ δίκαια vary, though not true without qualification, is true in a manner. It is positively untrue παρὰ τοῖς θεοῖς; but παρ' ἡμῖν, although there is a φύσει δίκαιον, every δίκαιον is variable.) In spite of what they say, there is a φύσει δίκαιον, as well as a νόμῳ δίκαιον.' I conceive τοῦτο δ' οὐκ ἔστιν—κινητὸν μέντοι πᾶν to be a parenthetical explanation of the author's views about his opponents' minor premiss, which he practically concedes. That is to say, the fact that δίκαια differ in different places (κινεῖται), and are therefore capable of arbitrary variation (κινητά), does not disprove the existence of an eternal, natural δίκαιον to which the before-mentioned δίκαια more or less conform. Hence δίκαια may be divided into (1) φύσει δίκαια, i.e. those which represent the eternal, natural δίκαιον, and (2) νόμῳ or συνθήκῃ δίκαια, which are wholly independent of it. "Ein unveränderliches Gerechte gibt es freilich unter Menschen nicht, wohl aber bei den Göttern. Dagegen ein Gerechtes, welches sich dem Menschen allenthalben durch eigene Kraft, wenn auch nicht mit unwiderstehlicher Nothwendigkeit aufdrängt, besteht allerdings." Hildenbrand's *Rechts- und Staatsphilosophie* p. 306. After the parenthesis the author resumes the main argument with a flat denial of their conclusion, leaving it to be understood that he demurs to their major—τὸ φύσει ἀκίνητον. If the sentence is not broken up in this way, the words ἀλλ' ὅμως seem strangely out of place.

δοκεῖ δ' ἐνίοις, κ.τ.λ.] Cf. Plat. *Laws* x. 889 E καὶ δὴ καὶ [sc. φασίν] τὰ καλὰ φύσει μὲν ἄλλα εἶναι νόμῳ δὲ ἕτερα· τὰ δὲ δίκαια οὐδ' εἶναι τὸ παράπαν φύσει, ἀλλ' ἀμφισβητοῦντας διατελεῖν ἀλλήλοις καὶ μετατιθεμένους ἀεὶ ταῦτα· ἃ δ' ἂν μετάθωνται καὶ ὅταν, τότε κύρια ἕκαστα εἶναι, γιγνόμενα τέχνῃ καὶ τοῖς νόμοις, ἀλλ' οὐ δή τινι φύσει. See also [Plat.] *Minos* 315 A—316 B, quoted by Grant, and *N. E.* I. 3 § 2.

§ 4. φύσει γάρ, κ.τ.λ.] Nature intends the right hand to be stronger than the left, but all men may become ambidextrous. In place of πάντας Bekker without remark reads τινάς: but as πάντας is found so far as I know in all the MSS. and gives a good sense, I have, with Fritzsche (who compares *M. M.* I. 34 § 21) and Zell, restored it to the text.

§ 5. ὠνοῦνται—πωλοῦσιν] sc. οἱ ἔμποροι.
ὁμοίως δὲ καί, κ.τ.λ.] Human δίκαια [as opposed to the eternal, natural δίκαιον] differ, inasmuch as the πολιτεῖαι to which they belong are all deviations from the one perfect πολιτεία.

§ 6. Each law stands to the variety of action included under it in the relation of universal to particulars: cf. *Polit.* II. 8. p. 44. 2 καθόλου γὰρ ἀναγκαῖον γραφῆναι, αἱ δὲ πράξεις περὶ τῶν καθ' ἕκαστον εἰσίν. This § and that which follows serve as a transition to another part of the inquiry—the justice and injustice of the individual.

§ 7. αὐτὸ δὲ τοῦτο] The editors write τὸ αὐτὸ δὲ τοῦτο in spite of the best MSS. Is the article necessary? 'This very thing when realized in fact is called an ἀδίκημα: until it is realized, it is only an ἄδικον.' This statement is qualified in 8 § 2, where we are told that every ἀδίκημα until it is committed is an ἄδικον: but not every ἄδικον when it is committed is an ἀδίκημα, because, to be an ἀδίκημα, an act must be ἑκούσιον.

καλεῖται, κ.τ.λ.] "It is not improbable," says Grant, "that Eudemus here is correcting the phraseology of Aristotle, who at all events in his *Rhetoric*, 1. 13 § 1, uses δικαίωμα as the opposite of ἀδίκημα, merely to denote a just action." See Cope on *Rhet.* l. 3 § 9. I have enclosed this sentence within marks of parenthesis to show that the original argument is continued in καθ' ἕκαστον δέ, κ.τ.λ.

ὕστερον] I.e. in the *Politics*, which treatise was evidently intended to include a book or books περὶ νόμων.

8 § 2.] See note on 7 § 7.

§ 3. πρότερον] The reference is to *E. E.* II. 9 § 3 ὅσα μὲν οὖν ἐφ' ἑαυτῷ ὂν μὴ πράττειν πράττει μὴ ἀγνοῶν καὶ δι' αὑτόν, ἑκούσια ταῦτ' ἀνάγκη εἶναι, καὶ τὸ ἑκούσιον τοῦτ' ἐστίν· ὅσα δ' ἀγνοῶν καὶ διὰ τὸ ἀγνοεῖν, ἀκών, rather than to *N. E.* III. 1 § 20 ὄντος δ' ἀκουσίου τοῦ βίᾳ καὶ δι' ἄγνοιαν, τὸ ἑκούσιον δόξειεν ἂν εἶναι οὗ ἡ ἀρχὴ ἐν αὐτῷ εἰδότι τὰ καθ' ἕκαστα ἐν οἷς ἡ πρᾶξις. Throughout this chapter we are reminded of the Eudemian, rather than of the Nicomachean, investigation of τὸ ἑκούσιον.

μήτε ὄν] Before or after this phrase Bernays (*Symb. Philol. Bonn.* I. 304) would add μήτε ὅ, comparing § 6. Would not this addition necessitate the further addition of ὅτι τύπτει καὶ before τίνα in the next clause? The list of particulars whereof ignorance is possible is not always given in full: even in *E. E.* II. 9 §§ 1, 2, where we should have expected the lists to be complete, we have in one place εἰδότα ἢ ὂν ἢ ᾧ ἢ οὗ ἕνεκα, and in another ἀγνοοῦντι καὶ ὂν καὶ ᾧ καὶ ὅ.

οὗ <ἕνεκα>] Bekker's addition of ἕνεκα appears to be necessary.

ὥσπερ εἴ τις λαβών, κ.τ.λ.] Cf. *E. E.* II. 8 § 10 ὥσπερ εἴ τις λαβὼν τὴν χεῖρα τύπτοι τινὰ ἀντιτείνοντος καὶ τῷ βούλεσθαι καὶ τῷ ἐπιθυμεῖν. On αὑτοῦ vide supra 5 § 13.

ὧν οὐθέν, κ.τ.λ.] So *E. E.* II. 8 §§ 4, 5 καθόλου δὲ τὸ βίαιον καὶ τὴν ἀνάγκην καὶ ἐπὶ τῶν ἀψύχων λέγομεν· καὶ γὰρ τὸν λίθον ἄνω καὶ τὸ πῦρ κάτω βίᾳ καὶ ἀναγκαζόμενα φέρεσθαι φαμέν. ταῦτα δ' ὅταν κατὰ τὴν φύσει καὶ καθ' αὑτὰ ὁρμὴν φέρηται, οὐ βίᾳ, οὐ μὴν οὐδ'

NOTES.

ἑκούσια λέγεται, ἀλλ' ἀνώνυμος ἡ ἀντίθεσις. ὅταν δὲ παρὰ ταύτην, βίᾳ φαμέν. Rassow however (*Forschungen* p. 95) corrects ὧν οὐθὲν οὔτ' ἐφ' ἡμῖν οὔθ' ἑκούσιόν ἐστιν, and Spengel (*Aristot. Stud.* I. 43) ὧν οὐθὲν ἑκούσιόν ἐστιν.

§ 4. διὰ φόβον] Cf. *N. E.* III. 1 §§ 4—6, where the conclusion is the same, though somewhat differently expressed.

§ 5. τῶν δὲ ἑκουσίων, κ.τ.λ.] Here, as in *E. E.* II., actions are classified as

$$\begin{array}{l}\text{ἀκούσια}\\ \text{ἑκούσια}\begin{cases}\text{ἀπροαίρετα}\\ \text{προαιρετά}\end{cases}\end{array}$$

Cf. *E. E.* II. 10 § 19 ἅμα δ' ἐκ τούτων φανερὸν καὶ ὅτι καλῶς διορίζονται οἱ τῶν παθημάτων τὰ μὲν ἑκούσια τὰ δ' ἀκούσια τὰ δ' ἐκ προνοίας νομοθετοῦσιν· εἰ γὰρ καὶ μὴ διακριβοῦσιν, ἀλλ' ἅπτονταί γέ πη τῆς ἀληθείας. ἀλλὰ περὶ μὲν τούτων ἐροῦμεν ἐν τῇ περὶ τῶν δικαίων ἐπισκέψει. In *N. E.* III. 1 § 13 οὐχ ἑκούσια are interpolated between ἀκούσια and ἑκούσια.

§ 6. τριῶν δὲ οὐσῶν, κ.τ.λ.] The three sorts of βλάβη are ἀτύχημα, ἁμάρτημα, and ἀδίκημα; but ἀδίκημα is afterwards subdivided into simple ἀδίκημα, and ἀδίκημα which implies ἀδικία in the doer. If we further include ὅσα βίαια καὶ μὴ ἐφ' αὐτῷ, we have the following classification:

$$\begin{array}{ll}\text{ἀκούσια}\begin{cases}(\alpha)\ \text{τὰ βίαια καὶ μὴ ἐφ' αὐτῷ}\\ (\beta)\ \text{τὰ μετ' ἀγνοίας, ὅταν παραλόγως ἡ}\\ \ \ \ \text{βλάβη γένηται, (ὅταν ἡ ἀρχὴ ἔξωθεν}\\ \ \ \ \text{ᾖ τῆς ἀγνοίας)}\end{cases} & \text{ἀτυχήματα}\\ \text{ἑκούσια}\begin{cases}(\gamma)\ \text{τὰ μετ' ἀγνοίας, ὅταν μὴ παραλόγως}\\ \ \ \ \text{ἄνευ δὲ κακίας, (ὅταν ἡ ἀρχὴ ἐν αὐτῷ}\\ \ \ \ \text{ᾖ τῆς ἀγνοίας)}\\ (\delta)\ \text{ὅταν εἰδὼς μὲν μὴ προβουλεύσας δέ}\\ (\epsilon)\ \text{ὅταν ἐκ προαιρέσεως, (ἐκ προνοίας)}\end{cases} & \begin{array}{l}\text{ἁμαρτήματα}\\ \\ \\ \text{ἀδικήματα}\\ \text{ἀδικήματα which}\\ \text{imply ἀδικία in}\\ \text{the doer}\end{array}\end{array}$$

The ἄγνοια here mentioned is of course ignorance of the circumstances of the act (τὰ καθ' ἕκαστα), not ignorance of rules (τὰ καθόλου): cf. *E. E.* II. 9 §§ 1, 2. *N. E.* III. 1 § 15. According to the above Eudemian list the act of the μεθύων is ranked under (γ), that of the θυμῷ ποιῶν under (δ), and that of the ἐπιβουλεύσας under (ε). In the *Rhet.* I. 13. p. 47. 29 ἔστι δ' ἀτυχήματα μὲν ὅσα παράλογα καὶ μὴ ἀπὸ μοχθηρίας, ἁμαρτήματα δὲ ὅσα μὴ παράλογα καὶ μὴ ἀπὸ πονηρίας, ἀδικήματα δὲ ὅσα μήτε παράλογα ἀπὸ πονηρίας τ' ἐστίν, (γ) and (δ) of the Eudemian list are classed together as ἁμαρτήματα: and in the same way in *N. E.* III. 1 § 14 the act of the μεθύων and the act of the ὀργιζόμενος are mentioned together as instances of ὅσα μὴ δι' ἄγνοιαν ἀλλ' ἀγνοῶν. Thus the θυμῷ ποιῶν according to Aristotle acts ἀγνοῶν ἀλλ' οὐ δι' ἄγνοιαν: according to Eudemus, εἰδὼς μὲν οὐ προβουλεύσας δέ. For this difference of statement Eudemus prepares us in II. 9 § 3 ἐπεὶ δὲ τὸ ἐπίστασθαι καὶ τὸ εἰδέναι διττόν, ἐν μὲν τὸ ἔχειν ἐν δὲ τὸ χρῆσθαι τῇ ἐπιστήμῃ, ὁ ἔχων μὴ χρώμενος δὲ ἔστι μὲν ὡς δικαίως <ἂν> ἀγνοῶν λέγοιτο, ἔστι δ' ὡς οὐ δικαίως, οἷον εἰ δι' ἀμέλειαν μὴ ἐχρῆτο. In the *Rhet. ad Alexand.* (c. 4. p. 24. 4. c. 36. p. 79. 27 Spengel) ἀδικία is said to be coextensive with τὰ ἐκ προνοίας, ἁμαρτία with τὰ δι' ἄγνοιαν, and ἀτυχία with τὰ δι' ἑτέρους τινὰς ἢ διὰ τύχην: but here τὰ δι' ἄγνοιαν is equivalent to Aristotle's ὅσα ἀγνοῶν ἀλλὰ μὴ δι' ἄγνοιαν. In *M. M.* I. 34 § 25, (γ), (δ), and (ε) of Eudemus's list are roughly thrown together under the title of ἀδίκημα: see note on § 7. The Eudemian terminology seems to be based upon that of Attic law: see Antiphon, *passim.*

ἁμαρτήματα] here includes ἀτυχήματα as well as ἁμαρτήματα in the narrower sense in which the word is used in § 7.

ᾧ] So Rassow *Forschungen* p. 61, on the authority of K[b]. Although the lists of particulars of which a man may be ignorant are not always the same, (see note on § 3,) it is reasonable to expect consistency in such a passage as the present, where the list occurs three times in the space of five lines. In *E. E.* II. 9 §§ 1, 2 the particulars are as here, ὅν, ᾧ, ὅ, and οὗ ἕνεκα, ὡς being suppressed and ὅν doing duty for the περὶ τί ἢ ἐν τίνι of *N. E.* III. 1 § 16.

§ 7. ἁμαρτάνει μὲν γάρ, κ.τ.λ.] It is plain that this sentence ought to restate the distinction already drawn between ἀτύχημα and ἁμάρτημα: but it is difficult to see how ὅταν ἡ ἀρχὴ ἐν αὐτῷ ᾖ τῆς αἰτίας—so the MSS. except H[a]M[b] (which have κακίας), and all the editors—can be equivalent to μὴ παραλόγως, and ὅταν ἔξωθεν to παραλόγως. Moreover, ἡ ἀρχὴ τῆς αἰτίας is a strange phrase. Hence I have supposed ΑΙΤΙΑΣ to be a corruption of ΑΓΝΟΙΑΣ, and I find the strongest possible confirmation of my conjecture both in the *N. E.* and in the *M. M.* Cf. *N. E.* III. 5 § 8 καὶ γὰρ ἐπ' αὐτῷ τῷ ἀγνοεῖν κολάζουσιν, ἐὰν αἴτιος εἶναι δοκῇ τῆς ἀγνοίας, οἷον τοῖς μεθύουσι διπλᾶ τὰ ἐπιτίμια· ἡ γὰρ ἀρχὴ ἐν αὐτῷ· κύριος γὰρ τοῦ μὴ μεθυσθῆναι, τοῦτο δ' αἴτιον τῆς ἀγνοίας: also § 7: and *M. M.* I. 34 §§ 27—28 ἔστω δὴ οὗτος ὁ διορισμός· ὅταν μὲν γὰρ ἡ ἄγνοια αἰτία ᾖ τοῦ πρᾶξαί τι, οὐχ ἑκὼν τοῦτο πράττει, ὥστε οὐκ ἀδικεῖ· ὅταν δὲ τῆς ἀγνοίας αὐτὸς ᾖ αἴτιος, καὶ πράττῃ τι κατὰ τὴν ἄγνοιαν ἧς αὐτὸς αἴτιός ἐστιν, οὗτος ἤδη ἀδικεῖ, καὶ δικαίως αἴτιος ὁ τοιοῦτος κληθήσεται. οἷον ἐπὶ τῶν μεθυόντων· οἱ γὰρ μεθύοντες καὶ πράξαντές τι κακὸν ἀδικοῦσιν· τῆς γὰρ ἀγνοίας αὐτοί εἰσιν αἴτιοι· ἐξῆν γὰρ αὐτοῖς μὴ πίνειν τοσοῦτον ὥστ' ἀγνοήσαντας τύπτειν τὸν πατέρα. ὁμοίως ἐπὶ τῶν ἄλλων ἀγνοιῶν ὅσαι μὲν γίνονται δι' αὑτούς, οἱ κατὰ ταύτας ἀδικοῦντες ἄδικοι· ὧν δὲ μὴ αὐτοί εἰσιν αἴτιοι, ἀλλ' ἡ ἄγνοια κἀκείνοις ἐστὶν αἰτία τοῖς πράξασι τοῦ πρᾶξαι, οὐκ ἄδικοι: and again § 29 ἡ γὰρ ἄγνοια αἰτία τοῦ πράττειν ταῦτα, τῆς δ' ἀγνοίας οὐκ αὐτὰ αἴτια. (I have already remarked on § 6 that the ἁμαρτήματα of the present passage are called ἀδικήματα in the *M. M.*) See also *E. E.* II. 9 § 3. With this change the sentence becomes perfectly intelligible: it is an ἀτύχημα when the doer does not know and could not have been expected to know, in other words when he is not answerable for his ignorance: but it is an ἁμάρτημα, when he might have been expected to know, in other words when he is answerable for his ignorance, οἷον ἐπὶ τῶν μεθυόντων. See Antiphon *Tetral. II.*, especially the defence, in which the father of the accused argues that the fatal accident was caused by the ἁμαρτία of the deceased, who ought not to have crossed the target.

With the received text the best rendering which I can devise is—'that is to say, a man ἁμαρτάνει when the origin of (the ignorance which is) the cause of the wrong is in himself; he ἀτυχεῖ when it is external to him.'

§ 8. εἰδώς] Thus ὁ θυμῷ ποιῶν is accounted εἰδώς. In the *N. E.* III. 1 § 14 he is classed with the μεθύων as an ἀγνοῶν: ἕτερον δ' ἔοικε καὶ τὸ δι' ἄγνοιαν πράττειν τοῦ ἀγνοοῦντα ποιεῖν· ὁ γὰρ μεθύων ἢ ὀργιζόμενος οὐ δοκεῖ δι' ἄγνοιαν πράττειν, ἀλλὰ διά τι τῶν εἰρημένων, οὐκ εἰδὼς δέ, ἀλλ' ἀγνοῶν. See note on § 6.

οἷον ὅσα τε, κ.τ.λ.] Thinking that the *second* ὅσα is the subject of συμβαίνει, I expunge the commas which Bekker places after πάθη and φυσικά. If the *first* ὅσα were the subject of συμβαίνει, τοῖς ἀνθρώποις would be unmeaning and superfluous. On the other hand these words are positively necessary to complete the sense of ὅσα ἀναγκαῖα ἢ φυσικά. Cf. § 12 διὰ πάθος δὲ μήτε φυσικὸν μήτ' ἀνθρωπικόν. See also *Polit.* III. 10. p. 75. 3 ἔχοντά γε τὰ συμβαίνοντα πάθη περὶ τὴν ψυχήν. V. (VIII.) 7. p. 142. 32 ὁ γὰρ περὶ ἐνίας συμβαίνει πάθος ψυχὰς ἰσχυρῶς, τοῦτο ἐν πάσαις ὑπάρχει, τῷ δὲ ἧττον διαφέρει καὶ τῷ μᾶλλον, οἷον ἔλεος καὶ φόβος, ἔτι δ' ἐνθουσιασμός. By φυσικὰ πάθη Eudemus means ὅσα κοινὰ πᾶσι καὶ ἐφ' ὅσον κοινά: the ἀναγκαῖα πάθη, which are a species of the φυσικὰ πάθη, include ἐπιθυμίαι αἱ περὶ τὴν τροφήν, κ.τ.λ. Opposed to the φυσικὰ καὶ ἀνθρωπικὰ πάθη are the θηριώδη and νοσηματώδη πάθη, which in the developed form of ἕξεις are described in *N. E.* VII. 5. See *N. E.* VII. 6 § 2 ἔτι ταῖς φυσικαῖς μᾶλλον συγγνώμη ἀκολουθεῖν ὀρέξεσιν, ἐπεὶ καὶ ἐπιθυμίαις ταῖς τοιαύταις μᾶλλον ὅσαι κοιναὶ πᾶσι καὶ ἐφ' ὅσον κοιναί· ὁ δὲ θυμὸς φυσικώτερον καὶ ἡ χαλεπότης τῶν ἐπιθυμιῶν τῶν τῆς ὑπερβολῆς καὶ τῶν μὴ ἀναγκαίων. VII. 4 § 2 ἀναγκαῖα μὲν [sc. τῶν ποιούντων ἡδονήν] τὰ σωματικά. λέγω δὲ τὰ τοιαῦτα, τά τε περὶ τὴν τροφὴν καὶ τὴν τῶν ἀφροδισίων χρείαν, καὶ τὰ τοιαῦτα τῶν σωματικῶν περὶ ἃ τὴν ἀκολασίαν ἔθεμεν καὶ τὴν σωφροσύνην. VII. 6. § 6 ὥσπερ γὰρ εἴρηται κατ' ἀρχάς, αἱ μὲν [sc. τῶν ἐπιθυμιῶν] ἀνθρωπικαί εἰσι καὶ φυσικαί, καὶ τῷ γένει καὶ τῷ μεγέθει, αἱ δὲ θηριώδεις, αἱ δὲ διὰ πηρώσεις καὶ νοσήματα. (In *N. E.* III. 11 § 1 the distinction between ἀναγκαῖαι and φυσικαὶ ἐπιθυμίαι is not recognized.)

οὐ γὰρ διὰ μοχθηρίαν ἢ βλάβη] After these words I have introduced 6 §§ 1, 2. See Introduction, On dislocations in the text.

6 § 1. ἢ οὕτω μὲν οὐδὲν διοίσει,...ὅταν δ' ἐκ προαιρέσεως, ἄδικος καὶ μοχθηρός;] I conceive that these clauses, of which the first belongs to 6 § 1, the second to 8 § 9, are to be read in close connection with one another, the intervening sentences being parenthetical. 'Or shall we say that it is not (as the question thus expressed assumes) the doing of certain acts, but the spirit of the doer, which makes him ἄδικος καὶ μοχθηρός?' Cf. 8 § 11 infra.

6 § 2. οἷον οὐ κλέπτης, ἔκλεψε δέ] On the authority of K^b P^b I have written οὐ κλέπτης in place of οὐδὲ κλέπτης, which is hardly intelligible even if with Münscher we expunge οὐδὲ μοιχός, ἐμοίχευσε δέ, so that οὐδέ may introduce an example supplementary to the one already discussed. As Bekker's text stands, οὐδέ cannot bear its proper meaning.

8 § 9. διὸ καλῶς, κ.τ.λ.] 'Hence the law is right in not accounting τὰ ἐκ θυμοῦ to be ἐκ προνοίας, because it is ὁ ὀργίσας who ἄρχει, not ὁ θυμῷ ποιῶν. Indeed it is a legal maxim that it is only an issue of fact on which it may be argued that one or other of the two parties is necessarily πονηρός [μὴ λανθανέτω δ' ὅτι ἀναγκαῖον ἐν ταύτῃ τῇ ἀμφισβητήσει μόνῃ τὸν ἕτερον εἶναι πονηρόν· οὐ γάρ ἐστιν ἄγνοια αἰτία, ὥσπερ

ἄν εἴ τινες περὶ τοῦ δικαίου ἀμφισβητοῖεν *Rhet.* III. 17. p. 143. 7],
whilst in the case of τὰ ἐκ θυμοῦ, done ἐπὶ φαινομένῃ ἀδικίᾳ, the
issue is not one of fact (περὶ τοῦ γενέσθαι), but one of justice (περὶ
τοῦ ποτέρως δίκαιον). Hence the angry man may plead ignorance.
On the other hand ὁ ἐπιβουλεύσας, i.e. the man who deliberately
attacks his neighbour, [whether by way of revenge or otherwise,]
cannot plead ignorance (οὐκ ἀγνοεῖ), and therefore must be punished
as an offender ἐκ προνοίας. Thus the difference between the θυμῷ
ποιῶν and the ἐπιβουλεύσας is that the one can plead that he thought
he had been wronged, the other cannot.' But what is the ἄγνοια
which in *Rhetoric* III. 17, quoted above, is said to be an αἰτία
or excuse in the ἀμφισβήτησις περὶ τοῦ δικαίου and not to be so
in the ἀμφισβήτησις περὶ τοῦ γενέσθαι? Clearly not ignorance of
the act done in anger, else the question περὶ τοῦ γενέσθαι would
have to be discussed, but ignorance or mistake about the supposed
provocation. Similarly in the passage before us, the θυμῷ ποιῶν may
plead ἄγνοια, not of his own action, for we have seen in § 8 that he
is εἰδὼς μὲν μὴ προβουλεύσας δέ, but of the φαινομένη ἀδικία which
he mistakes for a real ἀδικία. On the other hand the ἐπιβουλεύσας,
who takes time to retaliate, cannot plead ἄγνοια of this sort. The
action of the θυμῷ ποιῶν may be traced to the assumption, in this
case false, that he had been wronged, whilst the ἐπιβουλεύσας has
had time to consider the matter, and therefore cannot plead mistake
as an excuse. For example, *A*, wrongly thinking himself to have
been injured by *B*, strikes him in the heat of passion. Here *A* is
εἰδώς in respect of his own act, but ἀγνοῶν in respect of the supposed
injury. Hence his act is not held by the law to be ἐκ προνοίας. If
however *A* broods over his supposed wrong before he retaliates, he
can no longer plead that he supposed himself to have been unjustly
treated by *B*, because he has had time to discover his mistake. His
act is therefore ἐκ προνοίας. Cf. Antiphon p. 126 τὸν γὰρ ἐπιβουλεύ-
σαντα κελεύει [sc. ὁ νόμος] φονέα εἶναι.

The conclusion is then that the law is right in drawing a line
between ἀδικήματα done in the heat of passion and ἀδικήματα done
by way of revenge after an interval, the θυμῷ ποιῶν being entitled to
plead that he supposed himself to have provocation, the ἐπιβουλεύσας
not being entitled to do so. This result agrees very well (allowance
being made for differences in the use of the words ἑκούσιον and
ἀκούσιον) with Plato *Laws* IX. 867 A ὁ μὲν τὸν θυμὸν φυλάττων καὶ οὐκ
ἐκ τοῦ παραχρῆμα ἐξαίφνης ἀλλὰ μετὰ ἐπιβουλῆς ὕστερον χρόνῳ τιμω-
ρούμενος ἑκουσίῳ ἔοικεν, ὁ δὲ ἀταμιεύτως ταῖς ὀργαῖς καὶ ἐκ τοῦ παρα-

χρῆμα εὐθὺς χρώμενος ἀπροβουλεύτως ὅμοιος μὲν ἀκουσίῳ, ἔστι δὲ οὐδ᾽ οὗτος αὖ παντάπασιν ἀκούσιος ἀλλ᾽ εἰκὼν ἀκουσίου...βέλτιστον μὴν καὶ ἀληθέστατον εἰς εἰκόνα μὲν ἄμφω θεῖναι, τεμεῖν δὲ αὐτὼ χωρὶς τῇ ἐπιβουλῇ καὶ ἀπροβουλίᾳ, καὶ τοῖς μὲν μετ᾽ ἐπιβουλῆς τε καὶ ὀργῇ κτείνασι τὰς τιμωρίας χαλεπωτέρας, τοῖς δὲ ἀπροβουλεύτως τε καὶ ἐξαίφνης πραοτέρας νομοθετεῖν. Bywater (*Journal of Philology* 1874, v. 115) anticipates me in referring to the *Laws* for the explanation of the phrase ὁ ἐπιβουλεύσας; but I fancy that he takes the remarks made about ὁ θυμῷ ποιῶν to apply also to ὁ ἐπιβουλεύσας, as I did myself in a paper in the same journal (1876, VI. 109). Mich. Ephesius, the Paraphrast, and most of the editors seem to take ὁ μέν and ὁ δέ to be the two persons concerned in a quarrel, and ὁ ἐπιβουλεύσας to be equivalent to ὁ προκατάρξας.

On the ἀμφισβητήσεις or στάσεις (ὅτι οὐ γέγονεν, ὅτι οὐκ ἔβλαψεν, ὅτι οὐ τοσόνδε, ὅτι δικαίως: otherwise, στοχαστική, ὁρική, ποιότητος) vide *Rhet.* III. 17. p. 143. 1, and Cope's *Introduction* pp. 355, 397. That cases where the issue is περὶ τοῦ ποτέρως δίκαιον are not to be accounted ἐκ προνοίας is assumed in *Polit.* VI. (IV.) 16. p. 176. 20 περί τε τῶν ἐκ προνοίας, καὶ περὶ τῶν ἀκουσίων, καὶ ὅσα ὁμολογεῖται μὲν ἀμφισβητεῖται δὲ περὶ τοῦ δικαίου, τέταρτον δὲ ὅσα τοῖς φεύγουσι φόνου ἐπὶ καθόδῳ ἐπιφέρεται.

§ 10. ὧν] This relative has no expressed antecedent. Should we read οὐ γὰρ ὥσπερ <οἱ> ἐν τοῖς συναλλάγμασι? For the sense cf. *Rhet.* III. 17 quoted above.

ἂν μὴ διὰ λήθην αὐτὸ δρῶσιν] I think that the subject of δρῶσιν is ὅ τε ὀργίσας καὶ ὁ ὀργισθείς, who do not raise the issue of fact unless they do it through forgetfulness, i.e. the forgetfulness which results from anger. These words are commonly understood to refer to the two parties concerned in a συνάλλαγμα, "ubi fieri non potest quin eorum alter qui ita controversantur pravus sit, nisi forte oblivio intercessit" (Victorius on *Rhet.* III. 17): but (1) why is αὐτὸ δρῶσιν in the plural? and (2) what precise idea do these words convey? According to my interpretation they stand for περὶ τοῦ γενέσθαι ἀμφισβητῶσιν.

§ 11. ἀδικεῖ καὶ κατὰ ταῦτ᾽ ἤδη, κ.τ.λ.] All the editions with which I am acquainted place a full stop, or at least a colon, after ἀδικεῖ, thus completely destroying the sense. It is clear from the parallel statement in regard to ὁ δίκαιος and ὁ δικαιοπραγῶν which succeeds, and indeed from the whole argument of the passage, that if a man παρὰ τὸ ἀνάλογον ἢ παρὰ τὸ ἴσον βλάπτει another ἑκών, he ἀδικεῖ, but if a man παρὰ τὸ ἀνάλογον ἢ παρὰ τὸ ἴσον βλάπτει another προελόμενος, he ἀδικεῖ καὶ ἄδικός ἐστιν. Hence the words ἀδικεῖ καὶ κατὰ ταῦτ' ἤδη τὰ ἀδικήματα ὁ ἀδικῶν ἄδικος must be closely connected together, κατὰ ταῦτ' ἤδη τὰ ἀδικήματα representing ἂν ἐκ προαιρέσεως βλάψῃ. The words ὅταν παρὰ τὸ ἀνάλογον ᾖ ἢ παρὰ τὸ ἴσον do not refer exclusively to ὁ ἀδικῶν who is also ἄδικος, and therefore cannot constitute the distinction required: they are, in fact, part of the definition of τὸ ἐν μέρει ἄδικον. Cf. 4 §§ 2, 3, where it is stated that τὸ ἄδικον τὸ ἀντικείμενον τῷ διανεμητικῷ δικαίῳ is παρὰ τὸ ἀνάλογον, and that τὸ ἐν τοῖς συναλλάγμασιν ἄδικον is ἄνισον κατὰ τὴν ἀριθμητικὴν ἀναλογίαν, i.e. in the language of the passage before us παρὰ τὸ ἴσον.

δικαιοπραγῇ] After this word I have substituted a comma for a full stop.

§ 12. τῶν δ' ἀκουσίων] These words answer to τῶν δὲ ἑκουσίων in § 5: but it must be observed that the ἀκούσια of the present section include actions which do not appear at all in the foregoing classification. The ὅσα μὴ μόνον ἀγνοοῦντες ἀλλὰ καὶ δι' ἄγνοιαν ἁμαρτάνουσιν are the ἀτυχήματα of § 7: the ὅσα μὴ δι' ἄγνοιαν, ἀλλ' ἀγνοοῦντες μὲν διὰ πάθος δὲ μήτε φυσικὸν μήτ' ἀνθρωπικόν are neither the ἁμαρτήματα nor the ἀδικήματα of §§ 7, 8, but acts characteristic of the inhuman πάθη: see note on § 8 οἷον ὅσα τε, κ.τ.λ. and compare VII. 5. The acts in question are ἀκούσια because the perpetrators of them are not responsible agents, but they are not συγγνωμονικά, because they are even more detestable than ordinary vicious acts. (It may be worth while to note that τὰ ἔξω τῶν ὅρων τῆς κακίας are in VII. 5 classified as θηριώδη and νοσηματώδη, τὰ νοσηματώδη being subdivided into τὰ φύσει and τὰ ἐξ ἔθους.) Thus, as the πάθη here spoken of are such as are μήτε φυσικὰ μήτ' ἀνθρωπικά, it is a mistake to say that "the word [ἀκουσίων] is used less sternly here than it is by Aristotle in *Eth.* III. 1 § 21, &c., where acts of passion are excluded from the class of the involuntary." The acts done διὰ θυμὸν ἢ δι' ἐπιθυμίαν of which Aristotle speaks in the passage cited come under the head of ὅσα τε διὰ θυμὸν καὶ ἄλλα πάθη ὅσα ἀναγκαῖα ἢ φυσικὰ συμβαίνει τοῖς ἀνθρώποις § 8, and as we have seen (see note on § 6) are reckoned by Eudemus ἑκούσια. Mich. Ephes. and the Paraphrast similarly misconceive the passage.

ἀνθρωπικόν] I think that the passages cited in the Berlin Index favour ἀνθρωπικόν rather than ἀνθρώπινον. See especially *N. E.* VII. 6 § 6, quoted above on § 8.

9 §§ 1—7. The first of a series of ἀπορίαι is investigated: πότερον

ἔστιν ἑκόντα ἀδικεῖσθαι; 'It might be thought that as ἀδικεῖν and δικαιοπραγεῖν are πᾶν ἑκούσιον, so ἀδικεῖσθαι and δικαιοῦσθαι are either πᾶν ἑκούσιον or πᾶν ἀκούσιον. But no such symmetrical determination is possible: for δικαιοῦσθαι is sometimes ἑκούσιον, sometimes ἀκούσιον. Further, it may be asked πότερον ὁ τὸ ἄδικον πεπονθὼς ἀδικεῖται πᾶς; No: for in order that A may be said ἀδικεῖν, B ἀδικεῖσθαι, A must be ἑκών and B ἄκων. If A is ἄκων and B ἑκών, or both ἄκων, or both ἑκών, A may be said ἄδικα πράττειν but not ἀδικεῖν, B may be said ἄδικα πάσχειν but not ἀδικεῖσθαι. That A must be ἑκών we have assumed in the preceding chapter: that B must be ἄκων is necessary in order that there may be that contest of wills which we suppose when we say that A ἀδικεῖ B. Thus in either of the two alternatives contemplated by Phegeus in the quotation from Euripides Alcmaeon cannot be said ἀδικεῖν nor his mother ἀδικεῖσθαι.' The meanings here put upon the words ἀδικεῖν and ἀδικεῖσθαι are precisely those put upon them by the orators, with whom ἀδικεῖν is 'to owe compensation,' ἀδικεῖσθαι 'to be entitled to compensation.' It will be observed that in § 4 the author assumes that he will hereafter answer the question πότερον ἐνδέχεται αὐτὸν αὑτὸν ἀδικεῖν; in the negative. The results of these §§ are briefly summarized in the *Rhet.* I. 13. p. 46. 10 ἔστι δὴ τὸ ἀδικεῖσθαι τὸ ὑπὸ ἑκόντος τὰ ἄδικα πάσχειν... ἀνάγκη τὸν ἀδικούμενον βλάπτεσθαι καὶ ἀκουσίως βλάπτεσθαι. I have in §§ 1—3 departed from Bekker's punctuation on several occasions.

§ 1. μητέρα, κ.τ.λ.] Bekker reads with the MSS. κατέκτα and ἢ θέλουσαν, placing a comma at the end of the first, and a colon at the end of the second line. Nauck, Wagner, and others have altered κατέκτα into κατέκταν, and inserted οὐ before θέλουσαν, placing a full stop after λόγος, and a note of interrogation after οὐχ ἑκών. They suppose that these lines are part of a conversation between Alcmaeon and Phegeus in the Ἀλκμαίων ὁ διὰ Ψωφῖδος, a tragedy which is also referred to in *N. E.* III. 1 § 8. Mich. Ephes. says that these lines are from the Bellerophon; see Ellis's remarks in the *Journal of Philology* 1872, IV. 271. Adopting in the main the emendations above mentioned, I have further written ἢ οὐχ ἑκοῦσαν in place of the ἢ οὐ θέλουσαν of the editors. Cf. Eur. *Hippol.* 319 φίλος μ' ἀπόλλυσ' οὐχ ἑκοῦσαν οὐχ ἑκών, quoted by the commentators.

ὥσπερ καὶ τὸ ἀδικεῖν πᾶν ἑκούσιον] Nötel thinks that these words, which are repeated immediately afterwards, should be omitted. I do not see why they should not stand as part of the original question, as well as of the more comprehensive question which in καὶ ἆρα πᾶν, κ.τ.λ. is substituted for it.

§ 2. ὥστ' εὔλογον, κ.τ.λ.] The words ἢ ἑκούσιον ἢ ἀκούσιον εἶναι, grammatically regarded, are an awkward addition to this sentence. Compare however, for a similar supplementary explanation, 4 § 14. Rassow proposes to write καὶ instead of καθ'.

§ 4. ἐνδέχοιτο αὐτὸν αὑτὸν ἀδικεῖν] 'We should be obliged to answer in the affirmative the question "can a man ἀδικεῖν himself?" Whereas when the ἀπορία is discussed presently in § 8 sqq. and ch. 11 §§ 1—6, we shall see ourselves obliged to answer it in the negative.'

§§ 5, 6. 'A δι' ἀκρασίαν ἑκὼν ὑπὸ B ἑκόντος βλάπτεται. If then ἀδικεῖσθαι = ὑφ' ἑκόντος βλάπτεσθαι, the ἀκρατὴς ἑκὼν ἀδικεῖται. If however ἀδικεῖν presumes opposition from the βούλησις of the ἀδικούμενος, the ἀκρατής cannot be regarded simultaneously as ἀδικούμενος and ἑκών. For the ἀκρατής (who acts κατὰ τὴν ἐπιθυμίαν but παρὰ τὴν βούλησιν), (1) so long as his βούλησις resists is not ἑκών, and (2) when his ἐπιθυμία has its way, is not ἀδικούμενος, because his βούλησις has ceased to resist. [In fact in the case of the ἀκρατής the opposition offered by his βούλησις is overcome, not by the supposed ἀδικῶν, but by his own ἐπιθυμία, and therefore A οὐκ ἀδικεῖται ὑπὸ B, though, as we shall see in 11 § 9, κατὰ μεταφορὰν καὶ ὁμοιότητα, A's λόγον ἔχον may be said ἀδικεῖσθαι by his ἄλογον.] Thus the chief argument to show ὅτι εἴη ἂν ἑκόντ' ἀδικεῖσθαι is disproved.' The words οὐθεὶς γὰρ βούλεται—πράττειν πράττει explain the condition of the ἀκρατής when he proceeds ἀκρατεύεσθαι under the influence of ἐπιθυμία: he οὐ βούλεται βλάπτεσθαι, i.e. his ἐπιθυμία cannot induce his βούλησις to support it (as no one βούλεται that which he does not suppose to be good); but he πράττει παρὰ τὴν βούλησιν, i.e. when the struggle is over, his βούλησις retires from the field, and under the influence of ἐπιθυμία he does that which his better reason assures him he ought not to do. Cf. E. E. II. 7 § 5 βούλεται δ' οὐθεὶς ὃ οἴεται εἶναι κακόν· ἀλλὰ μὴν ὁ ἀκρατευόμενος οὐχ ἃ βούλεται ποιεῖ· τὸ γὰρ παρ' ὃ οἴεται βέλτιστον εἶναι πράττειν δι' ἐπιθυμίαν ἀκρατεύεσθαί ἐστιν, and E. E. II. 7 § 11 βούλεται μὲν γὰρ οὐθεὶς ἃ οἴεται εἶναι κακά, πράττει δ' ὅταν γίνηται ἀκρατής. According to Eudemus then we must distinguish in τὰ κατ' ἀκρασίαν two successive stages: (1) that in which the βούλησις resists, and therefore the man is ἄκων, and (2) that in which, the βούλησις having given way to the ἐπιθυμία, the man is ἑκών, but οὐθὲν παρὰ τὴν αὐτοῦ πάσχει βούλησιν. Thus the ἀκρατής is not *simultaneously* ἑκών and παρὰ τὴν βούλησιν πάσχων, and therefore the phenomena of ἀκρασία do not countenance the theory that a man may ἑκὼν ἀδικεῖσθαι. (For the successive predominance of βούλησις and πάθος cf. *N. E.* VII. 2 § 2 ὅτι γὰρ οὐκ οἴεταί γε ὁ ἀκρατευόμενος πρὶν ἐν τῷ πάθει γενέσθαι, φανερόν, and *E. E.* II. 7 § 4 quoted below.) The difficulty of the passage is due in large measure to the phrase ἀλλὰ παρὰ τὴν βούλησιν πράττει, which *seems* to surrender Eudemus's position: it will be well therefore to say a word or two more about it, even at the risk of iteration. In the earlier stage, during which *A* does not succumb to *B*'s seductions, *A*'s βούλησις directs his conduct, so that *B*'s action is παρὰ τὴν τοῦ A βούλησιν: but in the second stage *A*'s conduct is directed not by his βούλησις, but by his ἐπιθυμία, which plays into *B*'s hands; hence *B*'s action is no longer παρὰ τὴν τοῦ A βούλησιν, but κατὰ τὴν τοῦ A ἐπιθυμίαν. *A*'s ἐπιθυμία however is resisted by his βούλησις: and consequently, though *B*'s action is not παρὰ τὴν τοῦ A βούλησιν, *A* himself may be said πράττειν παρὰ τὴν ἑαυτοῦ βούλησιν. (Cf. *E. E.* II. 7 § 4 ὁ δ' ἀκρατὴς ὁ κατὰ τὴν ἐπιθυμίαν παρὰ τὸν λογισμὸν οἷος πράττειν, ἀκρατεύεται δ' ὅταν ἐνεργῇ κατ' αὐτήν, τὸ δ' ἀδικεῖν ἑκούσιον, ὥσθ' ὁ ἀκρατὴς ἀδικήσει τῷ πράττειν κατ' ἐπιθυμίαν· ἑκὼν ἄρα πράξει καὶ ἑκούσιον τὸ κατ' ἐπιθυμίαν.) Hence in the first stage *A* is not ἑκών, because βούλησις, being dominant, resists: in the second stage *A* is ἑκών but not ἀδικούμενος, because ἐπιθυμία, being dominant, assents to *B*'s solicitations, βούλησις having now given way.

The passage has been variously understood or misunderstood. The author of the *M. M.* I. 34 § 35 interprets—'the ἀκρατὴς βουλόμενος πράττει τὰ κατὰ τὴν ἀκρασίαν and therefore ἑκὼν βλάπτεται: but no one βούλεται ἀδικεῖσθαι, and therefore no one ἑκὼν ἀδικεῖται,' assuming apparently, in defiance of *E. E.* II. 7 § 10 (to say nothing of other passages), the identity of βούλεσθαι and ἑκὼν εἶναι. This view appears to be accepted by the Paraphrast, and by Hildenbrand, *Rechts- und Staatsphilosophie,* I. 315, who however recognizes the insufficiency of the argument. Mich. Ephes. boldly emends—ἀλλ' οὐδ' ὁ ἀκρατὴς παρὰ τὴν βούλησιν πράττει. Rassow virtually abandons the attempt to make sense of the passage (*Forschungen* p. 41). Nötel holds that the sentences οὐθεὶς γὰρ βούλεται, κ.τ.λ. do not justify the dictum οὐθεὶς ἑκὼν ἀδικεῖται, but declare a new dictum οὐθεὶς βούλεται ἀδικεῖσθαι. This interpretation leaves the case of the ἀκρατής unexplained: for the ἀκρατής is certainly ἑκών. It is no explanation to say that because he acts παρὰ τὴν βούλησιν he is not ἑκών. Moreover the γάρ which introduces the supposed new dictum needs explanation. Grant seems hardly to have realized the difficulty of the passage.

§ 6. ὃ οὐκ οἴεται, κ.τ.λ.] This reading seems to me to express Eudemus's meaning more clearly and correctly than οὐχ ἃ οἴεται, the reading which Bekker prefers on the authority of K[b]. Is it possible that the copyist was puzzled by the negative οὐκ in the relative sentence, and therefore transposed it? It is of course perfectly correct here, as the ἀκρατής does not do *those things* which he thinks to be wrong,' but *things* which he thinks to be wrong.' Cf. Plat. *Rep.* I. 330 ἐπειδάν τις ἐγγὺς ᾖ τοῦ οἴεσθαι τελευτήσειν, εἰσέρχεται αὐτῷ δέος καὶ φροντὶς περὶ ὧν ἔμπροσθεν οὐκ εἰσῄει (quoted by Madvig, *Gr. Synt.* § 203). In *E. E.* II. 7 § 5 however we have ὁ ἀκρατευόμενος οὐχ ἃ βούλεται ποιεῖ.

§§ 8—13. In these paragraphs the author raises two ἀπορίαι (1) πότερόν ποτ' ἀδικεῖ ὁ νείμας παρὰ τὴν ἀξίαν τὸ πλεῖον ἢ ὁ ἔχων, (2) εἰ ἔστιν αὐτὸν αὑτὸν ἀδικεῖν. They are put forward together, because it might at first sight seem that, if it is decided that ὁ νείμας ἀδικεῖ, the second question must be answered affirmatively, since the distributor may assign to himself too small a share. But on further consideration we see (1) that the distributor may assign to himself too small a share with a view to an equivalent, e.g. reputation, and (2) that, whether this is so or not, in the case supposed the distributor suffers nothing παρὰ τὴν βούλησιν and therefore οὐκ ἀδικεῖται. Having thus dissevered the two questions, the author proceeds to deal with the former of them in §§ 10—13. He remarks (1) that it is the distributor who ἀδικεῖ, as it is with him that the action originates: (2) that if the distributor is γινώσκων, he obtains by his unjust award either money or gratitude or revenge, and is therefore ἀδίκως πλέον ἔχων.

It will be seen from this summary that the question εἰ ἔστιν αὐτὸν αὑτὸν ἀδικεῖν, though mooted, is not discussed in these sections, whilst the words ἔτι δ' ὧν προειλόμεθα, κ.τ.λ. in § 8 show that the reference to the ἀπορία in § 4 is an anticipatory one. Hence the discussion of the question in 11 §§ 1—6 is not, as Grant and many others have thought, superfluous. On the contrary if these §§ are excised the second part of the programme announced in 9 § 8 remains unfulfilled. If then 9 §§ 14—17 and ch. 10 are removed, 11 §§ 1—6 immediately follow in their proper place. See Introduction, On dislocations in the text.

§ 8. ὧν προειλόμεθα] For this phrase cf. *Polit.* VIII. (V.) 1. p. 193. 21. Mich. Ephes. remarks that these ἀπορίαι have not been mentioned before, and that the sentence must therefore mean ὅτι τῆς προθέσεως ἡμῖν περὶ δικαιοσύνης εἰπεῖν οὔσης, ἐπεὶ ὁ περὶ αὐτῆς λόγος πεπλήρωται, ὑπόλοιπόν ἐστι περὶ δύο τινῶν εἰπεῖν. Although the second ἀπορία has been incidentally alluded to in § 4, the objection is a just one. The reference is perhaps, as Zell suggests, to the opening words of 9 § 1.

§ 9. τὸ πρότερον λεχθέν] Apparently by these words is meant the former of the two alternatives of the first question. But this is very awkward. Is it possible that the reading of K^b in § 8 represents ἀξίαν τὸ πλεῖον ἑκών?

τοῦτο] Sc. that the distributor in this case αὐτὸν ἀδικεῖ.

κατά] The editors write καὶ κατά against the authority of most, if not all, the MSS.

§ 10. ἀεί] I think that this word may stand in the sense of 'in every case.' Zell and Michelet translate 'nicht der, welcher jedesmal mehr hat.' Rassow supposes the word to be a corruption of the superfluous ἀδικεῖ which in K^b appears in place of it.

§ 11. This § is commonly understood to contain a distinct argument, which according to some refers to the distributor, according to others to the receiver. If the distributor is referred to, the § would naturally mean that 'the distributor, who may be regarded as an instrument, though he οὐκ ἀδικεῖ, ποιεῖ τὰ ἄδικα:' plainly this statement is anything but a proof that he ἀδικεῖ. Nor can it be regarded as an argument urged on the contrary part: for the author would then have written οὐκ ἀδικεῖ ἀλλὰ ποιεῖ τὰ ἄδικα. If again the argument is that the receiver οὐκ ἀδικεῖ and therefore the distributor ἀδικεῖ, the Greek is still questionable. The author would probably have written ποιεῖ μὲν τὰ ἄδικα οὐ μὴν ἀδικεῖ γε. Conceiving then that some change is necessary, I have bracketed ἔτι as a dittograph of the first two letters of ἐπεί, placing a colon instead of a full stop after λαμβάνοντι and removing the comma after ἐπιτάξαντος. I suppose the sentence thus altered to be a justification of the distinction just made between ᾧ τὸ ἄδικον [sc. ποιεῖν] ὑπάρχει and ᾧ τὸ ἑκόντα τοῦτο ποιεῖν. The Paraphrast seems to have understood the sentence as I do.

τὰ ἄψυχα κτείνει] Plat. *Laws* ix. 873 D ἐὰν δ᾿ ἄρα ὑποζύγιον ἢ ζῶον ἄλλο τι φονεύσῃ τινά...ἐὰν δὲ ἄψυχόν τι ψυχῆς ἄνθρωπον στερήσῃ. The commentators quote also Demosth. *Aristocrat.* 645. 16 and Aeschin. *Ctesiph.* § 244. Is it possible that the reading of P^b is something more than a mere blunder, and that we should read καὶ τὰ κτήνη in place of κτείνει?

§ 12. The argument is contained in the words εἰ γινώσκων ἔκρινεν ἀδίκως, πλεονεκτεῖ καὶ αὐτὸς ἢ χάριτος ἢ τιμωρίας. The words εἰ μὲν ἀγνοῶν—τὸ πρῶτον merely set aside the case of ignorance as irrelevant to our present remarks.

§ 13. 'If the judge secures to himself χάρις or τιμωρία by giving an unjust award, he is just as much a πλεονέκτης as if he were to share the plunder with the receiver. For it is not essential that the unjust distributor should take a share of the property distributed, since even if his share takes a more substantial form than χάρις and τιμωρία, he may receive it not in land (land being the article distributed), but in money.'

ἐπ' ἐκείνων] 'In such cases,' i.e. in cases where the distributor shares the profits with the receiver. I see no difficulty in the transition from the singular of εἴ τις μερίσαιτο τοῦ ἀδικήματος to the plural of ἐκείνων. Rassow however would read with K^b ἐπ' ἐκείνῳ τὸν ἀγρόν, κ.τ.λ., i.e. ἐπὶ τῷ μερίσασθαι τοῦ ἀδικήματος (*Forschungen* p. 62).

§§ 14—17. I have placed §§ 14—16 after 1 § 3, and 1 § 17 after 1 § 9. See Introduction, On dislocations in the text.

11 §§ 1—6. The second of the two ἀπορίαι raised in 9 § 8 'Can a man ἀδικεῖν ἑαυτόν?' is considered under two heads, first, when the ἀδικία is universal, and secondly, when it is particular.

Suicide is an ἀδίκημα of the first kind, because it is a violation of law, and as the suicide acts voluntarily (i.e. not under compulsion, and with full knowledge of the circumstances), he ἀδικεῖ. But whom? Not himself,—for οὐθεὶς ἑκὼν ἀδικεῖται,—but the state: wherefore the state exacts the penalty, and the penalty takes the form of a forfeiture of civil privileges.

That a man cannot ἀδικεῖν ἑαυτόν in the other sense of the word ἀδικεῖν, seems to be proved by the following considerations:

(1) the same thing cannot be subtracted from, and added to, the same thing at the same moment; in fact, the commission of particular ἀδικία implies two persons concerned, one who invades the rights of another, and a second whose rights are invaded:

(2) the commission of particular ἀδικία is always aggressive; whereas, when a man harms himself, he does and suffers the same thing at the same time, and therefore is not an aggressor:

(3) volenti non fit iniuria:

(4) no one can commit adultery with his own wife, burglary upon his own premises, or theft upon his own property, and without the commission of some such ἀδίκημα no one can ἀδικεῖν.

Thus in general the ἀπορία is resolved by a reference to the maxim οὐθεὶς ἑκὼν ἀδικεῖται, established in 9 §§ 5, 6.

§ 1. ἐκ τῶν εἰρημένων] I.e. from 9 §§ 1—13.

τὰ μὲν γάρ, κ.τ.λ.] Cf. 1 § 8. 2 § 6.

οὐ κελεύει] 'Does not allow,' i.e. forbids. Cf. the well-known use of οὐκ ἐᾶν as the correlative of κελεύειν. The words ἃ δὲ μὴ κελεύει, ἀπαγορεύει are explanatory of the phrase οὐ κελεύει. So Victorius, quoted by Cardwell. Eudemus wishes to say—'What the law *bids* is δίκαιον, what the law *forbids* is ἄδικον.' Cf. 1 § 14 προστάττει δ' ὁ νόμος καὶ τὰ τοῦ ἀνδρείου ἔργα ποιεῖν, οἷον μὴ λείπειν τὴν τάξιν... ὁμοίως δὲ καὶ τὰ κατὰ τὰς ἄλλας ἀρετὰς καὶ μοχθηρίας, τὰ μὲν κελεύων τὰ δ' ἀπαγορεύων. Not appreciating this idiomatic use of οὐ κελεύω, Grant remarks "The extraordinary assertion is made that 'whatever the law does not command it forbids.' We might well ask, Did the Athenian law command its citizens to breathe, to eat, to sleep, &c.?" This criticism is endorsed by Rassow (*Forschungen* p. 42), who regards the last section of the book (with the exception of ch. 10) as a very unsatisfactory piece of patchwork.

§ 2. ὅταν, κ.τ.λ.] The words μὴ ἀντιβλάπτων are parenthetical. Compare the parenthetical sentence ὁ γὰρ διότι ἔπαθε καὶ τὸ αὐτὸ ἀντιποιῶν οὐ δοκεῖ ἀδικεῖν. in § 5. It is obvious that, in spite of the editors, who place a comma before ἑκών, ἑκών should be connected with βλάπτῃ. It is necessary to specify that ὁ βλάπτων is ἑκών, as otherwise he would be, not ἀδικῶν, but ἄδικα πράττων (cf. 9 § 3); whilst with ἀδικεῖ, ἑκών is superfluous.

ἑκὼν δὲ ὁ εἰδὼς καὶ ὃν καὶ ᾧ] A man is ἑκών when he does ἑκούσια, i.e. ὅσα ἐφ' ἑαυτῷ ὂν μὴ πράττειν πράττει μὴ ἀγνοῶν καὶ δι' αὐτόν E. E. II. 9 § 2. Here as elsewhere the definition is abbreviated, as is also the list of circumstances in regard to which ignorance is possible. Cf. 9 §§ 4, 5.

§ 3. ἀτιμία] For the ἀτιμίαι of the suicide the commentators quote Aeschin. *Ctesiph.* § 244 and Plat. *Laws* IX. 873 D.

§ 4. ὅλως] I.e. κατὰ τὴν ὅλην ἀδικίαν.

τοῦτο γάρ—ἀδικεῖ] These sentences are manifestly parenthetical. They explain the difference between universal and particular justice, and declare the necessity of investigating the ἀπορία with regard to the latter as well as to the former.

§ 5. ἔτι δὲ ἑκούσιον τε καὶ ἐκ προαιρέσεως, καὶ πρότερον] The words ἑκούσιον τε καὶ ἐκ προαιρέσεως are not necessary to the argument. Indeed τὸ ἀδικεῖν is not necessarily ἐκ προαιρέσεως: I have therefore translated the phrase 'voluntary *or* deliberate, and aggressive.'

ὁ γὰρ διότι ἔπαθε, κ.τ.λ.] οὐ γὰρ ἄρχει ὁ θυμῷ ποιῶν, ἀλλ' ὁ ὀργίσας. 8 § 9.

§ 6. πρὸς δὲ τούτοις, κ.τ.λ.] 'If, instead of arguing from our conception of ἀδικία, we examine special cases of it, we come to the same conclusion.'

ὅλως, κ.τ.λ.] 'The maxim οὐθεὶς ἑκὼν ἀδικεῖται is decisive in both cases of the present ἀπορία.'

§§ 7, 8. I have placed these §§ after 5 § 18. See Introduction, On dislocations in the text.

§ 9. κατὰ μεταφορὰν δὲ καὶ ὁμοιότητα] 'There is a δίκαιον, οὐκ αὐτῷ πρὸς αὐτόν, but between the parts of the individual's ψυχή. This δίκαιον resembles that which subsists between master and slave, or that which subsists between husband and wife. The parts in question are τὸ λόγον ἔχον and τὸ ἄλογον, which, as we have seen in 9 §§ 5, 6, may be at variance.'

Fritzsche well compares the discussion in *E. E.* VII. 6 § 1 sqq. περὶ τοῦ αὐτὸν αὐτῷ φίλον εἶναι ἢ μή. See especially §§ 2, 3 καὶ ὅμοιον τὰ τοιαῦτα πάντα, εἰ φίλος αὐτὸς αὑτῷ καὶ ἐχθρός, καὶ εἰ ἀδικεῖ τις αὐτὸς αὐτόν. πάντα γὰρ ἐν δυσὶ ταῦτα καὶ διῃρημένοις. εἰ δὲ δύο πως καὶ ἡ ψυχή, ὑπάρχει πως ταῦτα· εἰ δ' οὐ διῃρημένα, οὐχ ὑπάρχει. In these discussions there is an allusion (as all the commentators from Mich. Ephes. downwards have seen) to Plato. See *Rep.* IV. 443 D, &c. In the same way in the *Gorgias*, 491 D, a man is said αὐτὸς ἑαυτοῦ ἄρχειν, when his reason controls his ἐπιθυμίαι.

ἐν τούτοις γὰρ τοῖς λόγοις, κ.τ.λ.] Mich. Ephes. ὃν λόγον ἔχει ὁ δοῦλος πρὸς <τὸν> δεσπότην, τὸν αὐτὸν καὶ τὸ ἄλογον μέρος τῆς ψυχῆς πρὸς τὸ λογιζόμενον. τοιαύτην γὰρ διέστηκε ταῦτα διάστασιν ἀπ' ἀλλήλων ὥσ<τε> εἶναι τὸ μὲν ἄρχον τὸ δὲ ἀρχόμενον. Thus he makes ἐν τούτοις τοῖς λόγοις διέστηκε equivalent to κατὰ τούτους τοὺς λόγους δ. Grant translates, "for in the theories alluded to there is a separation made between the reasonable and the unreasonable part of man's nature:" and Paley understands the sentence in the same way. As here Eudemus compares the relation of λόγον ἔχον and ἄλογον to the relations of master and slave, husband and wife, so Aristotle in *Polit.* I. 5. p. 7. 2 compares the relation of master and slave to the relation of νοῦς and ὄρεξις; but whereas Eudemus is careful to say (6 § 9) that the δίκαιον of the domestic relations is not identical with πολιτικὸν δίκαιον, Aristotle, less precisely, attributes to νοῦς an ἀρχὴ πολιτικὴ καὶ βασιλική.

καὶ δοκεῖ] 'People go on to assume.' Cf. *E. E.* II. 8 §§ 12, 13 ὥστε τὸ μὲν βίᾳ ἑκάτερον [sc. the ἐγκρατής and the ἀκρατής] φάναι ποιεῖν ἔχει λόγον, καὶ διὰ τὴν ὄρεξιν καὶ διὰ τὸν λογισμὸν ἑκάτερον ἄκοντα ποτὲ πράττειν· κεχωρισμένα γὰρ ὄντα ἑκάτερα ἐκκρούεται ὑπ' ἀλλήλων. ὅθεν καὶ ἐπὶ τὴν ὅλην μεταφέρουσι ψυχήν, ὅτι τῶν ἐν ψυχῇ τι τοιοῦτον ὁρῶσιν. ἐπὶ μὲν οὖν τῶν μορίων ἐνδέχεται τοῦτο λέγειν· ἡ δ' ὅλη ἑκοῦσα ψυχὴ καὶ τοῦ ἀκρατοῦς καὶ τοῦ ἐγκρατοῦς πράττει, βίᾳ δ' οὐδέτερος, ἀλλὰ τῶν ἐν ἐκείνοις τι, ἐπεὶ καὶ φύσει ἀμφότερα ἔχομεν.

ὅτι [ἐν] τούτοις] The preposition seems to me superfluous: compare εἶναι πρὸς ἄλληλα δίκαιόν τι καὶ τούτοις in the next sentence. The sentence evidently means: 'because there may be a struggle between the λόγον ἔχον and the ἄλογον' (κεχωρισμένα γὰρ ὄντα ἑκάτερα ἐκκρούεται ὑπ' ἀλλήλων. *E. E.* II. 8 § 12). Thus an ὄρεξις is loosely and κατὰ μεταφοράν attributed to the λόγον ἔχον: strictly speaking, βούλησις, which is ὄρεξις ἀγαθοῦ, though determined by the λόγον ἔχον, belongs to the ἄλογον, i.e. the φύσις ἄλογος μετέχουσα μέντοι πῃ λόγου of *N. E.* I. 13 § 15.

ὥσπερ οὖν ἄρχοντι καὶ ἀρχομένῳ] Cf. Plat. *Gorg.* 491 D. Aristot. *Polit.* I. 13. pp. 20, 21.

6 § 3. πῶς μὲν οὖν ἔχει, κ.τ.λ.] See Introduction, On dislocations in the text.

10 § 1. ὥστε καὶ ἐπὶ τὰ ἄλλα, κ.τ.λ.] For examples of this vague use of the word ἐπιεικής see *Berlin Index*. Grant aptly quotes 4 § 3.

τὸ ἐπιεικέστερον ὅτι βέλτιον δηλοῦντες] Does this mean (1) 'meaning by what is ἐπιεικέστερον what is βέλτιον' or (2) 'thus indicating that what is ἐπιεικέστερον is βέλτιον'?

ὁτὲ δὲ τῷ λόγῳ, κ.τ.λ.] 'There is an apparent inconsistency in the statement that τὸ ἐπιεικὲς παρὰ τὸ δίκαιόν τι ὂν ἐπαινετόν ἐστιν: for if ἐπιεικές is distinct from δίκαιον, and at the same time so commendable a thing, do we not deny the excellence of δίκαιον? If again we account both ἐπιεικές and δίκαιον excellent, do we not deny that there is any difference between them?' This must be the meaning of the sentence, but the ordinary text is perplexed by the words οὐ δίκαιον after ἢ τὸ ἐπιεικές. I think that Giphanius (on the authority of the V. A.) and Trendelenburg (on conjecture) are right in omitting οὐ δίκαιον. The words οὐ δίκαιον εἰ are omitted not only by the V. A., but also by N^b. Lambinus reads ἢ τὸ ἐπιεικὲς οὐκ, εἰ δικαίου ἄλλο: Michelet and Fritzsche punctuate ἢ τὸ ἐπιεικὲς οὔ, δίκαιον εἰ ἄλλο: finally, Nötel suggests ἢ τὸ ἐπιεικὲς οὐ σπουδαῖον.

§§ 3, 4. Vide *Polit.* II. 8. p. 44. 2. III. 10. p. 78. 1. 15. p. 87. 6. 16. p. 90. 10 and p. 91. 8. Plat. *Polit.* 294 A sqq. *Laws* IX. 875 C sqq.

§ 4. τοιαύτη] 'Such that it is not possible ὀρθῶς εἰπεῖν καθόλου.'

§ 5. ὃ κἄν, κ.τ.λ.] I prefer εἶπεν to εἴποι in this sentence, because it is distinctly assumed that the νομοθέτης is not present, and therefore does not pronounce. The tenses are of course quite correct: the lawgiver would pronounce in this manner (a single act in present time) if he were with us (a state in present time), and would have legislated accordingly (a single act in past time) if he had known the circumstances (a state in past time).

§ 6. οὐ τοῦ ἁπλῶς δέ, κ.τ.λ.] τοῦ ἁπλῶς i. q. τοῦ ἁπλῶς δικαίου, 'the just not limited in any particular way': διὰ τὸ ἁπλῶς i. q. διὰ τὸ ἁπλῶς εἰπεῖν, cf. ἁπλῶς εἰπών § 5 and διὰ τὸ καθόλου infra, 'because the statement is not limited in any particular way.' I am surprised that the editors do not suspect ἁμαρτήματος. I should have expected ἁμαρτάνοντος. The Paraphrast writes διὰ τοῦτο ἡ ἐπιείκεια δίκαιον μέν ἐστι βέλτιον <δέ> τινος δικαίου· οὐ τοῦ καθόλου δικαίου, ἀλλὰ τοῦ νομικοῦ τοῦ διὰ τὸ καθόλου ἁμαρτάνοντος.

§ 7. ὁ μολίβδινος κανών] "Quando murum construebant non ex quadratis et laeuibus, sed ex lapidibus polygoniis, in quibus alia eminerent alia essent concava, ut eiusmodi lapidi aspero et inaequali alium lapidem quam accuratissime (non interiectis lapidibus minoribus) coaptarent, norma utebantur plumbea, qua ad inaequalitatem saxi prioris inflexa, quod aliud saxum polygonium ad prius elegantissime accommodari posset, quaerebant. Eiusmodi accuratissima polygoniorum constructio lapidum est in muro quodam Cyclopio Mycenarum (Paus. II. 16). Cf. Forchhammer. in eph. *Allgem. Bauzeitung von Förster*, 9. Jahrg. 1844. p. 274. ibid. Förster p. 275: 'Noch jetzt baut man in Verona ähnliche Mauern aus polygonischen Steinen, und die Steinhauer bedienen sich gleichfalls einer beweglichen, aus mehreren Linealen zusammengesetzten Schmiege.'" Fritzsche.

www.ingramcontent.com/pod-product-compliance
Lightning Source LLC
Chambersburg PA
CBHW030318170426
43202CB00009B/1048